P9-DIY-676

FLORIDA

CONTENTS

DISCOVER 6

EXPERIENCE MIAMI 50

EXPERIENCE FLORIDA 106

NEED TO KNOW 314

Left: Art Deco architecture on Ocean Drive
Previous page: Downtown Miami skyline at sunrise
Front cover: Footbridge to Smathers Beach, Key West

DISCOVER

Vibrant sky over downtown Gainesville

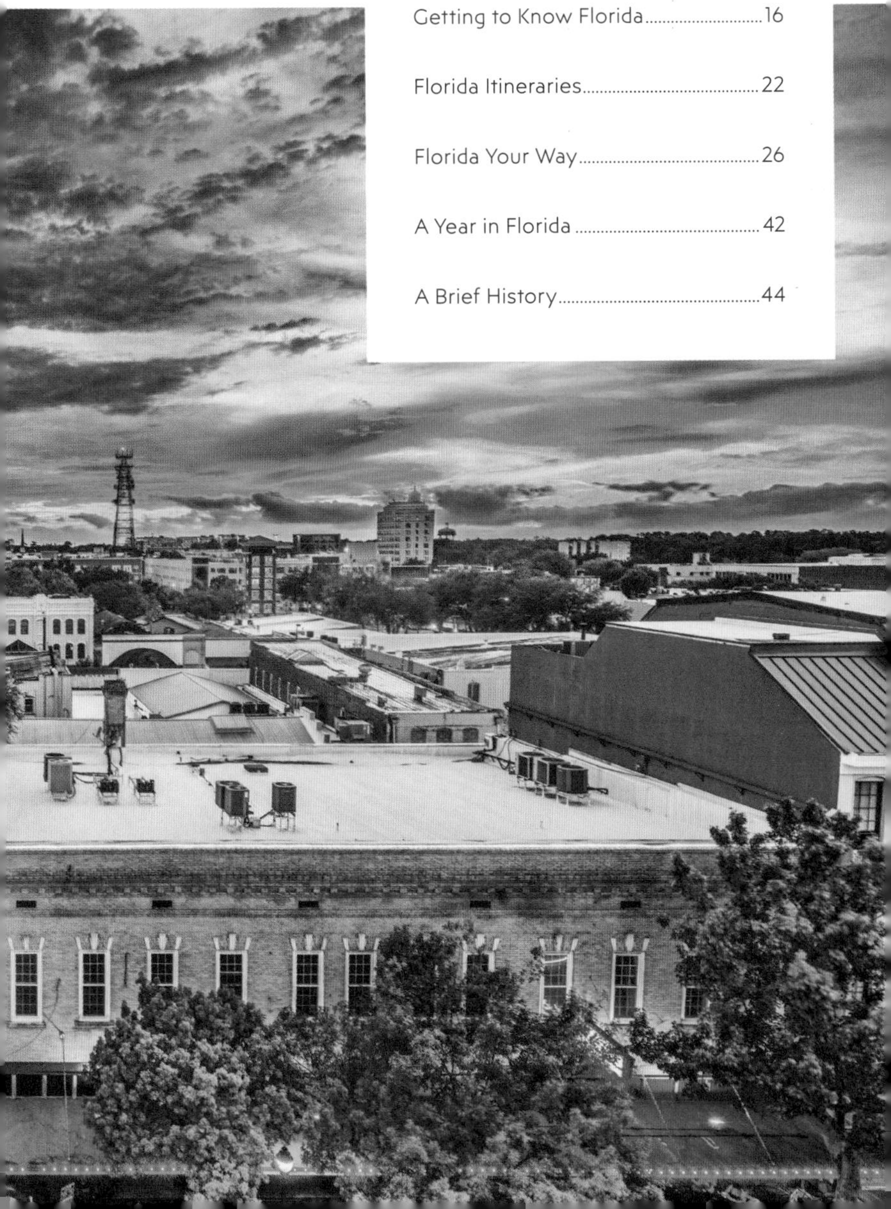

WELCOME TO
FLORIDA

Florida is well known for its theme parks and beautiful beaches, but there's so much more to experience here: nature trails and national parks, great food and nightlife, cosmopolitan cities and fascinating history. Whatever your dream trip to Florida includes, this DK Eyewitness travel guide is the perfect companion.

1 Riding the Astro Orbiter at the Magic Kingdom®.

2 Sunrise over a pristine beach at Fort Lauderdale.

3 Neon lights illuminating the street as evening falls over Miami's Ocean Drive.

Florida's beaches are second to none, and sun seekers flock to the scenic coastlines at places like St. Augustine, Naples, and down through the Florida Keys, the beautiful string of islands south of the peninsula. Nature lovers can get up close and personal with the state's flora and fauna at one of Florida's many national parks, the swamps and gators of The Everglades being the most well known, although the inland national forests and wildlife preserves add even more options.

Florida's cities offer food, culture, and nightlife in abundance, with each city giving off its own unique vibe: urban chic in Miami, historic beauty in Pensacola, and the laid-back seaside town feel of Fort Lauderdale and Tampa. Orlando, meanwhile, feels like a world apart with its acres of unique attractions. The twin giants of Walt Disney World® Resort and Universal Orlando Resort™ draw millions of visitors every year, and the city's neighboring Space Coast offers a whole new world of adventure in its own right.

From the historic towns of the northern Panhandle to the laid-back islands of the Keys over 500 miles (800 km) south, we've broken Florida into easily navigable adventures, with expert local knowledge, detailed itineraries, and colorful, comprehensive maps to help you plan the perfect visit. Whether you're here for the famous theme parks or want a vacation off the beaten path, this DK Eyewitness travel guide will help you make the most of all that the state has to offer. Enjoy the book, and enjoy Florida.

REASONS TO LOVE
FLORIDA

Bountiful beaches, delicious seafood, natural wonders, and sizzling nightlife - Florida has something for everyone. No matter what kind of trip you're planning, these are the highlights no visitor should miss.

1 BEACH LOVERS' PARADISE

An incredible 663 miles (1,067 km) of sandy shore rim the state *(p26)*, beckoning beach lovers from the placid Gulf of Mexico to the waves of the Atlantic Ocean.

THEME PARK THRILLS 2

Forget your age and let yourself be whisked away by the magic of Florida's amazing theme parks *(p30)*, all full of memorable rides and shows in fantastical settings.

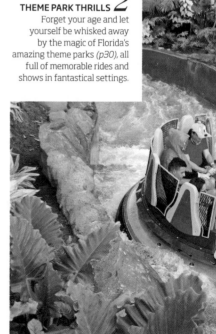

3 WONDERFUL WILDLIFE

For natural beauty and wildlife sightings, head to the state parks and preserves throughout Florida *(p36)*. The Merritt Island National Wildlife Refuges are some of the best.

ART DECO 4

Take a stroll along Miami Beach's Ocean Drive *(p68)* to beautifully preserved hotels that make the area feel like a chic outdoor design gallery.

KENNEDY SPACE CENTER 5

The Apollo space shuttle, a Mission Control Room, and a "garden" of giant rockets close up are just the start of the wonders awaiting at the Kennedy Space Center *(p190)*.

CUBAN FOOD 6

Sample regional dishes in the Cuban neighborhoods of Miami and Tampa *(p34)*. Look for tempting roast pork dishes, chicken with rice, and savory Cuban sandwiches.

DIVERSE MIAMI 7

From the historic feel of Coral Gables to the modern downtown skyline, the many moods of Miami *(p50)* make for good urban adventures full of brilliant food, fun nightlife, and culture.

THE EVERGLADES 8

Board an airboat ride above the swamps or take to a boardwalk trail to see alligators and great blue herons, among 1,000 other species living in this vast untouched wetland *(p292)*.

9 GOLF FOR EVERYONE

Florida boasts over 1,000 golf courses – more than any other state – from tournament level to affordable public facilities. No wonder so many golf pros live in Florida *(p40)*.

10 UNDERWATER ADVENTURES

John Pennekamp Coral Reef State Park (p306) was America's first underwater state park, and for good reason: here you can see the country's only living barrier reef.

FISHING IN THE KEYS 11

Snapper, redfish, tuna, mahi mahi: name a favorite and it's likely to be found in the rich fishing bounty off the Florida Keys. Tarpon tournaments are legendary for their big catches.

YEAR-ROUND SUNSHINE 12

They don't call it the "Sunshine State" for nothing! Even rainy days often break with periods of sun. The St. Petersburg coast set a record of 361 sunny days in a single year.

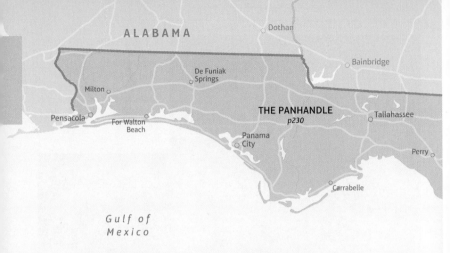

ALABAMA

Dothan

Bainbridge

De Funiak
Springs

Milton

THE PANHANDLE
p230

Tallahassee

Pensacola

For Walton
Beach

Panama
City

Perry

Carrabelle

*Gulf of
Mexico*

EXPLORE
FLORIDA

This guide divides Florida into eight color-coded
sightseeing areas, as shown on this map. Find out
more about each area on the following pages.

NORTH AMERICA

CANADA

Seattle

USA

Chicago

Boston

New York

San Francisco

Washington, DC

*Atlantic
Ocean*

Los Angeles

Atlanta

Houston

FLORIDA

*Gulf of
Mexico*

Miami

*Pacific
Ocean*

MEXICO

CUBA

0 kilometers 100
0 miles 100

N

GEORGIA

Brunswick

Valdosta

Fernandina Beach

Atlantic Ocean

Jacksonville

Lake City

Jacksonville Beach

Suwannee

THE NORTHEAST
p204

St. Augustine

Alachua

Steinhatchee

Palatka

Gainesville

Palm Coast

Bronson

Daytona Beach

Ocala

DeLand

Homosassa Springs

Deltona

Sanford

WALT DISNEY WORLD® RESORT
p138

Orlando

Titusville

Cape Canaveral

Kissimmee

Cocoa

Lakeland

ORLANDO AND
THE SPACE COAST
p170

Melbourne

Clearwater

Tampa

Brandon

Winter Haven

St. Petersburg

Yeehaw Junction

Vero Beach

THE GULF
COAST
p254

Bradenton

Fort Pierce

Sarasota

Arcadia

Port Saint Lucie

THE GOLD AND
TREASURE COASTS
p108

Stuart

Port Charlotte

Lake Okeechobee

Jupiter

Punta Gorda

Clewiston

Belle Glade

Palm Beach

Fort Myers

Delray Beach

Cape Coral

Boca Raton

Fort Lauderdale

Naples

THE EVERGLADES
AND THE KEYS
p288

Marco

Miami

Miami Beach

MIAMI
p50

Florida City

Islamorada

Marathon

Key West

GETTING TO KNOW
FLORIDA

There's an incredible regional diversity to the Sunshine State, with its stunning beaches acting as the common thread that ties it all together. The scenery changes from moss-draped oaks in the north to tropical palms in the south, and even the beaches have distinct personalities.

PAGE 50

MIAMI

A big city with Latin American influences, Miami has many moods. Experience the different atmospheres of its neighborhoods like the historic Coral Gables, lively Little Havana, and the offbeat art mecca of Wynwood. Downtown Miami feels like a real modern metropolis, and is enriched with a growing emphasis on museums and culture to add to its shops and restaurants. While central areas like Miami Beach draw crowds to enjoy Art Deco architecture, thrilling nightlife, and action-packed beaches, farther afield there are places like Key Biscayne offering a calm escape on its long, sandy shoreline.

Best for
Nightlife, arts, and architecture

Home to
Ocean Drive, Little Havana, Vizcaya Museum and Gardens, and the Ancient Spanish Monastery

Experience
Touring South Beach's amazing Art Deco architecture

THE GOLD AND TREASURE COASTS

Sun-kissed beaches and seaside resorts line the coast north of Miami, a much-loved destination for both vacationers and retirees. Fort Lauderdale, with its cruise port, is the busiest place along the Gold Coast, while Palm Beach is the wealthiest, known for its mansions and luxury shopping. The Treasure Coast begins with Jupiter, a favorite place for the golfing world, then turns more rural with unspoiled beaches heading north to Sebastian Inlet.

Best for
Beach resorts and golf

Home to
Palm Beach, Boca Raton, and Fort Lauderdale

Experience
Joining a boat cruise to see hidden mansions in Fort Lauderdale

$\longrightarrow$

PAGE 138

WALT DISNEY WORLD® RESORT

There may be other Disney parks across the globe, but there's nothing quite like this vast complex on the outskirts of Orlando. Escape from the real world into four fantastic theme parks and two wild water parks – or enjoy the laid-back campgrounds, multiple golf courses, or the exciting shopping and dining on offer at Disney Springs®. There's enough for days of diversions for all ages, so everyone can find a place where they belong in this enchanting kingdom.

Best for
Quality family time and magical memories

Home to
Magic Kingdom®, Disney's Hollywood Studios®, EPCOT®, and Disney's Animal Kingdom®

Experience
A charming tour around the globe on the "it's a small world"® boat ride in the Magic Kingdom®

ORLANDO AND THE SPACE COAST

In contrast to the high-energy and excitement found at Universal Orlando®, the city's peaceful downtown, with its many museums and gardens, offers a pleasant change of pace. Its upscale neighbor Winter Park is well worth exploring, as are the futuristic wonders at the Kennedy Space Center. Beach breaks on the Space Coast can be laid-back affairs at the Canaveral National Seashore or full of surfing action on Cocoa Beach.

Best for
Families, theme parks, and charming cities

Home to
Universal Orlando®, LEGOLAND®, Central Orlando, Kennedy Space Center

Experience
The thrilling speed and jaw-dropping effects of the Harry Potter and the Forbidden Journey™ ride at Universal Orlando®

THE NORTHEAST

Daytona Beach is known to car racing fans and students on spring break, and the state's oldest town – the charming St. Augustine – attracts history buffs, but many visitors overlook the rest of this quiet coast. To do so means missing out on a long string of fine beaches, and the lovely city of Jacksonville, with its revitalized downtown along the St. John's River. Further inland there are sprawling horse farms near Ocala and, to the north, peaceful quaint Fernandina Beach on Amelia Island, another great find for beach lovers.

Best for
Quaint country towns and history

Home to
Jacksonville and St. Augustine

Experience
Driving a real NASCAR race car at Daytona Speedway

$\rightarrow$

PAGE 230

THE PANHANDLE

This quiet northern region has more ties to Southern traditions than the main Florida peninsula. This heritage is strong in cities like the state capital of Tallahassee and the historic districts of Pensacola. The coastline is a beach-lover's dream, accompanied by buzzing beach towns such as Panama City and Destin. Fishing villages such as Cedar Key and Apalachicola offer a different side of Florida, more removed from the touristy vacation spots, and there are national parks and islands to escape the crowds and get back to nature.

Best for
Nature, beaches, and Old South flavor

Home to
Pensacola and Tallahassee

Experience
Strolling the wooden boardwalks to reach the pristine beaches of Grayton Beach State Park

PAGE 254

THE GULF COAST

Along with stunning beaches along the Gulf of Mexico, this region is rich with both city pleasures and unspoiled nature. Upscale Sarasota is a wonderful cultural center with two museums created by the famous Ringling brothers. Meanwhile, St. Petersburg has the largest Dalí Museum in the US, and in growing high-rise Tampa, the Ybor City district provides both history and nightlife. To the south, shell collectors flock to the Lee Island Coast off Fort Myers. Farther north, the scene shifts to natural springs and state parks perfect for outdoor activities.

Best for
Seaside fun, museums, and city life

Home to
St. Petersburg, Tampa, Lee Island Coast, Ringling Musuem of Art, Ringling Museum Cà' d'Zan

Experience
Watching performing mermaids dance underwater at Weeki Wachee Springs

PAGE 288

THE EVERGLADES AND THE KEYS

On the southern tip of the peninsula, the vast wilderness of the Everglades acts as a fascinating natural counterpoint to the beach and city tourism focus in the rest of the state. And beyond the mainland are the Keys, where laid-back island communities are reached via 42 bridges on the Overseas Highway. The Keys are loved by divers and snorkelers for North America's only live coral reef, and by fisherman for bountiful deep-sea catches of marlin and tarpon.

Best for
Wildlife, boat trips, snorkeling, and fishing

Home to
Everglades National Park and Key West

Experience
Spotting alligators and rare birds on a boat tour through the Everglades

←

 The sandy shores of Panama City Beach.

2 A family kayaking in Ocala National Forest.

3 A manatee at Crystal River.

4 Dinner at The Fish House.

Much of Florida is overlooked by visitors in favor of the main spots like Orlando and Miami Beach, but even a few days exploring offers a wealth of exciting Floridian experiences.

5 DAYS
in Northern Florida

Day 1

Starting your trip in Jacksonville *(p208)*, grab an early breakfast at one of the many dining options at Jacksonville Landing and spend the morning at the Museum of Contemporary Art. Head to St. Augustine *(p212)* for lunch at the water at Harry's Seafood Bar & Grille *(hookedonharrys.com)*, then wander the town's beautiful narrow streets. Dine in the vicinity of Flagler College before enjoying the downtown nightlife.

Day 2

After breakfast, drive to Daytona and tour the Daytona International Speedway *(p220)* before lunch at Daytona Beach – Caribbean Jack's *(www.caribbeanjacks. com)* is a great, casual spot with waterfront views. Switch it up in the afternoon by heading out to enjoy Florida's natural beauty at Ocala National Forest *(p226)*, which has plenty of trails for an afternoon hike. Spend the night in Ocala, with classic Southern fare at historic Ivy on the Square *(ivyhousefl.com)*.

Day 3

In Weeki Wachee *(p278)* you can see one of Florida's most enduring road-side attractions: an underwater theater complete with live "mermaids." For some more authentic aquatic creatures, spend the late afternoon at Crystal River *(p278)*, which has manatees around the Three Sisters Springs Wildlife Refuge.

Spend your evening enjoying the local seafood at a Fish Shack or an outdoor dining spot.

Day 4

Cedar Key *(p250)* is one of the cutest seaside towns in northern Florida. Arrive early to take an island tour then lunch on the town's famous clams. Drive on to the state capital of Tallahassee *(p240)* – the journey is about two and a half hours from Cedar Key, but you should still have time to enjoy Tallahassee Museum in the late afternoon. For dinner, sample Southern cooking at one of Tallahassee's many restaurants.

Day 5

Today is all about beaches, and St. Andrews *(p245)* is one of the best. Head there early and camp out on the sand for a long, luxurious morning of sunbathing and swimming. If you can tear yourself away, there are many options for lunch in nearby Panama City Beach *(p244)*. An hour's pleasant drive along the coastal road lands you in Destin *(p246)*, one of the Gulf Coast's most popular beach resorts, with lots of opportunities for diving, snorkeling, and fishing. In the evening visit Pensacola *(p234)*, a larger seaside town with plenty of nightlife. Reap the benefits of the incredibly fresh seafood by dining dockside at The Fish House *(www.fishhousepensacola.com)*.

7 DAYS
in Southern Florida

Day 1

Start your trip in southern Florida with the must-see city of Miami. Treat yourself to breakfast at the legendary Biltmore Hotel *(p92)*, then explore the architecture, galleries, and Miracle Mile shopping in posh Coral Gables *(p80)*. Spend the afternoon exploring Vizcaya Museum and Gardens *(p86)*, Florida's grandest residence. Follow a Cuban dinner at Versailles *(p84)* with a walk along Calle Ocho *(p84)*, the heart of Little Havana.

Day 2

After breakfast in Downtown Miami, take a full day to explore the city's museums. Start with the exhibits, planetarium, and aquarium at the Phillip and Patricia Frost Museum of Science *(p88)*. Have a light lunch at the on-site Food@Science, then visit the nearby Perez Art Museum *(p88)* for contemporary international art. Afterward take a stroll along the waterfront Baywalk and check out the stores at Bayside Marketplace *(p88)* before sitting down for dinner.

Day 3

Breakfast al fresco at one of the cafes in South Beach, before taking a stroll on Ocean Drive to enjoy the area's stunning Art Deco architecture *(p68)*. Follow it up with exhibits on decorative arts at The Wolfsonian-Florida International University *(p74)* and paintings at The Bass *(p76)*. Lunch at a cafe along Lincoln Road Mall *(p76)*, browse the stores, then kick back on Miami's famous beach. Refresh later with dinner at the legendary Joe's Stone Crab Restaurant *(p77)*, before sampling some sizzling South Beach nightlife at Story *(www.storymiami.com)*.

Day 4

Just an hour's drive south, the vast Everglades National Park *(p292)* promises a full day of discoveries, with many visitor centers to supply information and maps. For casual exploring there are plenty of easy walks on elevated boardwalks, paved cycle routes, and short kayak trips to enjoy. There are also longer routes for the more adventurous. Everglades City is the closest place for an overnight

1. Palm trees in Miami.

2. Preparing a cocktail at Muse at the Ringling in Sarasota.

3. The Everglades National Park.

4. Viewing contemporary art in Miami's Perez Art Museum.

5. Exotic plants in Vizcaya Gardens.

stay, and Camellia Street Grill *(202 Camellia St E)* is recommended for a seafood dinner by the river.

Day 5

Fortify yourself with breakfast before the two-and-a-half hour drive to Sarasota *(p276)*, on Florida's Gulf coast. You can easily spend the entire day exploring the exceptional Ringling complex, the legacy of the famous family of circus owners of the early 19th century. Start with the Museum of Cà' d'Zan *(p274)*, the 56-room villa on the bay which is a work of art both inside and out. After lunch at the Marble's Coffee and Tea *(5401 Bay Shore Rd)*, see the treasures of the Ringling Museum of Art *(p272)*. Head to Downtown Sarasota for dinner in one of the many restaurants along Main Street, followed by an evening stroll around Bayfront Park.

Day 6

Start the day at First Watch *(firstwatch. com)* and a walk along Sarasota's appealing Main Street. Spend the morning admiring the rare orchids at Marie Selby Botanical Gardens overlooking the bay. Have a scrumptious lunch at O'Leary's Tiki Bar & Grill *(www. olearystikibar.com)* before heading to Long Boat Key and the beaches for an afternoon of lounging on talcum-soft sand. Later, head back across the bay to check out the stores along delightful St. Armands Circle and enjoy dinner at one of the fine restaurants here.

Day 7

An hour's drive – via the soaring Skyway Bridge, through St. Petersburg, and over another bridge across Old Tampa Bay – brings you to the young, vibrant city of Tampa *(p268)*. Have a late breakfast in Downtown before taking a pleasant boat cruise along the Hillsborough River and around the bay in the afternoon. Move on from here to visit Ybor City, Tampa's Cuban quarter and wind up the week with dinner at the beautiful Columbia restaurant *(www.columbiarestaurant.com)*.

Remote Escapes
Beaches with a sense of isolation include St. George Island *(p252)*, with 22 miles (35 km) of unspoiled sands and the Canaveral National Seashore *(p202)* just 30 miles (48 km) east of Orlando – the longest undeveloped beach on the East coast. The Gulf Coast, too, has havens such as Caladesi Island State Park *(p282)*, only accessible by boat from Honeymoon Island State Park.

Sunrise over the rolling surf of the Canaveral National Seashore

FLORIDA'S
BEACHES

Florida is blessed with world-class, globally renowned beaches. Each region offers something different, from all-day partying to top-class water sports, exotic local wildlife to romantic seclusion. From the Panhandle to the Keys, there's a beach to suit everyone – you just have to know where to look.

Family-Friendly Beaches
Beaches to please energetic youngsters include Fort Lauderdale *(p120)*, with banana boats and paddle boards, Sanibel Island *(p270)*, awash with seashells, and Palm Island, with bike trails, and shark's teeth and sand dollars buried in the sand.

↑ Families playing on Fort Lauderdale's spacious, uncrowded beach

City Beaches

Even Florida's biggest cities have that laid back coastal vibe, and you're never far away from white sands. Miami has South Beach *(p78)*, with its high-rolling glamor, Art Deco architecture, and partying. Sarasota has two island beaches that welcome families by day and a party crowd at night. St. Pete Beach *(p265)*, off St. Petersburg, is famous for retro chic Don Cesar Hotel.

> INSIDER TIP
> ### Beach Camping
> To enjoy Florida's sun, sea, and sand to the full, book a spot at one of the hundreds of camp grounds near your favorite beach. There are plenty of options for RVs and tents up and down the coast.

←

Miami's South Beach, backed by iconic Art Deco architecture and city high-rises

←

Kayaking around the backwaters behind the beach at Fort de Soto Park

Hidden Gems

Finding a slower pace and a little more breathing room is easy in Florida. A short walk south from St. Pete Beach, for instance, is Pass-a-Grille *(p264)*, a quieter spot to sunbathe before enjoying the boutiques and ice-cream parlors in town. Farther south, Fort de Soto Park *(p284)* has five beaches, water sports, fishing, and scenic sands. North of Miami and Fort Lauderdale is arty Delaray Beach (p128), with striking views.

→

A flock of red knots in search of tasty morsels on Delray Beach

A Sporting Chance

Florida has some of the most exciting teams in the US, and family-friendly venues make it fun for all. Football is huge, with top teams such as the Miami Dolphins, Jacksonville Jaguars, and Tampa Bay Buccaneers. The Miami Heat and Orlando Magic are in the top basketball league, and the Miami Marlins and Tampa Bay Rays are the baseball teams. Ice Hockey is popular, too, with the Tampa Bay Lightning and Florida Panthers. The best place to get tickets to any game is on individual team websites.

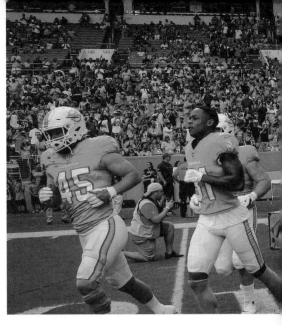

Miami Dolphins players running onto the field at an NFL football game in Miami

FLORIDA FOR
FAMILIES

If you had to rank the world's most family-friendly places, Florida would surely be among the best. Orlando's theme parks *(p30)* are clear stand-outs, but there are also weird and wonderful roadside attractions, fascinating museums, days out at the beach, and world-class sporting events.

Rainy-Day Activities

Florida's summer afternoon rains are the perfect time to explore kid-friendly indoor attractions. Miami's Phillip and Patricia Frost Museum of Science *(p88)* is home to the Gulfstream Aquarium and a spectacular planetarium. The Orlando Science Center *(p188)* has hands-on exhibits, animal encounters, and IMAX films. In Orlando, there are some great family-friendly attractions on International Drive *(p198)*, and lots of shops to explore at Disney Springs® *(p168)*.

Gigantic space exhibits suspended aloft at the Orlando Science Center

Roadside Attractions

Road trips are a great way to explore Florida, and with quirky roadside attractions along many routes there are lots of great places to stretch your legs while enjoying some family fun. Don't miss a stop at the fantastical Weeki Wachee Springs State Park *(p278)* if you're passing by.

→

A mermaid in a Weeki Wachee Springs State Park underwater theater show

Fun in the Sun

Florida has miles of family-friendly beaches, from the white sands of Siesta Key *(p276)* to the serene stretches of Amelia Island *(p219)*. Florida's spring pools – like those at Alexander Springs and Silver Glen Springs in the Ocala National Forest *(p226)* – are fabulous spots for a dip and a picnic.

↑ Children playing in the cool water of Alexander Springs

Live Entertainment

If you're only focused on the rides, you'll end up missing half the fun at Florida's theme parks. Expect Broadway-style musicals with rousing scores throughout the parks, especially in Orlando where film and cartoon characters walk the streets. Both Walt Disney World® Resort and Universal Orlando Resort™ come alive after dark, when The Nighttime Lights At Hogwarts™ Castle brings magical revelry to The Wizarding World of Harry Potter™, and fireworks soar atop the Cinderella Castle during Happily Ever After in Disney's Magic Kingdom®.

→

The colorful parade – a daily event at Disney's Magic Kingdom®

FLORIDA'S
THEME PARKS

With this much fun packed into one area, Orlando is essentially the unofficial theme park capital of the world, with Walt Disney World® Resort's mix of storybook splendor and pop-culture adventure; Universal Orlando® Resort's on-screen experiences; plus LEGOLAND® and SeaWorld®.

Wild Rides

Brave the eye-popping inversions of The Incredible Hulk Coaster® in Universal's Islands of Adventure™ and the blood-curdling drop of the The Twilight Zone Tower of Terror at Disney's Hollywood Studios®. The fastest coaster is SeaWorld® Orlando's Mako, but rides like Harry Potter and the Escape from Gringotts™ at Universal Studios Florida™ guarantee something for every type of adrenaline junkie.

STAY

When you stay at a hotel in one of Orlando's theme park resorts, the fun never has to end. The exotic fantasy worlds and the magic of the movies extend far beyond the theme park gates and right to your room.

Universal's Cabana Bay Beach Resort
Ⓐ F3 Ⓝ 6550 Adventure Way, Orlando
Ⓦ loewshotels.com/ cabana-bay-hotel

Ⓢ Ⓢ Ⓢ

Disney's Animal Kingdom Lodge
Ⓐ F3 Ⓝ 2901 Osceola Pkwy, Orlando
Ⓦ disneyworld.disney. go.com/resorts

Ⓢ Ⓢ Ⓢ

← Mickey Mouse in his party attire on a Disney parade float

← The Incredible Hulk Coaster® on Marvel Super Hero Island

Movie Magic
See blockbusters come to life with special effects shows, ground-breaking attractions, and entire themed lands to explore. Walk below the floating mountains of Avatar's otherworldly Pandora in Disney's Animal Kingdom®, explore the thrills of Jurassic Park® at Universal's Island of Adventures™, or board the Hogwarts Express™ for a journey to the magical village of Hogsmeade™.

↑ Live action performers thrilling spectators at Universal Studios Florida™

The Cracker Style

Early pioneers built houses mainly from wood, and employed designs that maximized ventilation. One of the best surviving examples is the McMullen Log House, in Pinellas County Heritage Village (p264). Original "Cracker" homes, as the style was called, do not survive in great numbers, but the style was a huge influence on Florida's architecture.

←

The McMullen Log House, a typical "Cracker" home in Florida

FLORIDA'S
ARCHITECTURE

Although most people associate Floridian architecture with the Art Deco facades of South Beach, the state boasts a diverse range of styles. Often quirky and striking, the trends reflect Florida's waves of settlement and the aspirations of local luminaries, as well as adaptions for the warm climate.

Boom Years

From the 1920s, a new wave of buildings was designed, setting out to evoke the romance of faraway lands. The movement was comprised of various styles, from the Spanish Revival best represented in the mansions of Palm Beach (p112) to the famous Art Deco buildings (p68) such as The Raleigh, The Delano, and the Carlyle that characterize Miami's South Beach district.

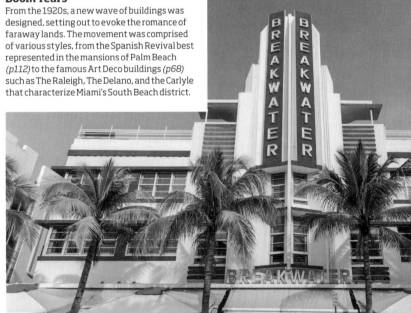

↑ Spiral staircase and the Glass Enigma at the Salvador Dalí Museum

Contemporary Constructions

The last 50 years have seen large-scale projects with daring designs, including shopping malls, public buildings, and sports stadiums. There are also plenty of wonderful, design-forward examples of contemporary architecture, like the Glass Enigma at the Salvador Dalí Museum *(p262)*.

↑ Breakwater Hotel and The Carlyle hotel *(inset)* in South Beach, both fine examples of Art Deco style

The Gilded Age

Toward the end of the 19th century, the railroads and growing tourism industry brought money and new ideas into the region. A more decorative approach reflected the times, and a penchant for Mediterranean Revivalism took hold. The pinnacle of this Gilded Age look is perhaps the Flagler Museum *(p114)* in Palm Beach, a 75-room mansion and exercise in extravagance.

↑ Visitors walking up the palm-lined entrance to the Flagler Museum

Preparing chicken at an annual Hispanic festival in Little Havana ↑

FLORIDA FOR
FOODIES

The Sunshine State has more culinary diversity and depth than you might imagine. The Cuban influence is strong, especially in areas like Little Havana in Miami. Fresh seafood abounds across the state, as do regional classics such as Key lime pie.

Regional Specialties

The most famous example of a true Floridian classic is probably the Key lime pie, a dessert pie made with Key lime juice and topped with meringue. As the name suggests, it's especially popular in the Keys *(p288)* – you'll find one of the best slices at the Old Town Bakery *(930 Eaton St, Key West)*. Florida's alligators also pop up on menus, served as nuggets or the classic gator tail. The Tarpon Springs Greek Salad is also worth trying, made with potato salad, tomatoes, kalamata olives, feta, cucumbers, and pepperoncini.

→

Florida's legendary and tempting Key lime pie, served with fresh lime

Latin American Cuisine

You'll find Caribbean, and Central and South American food in most of the larger cities in Florida, but Miami is certainly the epicenter. In and around the Little Havana neighborhood *(p84)*, there's everything from casual sandwich and coffee shops to food trucks and fine dining restaurants, all selling classic Cuban cuisine. This could be anything from a sandwich – Enriqueta's Sandwich Shops *(186 NE 29th S, Miami)* serves up the best – to *croquetas* (a fried breadcrumbed roll with meat or vegetable filling).

Cuban sandwich filled with pork, ham, Swiss cheese, and dill pickle

INSIDER TIP
Seafood Seasons

Florida's famous stone crab can be enjoyed from October through May. For lobster, it's best to visit between September and December.

EAT

There's a wealth of seafood restaurants all across the Sunshine State, but some are destinations in themselves. Here are some long-time seafood institutions.

Hunt's Oyster Bar & Seafood Restaurant
🏠1150 Beck Ave, Panama City
ⓦfacebook.com/ pearlofhunts

Ⓢ$$

Walt's Fish Market Restaurant
🏠4144 S Tamiami Trail, Sarasota
ⓦwaltsfishmarket restaurant.com

Ⓢ$$

A platter of stone crab claws, oysters and other fresh fish

Fresh Seafood

With its vast coastlines, Florida enjoys an abundance of fresh seafood. All tastes are catered for, with crab, clams, mahi-mahi, oysters, grouper, and rock shrimp to name just a few of the tempting local catches. The Floridian "fish shack" (typically a casual, somewhat weathered small restaurant serving up seafood bought fresh that day) is a true state-wide institution. For the freshest seafood, seek out a fish shack right on the coast, where you'll also be rewarded with stunning ocean views.

DISCOVER Florida Your Way

Freshwater Swamps

We rightly associate this habitat with the Everglades, but swamps can be found all over Florida, including the Ocala National Forest *(p226)*. Bobcats and white ibises are among the local wildlife that can be spotted around the swamplands, as well as small anole lizards and beautiful flowering water lilies. A trip to the wild and wonderful Everglades National Park *(p292)* is an essential Florida experience, whether you take to the water or hike the trails.

→

Stunning native water lilies, most commonly found around Florida's swamplands

FLORIDA'S
WILDLIFE

Florida's varied landscapes are split by two distinct climates – the temperate north and the subtropical south. The result is a fascinating mix of scenery, with coastal areas, forests, and swamps. The animal and plant life are similarly diverse, and migratory birds flock here in the winter.

Pine Flatwoods

Myakka River State Park *(p286)* is a classic example of this common Floridian landscape. Around half of the state is covered in these areas of tall pine trees towering over plants and shrubs. White-tailed deer can be spotted in pine flatwood areas (if you're lucky), as well as pygmy rattlesnakes and red-bellied woodpeckers.

←

A fortunate sighting of a white-tailed deer exploring pine flatwood areas

The American white ibis with its beautiful white feathers and red bill

Deep in the Forest

Besides the beaches, Florida is also surrounded by verdant regions of forests. There are some quirky North American animals to be spotted in these environments, such as wild turkeys, armadillos, and opossums. Florida's State Forests, such as Blackwater River State *(p247)* are typically well-maintained with easy-to-follow trails and recreational activities on offer.

A nine-banded armadillo surveying the land

💬 **INSIDER TIP**
Visiting the Everglades
The best time to visit the Everglades National Park is in the dry season, from December through April. There are various park entrances with visitor centers where you can pick up information about hiking trails or boat trips.

Coastal Critters

Florida's coastal regions can be exposed to extremes of weather, but this doesn't diminish the richness of landscapes and the truly beautiful scenery. Wading birds are a familiar sight along the sand dunes and lagoons around the coast, but look up to catch bald eagles, particularly around Cape Canaveral *(p202)*. Horseshoe crabs are among the more unusual local shellfish, emerging from the ocean to breed in the springtime around the Nature Coast of Florida, south from the Panhandle *(p230)*.

← The iconic American bald eagle perched on a mangrove bush in Florida

FLORIDA FOR
CULTURE

There's a rich cultural life beyond the theme parks, spring break parties, and sporting events. Statewide there are arts, music, food, and heritage festivals, plus world-class performance venues. From Art Basel to jazz clubs and a wealth of museums, it's easy to find your cultural fix.

Fascinating Museums

From the academic and serious to the fun and whimsical, Florida is peppered with a generous helping of great museums. The Jewish Museum of Florida *(p74)* is a wonderful tour through local Jewish history and culture. On the quirkier side is the Pirate and Treasure Museum in St. Augustine *(p210)*. To the south, the WonderWorks Orlando *(p198)* and Orlando Science Center *(p188)* are interactive educational alternatives to the city's theme parks.

→

The intriguing and photo-worthy facade
of WonderWorks Orlando

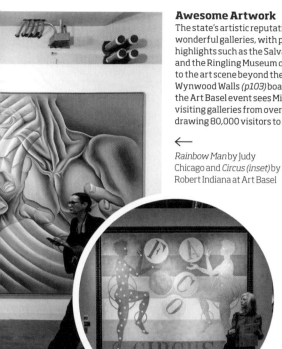

Awesome Artwork

The state's artistic reputation is thanks in part to its wonderful galleries, with prestigious and unmissable highlights such as the Salvador Dalí Museum *(p262)* and the Ringling Museum of Art *(p272)*. But there's more to the art scene beyond the brilliant institutions. The Wynwood Walls *(p103)* boast exciting street art, and the Art Basel event sees Miami play host to over 300 visiting galleries from over 30 countries around the world, drawing 80,000 visitors to the city every December.

←

Rainbow Man by Judy Chicago and *Circus (inset)* by Robert Indiana at Art Basel

ART DISTRICTS

Miami has a robust art scene, and two of its neighborhoods characterize different art movements. The Miami Design District, in the Buena Vista neighborhood, boasts a number of high-end galleries among the designer boutiques. Here, the Institute of Contemporary Art is a venue for cutting edge exhibitions. Nearby, Wynwood is an up-and-coming neighborhood known for its street art.

Fantastic Festivals

Florida's warm climate makes it the perfect place to enjoy festivals at any time of year *(p42)*. Music lovers should visit in March, for the acclaimed Orlando Jazz Festival and Miami's Winter Music Conference, a week of electronic music. There's the huge South Beach Food and Wine Festival in February for foodies, and for a romantic evening the St. Augustine Night of Lights sees the city aglow November through January.

↑ The glittering St. Augustine Night of Lights festival illuminating the city

Hike the Trails

Woodlands and forests cover a large proportion of Florida's landscape, so it's little wonder that hiking is such a popular activity. The state has 5,000 miles of hiking trails, with something for all abilities and interests. For spectacular scenery, Big Cypress National Preserve *(p305)* has raw beauty and a chance to spot the rare Florida panther.

Hiking in Big Cypress Swamp National Preserve

FLORIDA
OUTDOORS

The state's warm climate means that most of Floridian life is led outdoors. Days lounging at the beach are hugely popular, but there are plenty of opportunities to be more active, with water sports aplenty. For inland activities, you can discover world-class golf courses or scenic hiking trails.

Wet and Wild

Florida's abundant coastline and inland waterways mean that there's plenty of opportunities for swimming and deep-sea fun. Scuba divers and snorkelers can explore clear waters and shipwrecks, Key Largo *(p306)* being generally regarded as one of the best dive sites in the United States.

→

Diver exploring the incredible Benwood Wreck site at Key Largo

INSIDER TIP
Take a Paddle

The mangroves, reefs, and beaches of the Florida Keys are great for paddle-boarding. Enjoy sublime experiences *(www.paddle thefloridakeys.com)* in Key Largo and Islamorada.

Set Sail

Most coastal cities and towns around Florida have boat trips on offer, and you can enjoy everything from dolphin watching to relaxing on luxury yachts. Pensacola *(p234)* is one of the state's main sailing centers, with lots of opportunities for fun out on the water.

→

Enjoying the beautiful sunset from a sail boat in the Gulf of Mexico

A Golfer's Paradise

Florida has more golf courses than any other state, and the climate makes it a joy to play at any time of year. Many clubs are open to the public and some have wonderful coastal views. Check out TCP Sawgrass (Ponte Vedra Beach) and World Woods (Brooksville).

←

Young golfer playing on a sunny day

Fishing Fever

Florida is a hotspot for fishing fans from all over the word, offering high-adrenaline sports fishing out on the ocean, to more tranquil days fishing off a pier or jetty. Islamorada *(p308)* is one of the best spots in the state, while Key West *(p298)* and Key Largo *(p306)* are good for tarpon and even sharks.

→

Offshore deep-sea fishing off Key West

A YEAR IN
FLORIDA

JANUARY

△ **Art Deco Weekend** (mid-Jan). A street party in the art deco area of Miami Beach.

Downtown Venice Craft Festival (late Jan). Venice spruces up its downtown streets for this popular crafts bazaar.

FEBRUARY

Florida State Fair (early Feb). This fair in Tampa features a range of carnival rides and big-name performers.

△ **Coconut Grove Arts Festival** (mid-Feb). An avant-garde art show in Miami that's one of the country's largest.

MAY

△ **Jacksonville Jazz Festival** (late May). Art and craft exhibitions mixed with three days of international jazz.

Tampa Bay Margarita Festival (late May). Performances by renowned artists and plenty of margaritas, as well as tasty bites to soak them up.

JUNE

Fiesta of Five Flags (early Jun). Pensacola plays host to two weeks of parades, marathons, and rodeos, plus the reenactment of Tristán de Luna's beach landing in 1559.

△ **Watermelon Festival** (3rd weekend). The harvest in Monticello is celebrated with barbecues and hoedowns.

SEPTEMBER

△ **St. Augustine's Founding Anniversary** (1st or 2nd Sat). A period-dress reenactment of the Spanish landing in 1565 is held near the spot where the first European settlers first set foot.

OCTOBER

△ **John's Pass Seafood & Music Festival** (late Oct). This popular festival attracts seafood lovers to John's Pass Village at Madeira Beach.

MARCH

△ **Carnaval Miami** (*early Mar*). Ten days of Latin American Miami festivities, with beauty pageants, sports, food, and concerts. The Calle Ocho street festival finale is the largest in the world.

Miami International Film Festival (*early Mar*). The Miami Film Society showcases independent American and international movies over 10 days.

APRIL

△ **Easter** (*Mar/Apr*). Take carriage rides around St. Augustine and celebrate sunrise services at the Castillo de San Marcos.

Conch Republic Celebration (*mid-Apr*). Party all week in Key West with parades, bed races, and dancing – all in honor of the town's founding fathers.

JULY

△ **America's Birthday Bash** (*Jul 4*). Picnics and family fun in Miami are followed by midnight fireworks at south Florida's largest Independence Day celebration.

Hemingway Days (*mid-Jul*). Key West offers a week of author signings, short-story contests, theatrical productions, and an entertaining Hemingway look-alike contest.

AUGUST

△ **Key West Lobsterfest** (*early Aug*). Live music, cold drinks, and fresh lobster at this end-of-summer party, wrapped up with Sunday brunch.

Boca Festival Days (*throughout Aug*). A fun-filled month in Boca Raton, with highlights including an arts-and-craft fair, barber-shop quartet performances, and a sand castle-building contest.

NOVEMBER

Florida Seafood Festival (*1st weekend*). A blessing of the fishing fleet, oyster-shucking contests, and plenty of seafood in Apalachicola.

△ **Miami Book Fair** (*mid-Nov*). Publishers, authors, and bookworms congregate for this cultural highlight.

DECEMBER

△ **Winterfest Boat Parade** (*early Dec*). Boats decked with lights cruise the Intracoastal Waterway at Fort Lauderdale in a magical night-time display.

St. Augustine Colonial Night Watch (*early Dec*). A torchlight parade through the old town, from the Castillo de San Marcos to the City Gate.

1

A BRIEF
HISTORY

Behind Florida's modern veneer lies a long and rich past, molded by many different nationalities and cultures. Tourism has driven development since the mid-20th century, but not without consequences for the Sunshine State's rich natural environment.

First Inhabitants

Humans first arrived in Florida after the last Ice Age and for some 11,500 years were split into many small groups. Some remained nomadic hunter-gatherers, while others developed permanent settlements along Florida's rivers and rich seaboard.

Spanish Florida

After sighting Florida in 1513, the Spanish were the first Europeans to colonize the region, introducing Christianity, horses, and cattle. The brutality of the conquistadors, plus

1 An illustration of West Palm Beach from 1915.

2 General Andrew Jackson with members of his troop.

3 Seminoles during the First Seminole War.

4 *Building of Castillo de San Marcos,* Mort Künstler (1966).

Timeline of events

8000–1000 BC

Horr's Island is the largest of numerous communities in Florida during the Archaic period.

500 BC

The Archaic culture begins to develop into regional tribes, the ancestors of the Ais, Calusa, Jaega Apalachee, Tequesta, Timucua and other Indigenous peoples.

1200–1500

Fort Walton and Pensacola cultures flourish on the Panhandle, antecedents of the Apalachee.

1513

Ponce de León becomes the first European to lay eyes on Florida; he unsuccessfully tries to establish a Spanish colony eight years later.

1565

Spanish Conquistador Pedro Menéndez de Avilés establishes St. Augustine, the first permanent European settlement in the Americas.

European diseases, decimated the Indigenous population. Florida changed hands several times between the Spanish and British throughout the 18th century, returning under Spanish control by the end of the American Revolution.

The Seminole Wars and Civil War

During the 1800s, the US saw conflict with Florida's Seminoles three times. In 1816 American Andrew Jackson attacked the Seminoles people for harboring those who escaped slavery, a war that led to Florida becoming part of the US by 1821. As American settlement quickened pace, the government passed the Indian Removal Act, which aimed to forcibly move all Native Americans west of the Mississippi River. The resulting conflicts developed into the Second and Third Seminole Wars.

By the mid-1800s, enslaved people formed over a third of Florida's population, most working on cotton plantations. After Abraham Lincoln – an opponent of slavery – was elected president in 1860, Florida seceded from the Union, helping to form the Confederate States. The ensuing Civil War saw victory for the Union and the end of slavery in Florida.

↑ Statue of Pedro Menéndez de Avilés, founder of St. Augustine

1816–19
The First Seminole War. The Second and Third Seminole Wars followed in 1835-42 and 1855-8 respectively.

1821
Florida is transferred from Spain to the US; Andrew Jackson is the first governor.

1845
On July 4 Florida becomes the 27th state of the USA.

1763
The Spanish trade Florida with Britain in return for Havana, Cuba.

1775–83
The American Revolutionary War; British-held Florida is ceded to the Spanish once again.

Florida's Golden Age

Florida's economy was devastated after the Civil War, but its fine climate and small population made it ripe for investment. Railroad barons Henry Flagler and Henry Plant forged their lines down the east and west coasts of Florida during the late 1880s and 1890s, and luxurious hotels attracted tourists in increasing numbers, stimulating the economy. A diverse agricultural base also sheltered Florida from the depression of the 1890s. However, beginning in the 1870s, segregation was imposed in Florida, and the Ku Klux Klan was revived in Tallahassee in 1915.

Boom, Bust, and Recovery

During the first half of the 20th century, Florida experienced both rapid growth and depression. Northerners poured in, excited by the rampant development during the 1920s land boom, but a real estate slump ruined many in the state in 1926, followed by further financial disasters during the Great Depression a few years later. Economic recovery came earlier than in the rest of the US, however, with the growth of tourism and the introduction of Federal relief schemes.

1 A Florida East Coast Railway engine.

2 A family in a migrant camp during the Great Depression.

3 Apollo XV launching from the Kennedy Space Center.

Did You Know?

In the 20th century Florida became the largest citrus producer in the country, helping it to survive the Great Depression.

Timeline of events

1886
Flagler starts construction of the Florida East Coast Railway.

1926
Florida land prices crash, two banks collapse, and a hurricane hits the southeast and the Everglades, devastating Miami 1939.

1958
The first Earth satellite, Explorer I, is launched from Florida after NASA chooses Cape Canaveral as the site of its NASA satellite and rocket programs.

1964
Civil rights activist Martin Luther King Jr. is arrested and imprisoned in St. Augustine.

3

The 1960s and Beyond

Tourism expanded at an unprecedented rate from 1960. Attractions such as Walt Disney World®, Universal Studios®, and the Kennedy Space Center – home to NASA's space program – brought worldwide fame and crowds of visitors. The population also grew rapidly, through migration from within the US and from abroad, particularly Cuba, as many Hispanic people fled to Florida during the Castro regime (1959–2016).

Florida Today

Tourism continues to boom, with the state welcoming record numbers almost every year. Economic inequalities have led to social problems, however, and the state's urbanization has put a severe strain on the environment. Conservation has become a major issue, as year-on-year the state witnesses the results of climate change – all of which have immediate and long-term effects on the state's economic foundations: tourism and agriculture. Despite this, Florida is still known for fun, beaches, and sunshine, and draws in vacationers from near and far.

THE CIVIL RIGHTS MOVEMENT

The 1956 Tallahassee bus boycott started the Civil Rights Movement in Florida, with protests taking place throughout the state. Though Florida was desegregated after 1965, racist attitudes remained. In 2013, George Zimmerman was acquitted of killing 17-year-old African American Trayvon Martin, leading to a national debate about racial profiling.

1971

The Magic Kingdom®, Walt Disney's first venture in Florida, opens in Orlando at a cost of $700 million.

2000

Florida becomes the focus of the entire nation during the presidential election; various controversies result in a vote recount in several counties.

2018

17 people were killed in a mass shooting at Stoneman Douglas High School - Florida enacts stricter gun controls.

2017

Hurricane Irma wreaks havoc in Florida; over 6 million people evacuate their homes, the largest evacuation in the state's history.

← Martin Lawrence and Will Smith in the action comedy film *Bad Boys*

A BRIEF HISTORY
ON SCREEN

Florida has provided a backdrop to a plethora of iconic and beloved films and TV series over the years. While exploring Florida's cities, beaches, and cultural offerings, you'll no doubt be reminded of a favorite old flick or find inspiration for a new series to binge-watch back at home.

The blue skies, scenic natural landscapes, and cool beach-side cities provide a serene backdrop that contrasts perfectly with Florida's on-screen bread and butter: crime and action. If explosions aren't really your thing, you'll likely still recognize Florida from many family favorites or TV sitcoms.

There's so much variety in the culture and landscapes of Florida that the state is equally perfect playing party central in films like *Magic Mike* (2012), as well as being home to personal dramas including the Oscar-winning *Moonlight* (2016).

↑ Nathan Lane and Robin Williams working on *The Birdcage*

TV and movie guide

1946
The Yearling

1964
Flipper

1983
Scarface

1984–89
Miami Vice

1994
Ace Ventura: Pet Detective

1996
The Birdcage

FILMING LOCATIONS

① *Ace Ventura Pet Detective*, Marlins Park

② *Moonlight*, Virginia Key Beach

③ *Scarface*, Ocean Drive

④ *There's Something About Mary*, Matheson Hammock Park

⑤ *Miami Vice*, South Beach

⑥ *The Birdcage*, Lincoln Road

⑦ *Bad Boys*, The Biltmore Miami - Coral Gables

⑧ *Goldfinger*, Fontainebleau Miami Beach

⑨ *2 Fast 2 Furious*, South Miami Avenue Bridge

0 kilometers 4
0 miles 4

N ↑

MIAMI VICE

Miami Vice, a hit TV series about a pair of undercover cops, is an icon of its time. The show had a huge impact on contemporary culture and greatly influenced the future of television with its use of a cool pop soundtrack and cinematic style. The series was largely filmed in Miami, unlike a lot of recent TV shows that are set here but filmed in LA.

2003
2 Fast 2 Furious

2002–12
CSI: Miami

2017
The Florida Project

1998
There's Something About Mary, Wild Things, Great Expectations (Ca' d'Zan)

2008
Marley & Me

2016
Moonlight

2013
Spring Breakers

EXPERIENCE
MIAMI

Ocean Drive illuminated at night

EXPLORE
MIAMI

This guide divides Miami into two color-coded sightseeing areas, as shown here, and an area beyond the city center. Find out more about each area on the following pages.

LITTLE HAITI

WYNWOOD

OVERTOWN

LITTLE HAVANA

WEST MIAMI

Woodlawn Cemetery

DOWNTOWN AND CORAL GABLES
p80

Coral Gables City Hall

Miracle Mile

Vizcaya Museum And Gardens

Biltmore Hotel

CORAL GABLES

Cocowalk

COCONUT GROVE

Miami City Hall

University of Miami

Lowe Art Museum

Biscayne Bay

SOUTH MIAMI

SUNSET ACRES

0 kilometers   2

0 miles   2

N ↑

MORNINGSIDE

CENTRAL
MIAMI BEACH

BAYSHORE

Bass Museum
of Art

*Miami
Beach*

*Venetian
Islands*

MIAMI BEACH
p64

Pérez Art
Museum Miami

SOUTH
BEACH

*Atlantic
Ocean*

Bayside
Market Place

*Miami
Beach*

DOWNTOWN

*Dodge
Island*

South Pointe
Park

BRICKELL

*Virginia
Key*

FLORIDA

*Crandon
Park*

*Key
Biscayne*

KEY
BISCAYNE

MIAMI

*Bill Baggs
Cape Florida
State Park*

GETTING TO KNOW
MIAMI

With its world-class beaches, pastel-colored Art Deco architecture, and pulsating nightlife, Miami is Florida's most glamorous city. There's also a robust cultural scene, with Little Havana adding a vibrant Cuban influence, and up-and-coming neighborhoods like Wynwood keeping things exciting.

MIAMI BEACH

PAGE 64

Technically a separate city, this island is still a Miami area highlight. The stunning Art Deco buildings along Ocean Drive are as colorful as the people you're likely to see here, where the young and the beautiful flock to enjoy beaches, shopping, food, and nightlife. South Beach (or SoBe) is particularly famous for the retro look, the alluring sands, and the high-end fashion boutiques. But it's not all frivolous fun here: there's some depth to the area, too, with an array of thought-provoking museums and annual art festivals to add to the cultural life of the neighborhood.

Best for
Sun, art, and Art Deco architecture

Home to
Ocean Drive

Experience
Strolling down Collins Avenue before spending an evening in a hip SoBe bar

PAGE 80

DOWNTOWN AND CORAL GABLES

The modernity of Downtown Miami with its steel-and-glass skyscrapers and neon skyline eventually gives way to the charm of Little Havana. Here, in a neighborhood that dates back to the late 1950s, Cuban music, food, and culture take over. To the south, Coral Gables – a separate city but a key part of Miami's history – is an elegant escape full of Mediterranean-style buildings and scenic streets, a city dreamed up by real estate developer George Merrick in the 1920s.

Best for
Nightlife, culture, and food

Home to
Little Havana and Vizcaya Museum and Gardens

Experience
Enjoying the perfect Cuban sandwich as you listen to live Latin music in Little Havana

PAGE 98

BEYOND THE CENTER

There are plenty of reasons to set out beyond the confines of the central districts and explore Miami's outer neighborhoods. Wynwood Arts District is a case in point, its vibrant street art scene having given rise to a cool, up-and-coming area with an array of eclectic galleries, bars, and restaurants. Bal Harbour and the North Beaches offer relative respite from the crowds of South Beach, and near the latter is the impressive reconstructed Ancient Spanish Monastery.

Best for
Beautiful views and history

Home to
The Ancient Spanish Monastery

Experience
Admiring the Downtown Miami skyline from Rickenbacker Causeway as you head to the beaches at Key Biscayne

→

1 Soaring palm trees and buildings at Miami Beach.

2 A South Beach lifeguard station.

3 Palm-shaded al fresco restaurant.

4 Installation by Julio Le Parc at the Perez Art Museum during the 2016 Art Basel Miami.

3 DAYS
in Miami

Day 1

Morning Start your day on Ocean Drive (p68) to marvel at the vividly restored Art Deco buildings that line the street. Call in at The Wolfsonian-Florida International University (p74) on Washington Avenue, once a warehouse where, in the 1920s, the wealthy stored their valuables during hot, humid summers when they fled north. Now it's a museum of the decorative arts.

Afternoon Spend some time walking along the shore of Miami's stunning beach (p76), admiring the colorful lifeguard stations and beautiful ocean vistas. Pick a spot and settle in for a few hours of soaking up the sun – maybe taking a dip in the water if you can tear yourself away from the luxury of doing nothing at all.

Evening Find a hotel with seafront dining to end your day, like the Ocean Grill at the Setai Hotel (p74), then take a walk along the shoreline to commune barefoot with the surf.

Day 2

Morning Breakfast in Little Havana (p84) at El Rey De Las Fritas on Calle Ocho, then head west to Brickell Key, a perfect artificial triangular island of jogging tracks. Look out over the water for superb skyscraper views of downtown Miami.

Afternoon Find lunch in the charming old Financial District at Eurostars Langford Hotel (www.eurostarshotels.com), built in the 1920s for the Miami Bank & Trust. Then travel north to the Perez Museum (p88) on Biscayne Boulevard, with its 2,000 works of art and then take the bus to the modern Institute of Contemporary Art (p104), one of Miami's most experimental art spaces.

Evening Head back into Little Havana for genuine Cuban nightlife at the Cubaocho Museum & Performing Arts Center (p84), before popping into Versailles (p85) for some late night coconut flan or guava cheesecake.

Day 3

Morning Start with breakfast in the Fontana at the Biltmore (p92), a great opportunity to look around this classic Prohibition-era hotel, now restored to its splendid 1920s color scheme. Afterward, take your time driving around the Coral Gables estate (p96). There's a wider range of architectural styles han first seems apparent – seven in all, including Chinese and South African. Be sure to stop by George Merrick's own house and take time out for a dip in the Rococo Venetian Pool (p90).

Afternoon Pull in by Coral Gables City Hall (p90) to snap the statue of George Merrick, the visionary who created this inland resort from a swamp. Then head east down his Miracle Mile (p90) and on to Vizcaya (p86), Miami's finest stately home, where James Deering, owner of the famous Deering farm equipment company, once lived.

Evening Enjoy dinner al fresco with splendid views over the Dinner Quay Marina and The Barnacle Historic State Park (p94) at the Panorama Restaurant & Sky Lounge, which sits atop Hotel Arya Coconut Grove (www.hotelaryacg.com). On a clear evening you can see all the way back to the Biltmore.

→
Saks Fifth Avenue, in a tropical setting on Collins Avenue in Bal Harbour

MIAMI FOR
SHOPPERS

Miami is all about glamour, and beyond the beaches and nightlife is a chic shopping scene, from the designer names of South Beach to the independent boutiques of Coconut Grove. Find quirky bargains around Wynwood or head for one of the city's huge shopping malls.

Classic Malls

Renowned shopping malls include Aventura Mall (www.aventuramall.com), one of the most visited in the country, with over 300 stores – designer names and high street brands – farmers' markets, and 40 restaurants. Lincoln Road Mall (p76), a pedestrian road between 16th and 17th streets in Miami Beach, has ten blocks of shopping, dining, and entertainment, and is also the city's oldest mall. Expect discount retailers as well as high street favorites.

Miami's Dadeland Mall, on North Kendall Drive, with around 185 stores ↑

Ultra Chic

Miami Beach is the epicenter for high-end, designer stores. To the north, Bal Harbour Shops (p102) is a three-story mall that boasts such familiar names as Neiman Marcus, Prada, and Versace. There are luxe spots across the bridge, too, such as En Avance (www.enavance.co), an elegant showcase of global designers. This store is part of Miami's rapidly growing Design District (p39), which has been populated in recent years by the likes of Cartier and Louis Vuitton. To the south, Coconut Grove (p92) is more laid back, reflected in the beachwear at Nikki's Beachhouse Boutique (nikkisbeachhouse. com). Here too is Brickell City Centre (www. brickellcitycentre. com), with outlets for Hugo Boss and Saks Fifth Avenue among other premium brands.

← The tropical al fresco Bal Harbour Shops, full of flora

SHOP

You'll want to pick up some great souvenirs to remind you of your time in Florida, and these classic stores in Miami have a particularly good selection of items to take home.

Art Deco Welcome Center
🅐G6 🅐1001 Ocean Drive 🅦artdeco welcomecenter.com

Caribbean Life
🅐G6 🅐401 Biscayne Blvd 🅒(305) 416-9695

Edwin Watts Golf
🅐G6 🅐15999 Biscayne Blvd 🅦worldwidegolf shops.com

El Titan de Bronze
🅐G6 🅐1071 SW 8th St 🅦titandebronze.com

INSIDER TIP
Weekend Rush

Miami's biggest malls are best enjoyed on weekdays – not only to avoid the crowds and exasperatingly long lines, but also to ensure a parking spot. If you can't avoid weekend shopping, head out early.

Quirky Boutiques

The city's artsy areas have unusual finds. Wynwood (p103) has great places like Boho Hunter (www.boho hunter.com), with fashions from Latin American designers. Frangipani (www. frangipanimiami.com) has handmade accessories, while the Mimo Market Clothing Boutique (www.mimomarket. com) carries eclectic clothing. Sweat Records (www.sweat recordsmiami.com) in Little Haiti has hip vinyl.

↑ Visitors shopping at one of the whimsical shops in the Wynwood neighborhood

Performing Arts

Miami's rich arts scene has top productions year round. The Adrienne Arsht Center for the Performing Arts *(www.arshtcenter.org)* is home to Miami City Ballet; the Olympia Theater *(www.olympiatheater.org)* retains its 1920s architecture; and for classical music, the New World Center *(www.nws.edu)* is as good as it gets.

A performance at the Frank Gehry-designed New World Center

MIAMI
AFTER DARK

Miami's nightlife is legendary. Visitors come from all over the world to sample the city's many nightclubs, and the party atmosphere permeates the city after dark. There's much more to discover, though, with all kinds of performing arts, from live Latin bands to opera and ballet.

Late Night Parties

Brave the long lines and strict door policies and you'll get to experience the full Miami nightclub experience. The city is rightly known as a place to party, and the clubs do not disappoint, with state-of-the-art hospitality and world-famous DJs. Some clubs start in the daytime - Nikki Beach *(www.nikkibeach.com)* is the place where the young lounge and dance all day. After dark, the crowds head to any of the nightclubs around South Beach, Downtown, and Coconut Grove. Among the most popular is LIV, a "mega" nightclub at the Fontainebleau Hotel *(www.fontainebleau.com)*. STORY *(www.storymiami.com)* is an equally opulent venue, with spectacular lighting.

Live Music

Ocean Drive has a host of bars that have live bands, and on any one night you'll hear jazz, reggae, salsa, and Latin music. The best venues for jazz are The Globe *(www.theglobe cafe.com)* in Coral Gables and the High Note Jazz Club *(www.thehighnotejazz.com)* at Cuba Ocho. For Latin music great Cuban musicians play at Mango's Tropical Cafe *(www.mangos.com)* in South Beach.

→

Mango's Tropical Cafe and one of their popular live reggae music sets *(inset)*

DRINK

While the city offers plenty of cool, late night spots, these are some of the best. Expect a lively atmosphere and a range of brilliant drink options at all of these locations.

Bodega Taqueria y Tequila
Ⓐ G6 Ⓐ 1220 16th St
Ⓦ bodegataqueria.com

La Sandwicherie
Ⓐ G6 Ⓐ 229 14th St
Ⓦ lasandwicherie.com

Lost Weekend
Ⓐ G6 Ⓐ 218 Española Way Ⓦ sub-culture.org/lost-weekend-miami

↑ STORY nightclub has top DJs and state-of-the-art sound and light systems

New Perspectives

Every city has its over-touristy viewpoints and Miami is no different. Seek out these little-known spots for a new perspective on the city. Bayside Marketplace *(p89)* has great city views, especially when there are fireworks at night. The best sunset views are generally at Maurice Gibb Memorial Park *(18th St & Purdy Avenue)*, though South Pointe Park *(p68)* and Pier are also spectacular. Cityscapes from the Venetian Causeway never fail to be impressive, nor do the sensational views from Hobie Island Beach Park, on Virginia Key.

→

Waterfront at Bayside Marketplace, overlooked by the city's buildings

MIAMI'S
HIDDEN GEMS

Many visitors to Miami head for its most famous spots, meaning that the main thoroughfares in South Beach and Downtown can get crowded. If you're looking for a little more personal space, then it's well worth breaking away from the masses and seeking out these lesser-known locations.

Secret Escapes

Compared to other large American cities, Miami isn't particularly blessed with green spaces, but, with a little effort, some beautiful spots can be found. South of Coral Gables are the Pinecrest Gardens *(www.pinecrestgardens. org)*, and Crandon Park Gardens on Key Biscayne *(p102)* is a tranquil, leafy escape. Brickell Park and Morningside Park are also worth visiting.

→

The idyllic and peaceful Hammock Pavilion at the Pinecrest Gardens

← Entrance of the Bayside Marketplace, dotted with kiosks

↑ Part of Simon Ma's *Heart, Water, Ink* exhibition at the Frost Museum of Art

Culture Spots

There's culture to be found beyond the larger museums in Miami, and some of the lesser-known institutions round out the city's arts scene nicely. The Patricia & Phillip Frost Art Museum *(www.frost.fiu.edu)* showcases Latin American and American art, while the World Erotic Art Museum *(www. weam.com)* contains 400 exhibits ranging from Rembrandt to Mapplethorpe. The Museum of Art and Design at Miami Dade College *(www.mdcmoad.org)* shows cutting-edge visual art.

MIAMI BEACH

Often referred to as the American Riviera, Miami Beach was once a sandbar accessible only by boat. It was the building of a bridge to the mainland in 1913 that enabled real estate investors such as millionaire Carl Fisher to begin developing the island. The resort they created took off in the 1920s, becoming a spectacular winter playground. The devastating hurricane of 1926 and the 1929 Wall Street Crash signaled the end of the boom, but Miami Beach bounced back in the 1930s with the erection of hundreds of Art Deco buildings.

As a result of a spirited preservation campaign, South Beach has been given a new lease on life. It boasts the world's largest concentration of Art Deco buildings, a beautiful array of structures made of clean lines, bright colors, and neon lights. Anything goes in South Beach, where the mood veers between the chic and the laid-back, hence its nickname SoBe – after New York's hip SoHo district. The Art Deco hotels along Ocean Drive are everyone's favorite haunt, but there are other diversions, from trendy shops to art museums. The district north of SoBe is less popular as a leisure spot, but what the two areas do share is a superb sandy beach, unbroken for miles.

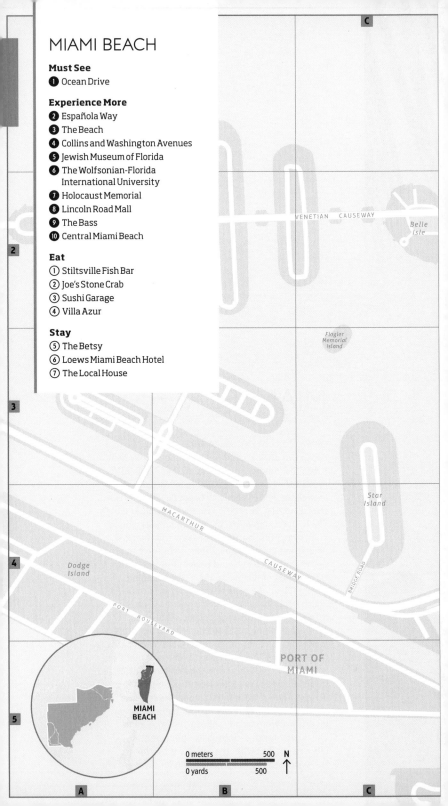

MIAMI BEACH

Must See

① Ocean Drive

Experience More

② Española Way
③ The Beach
④ Collins and Washington Avenues
⑤ Jewish Museum of Florida
⑥ The Wolfsonian-Florida
   International University
⑦ Holocaust Memorial
⑧ Lincoln Road Mall
⑨ The Bass
⑩ Central Miami Beach

Eat

① Stiltsville Fish Bar
② Joe's Stone Crab
③ Sushi Garage
④ Villa Azur

Stay

⑤ The Betsy
⑥ Loews Miami Beach Hotel
⑦ The Local House

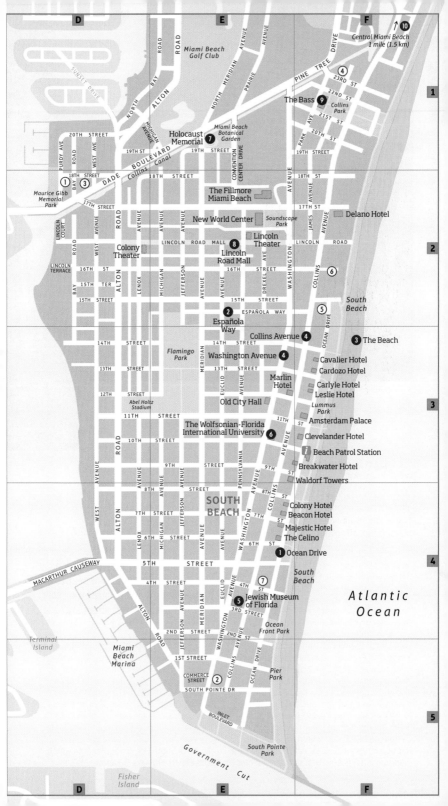

1 🍴 🖥 🛍

OCEAN DRIVE

⚠ E4 ℹ **Art Deco Welcome Center, 1001 Ocean Drive;**
www.mdpl.org

One of the city's best known boulevards, Ocean Drive is home to Miami's best examples of its famous Art Deco architecture *(p70)*. There are some wonderful residences and hotels all within a few blocks that offer fantastic photo opportunities.

Spending time at one of the bars or cafes on the waterfront is arguably the best way to experience Ocean Drive. It is effectively a catwalk for a constant procession of beautiful people and avant-garde outfits; even the street cleaners look cool in their white uniforms, while police officers in skintight shorts cruise past on mountain bikes. But a more active exploration need not involve more than a stroll. At No. 1114 is the 1930 Mediterranean Revival Amsterdam Palace, also known as Casa Casuarina, which the late designer Gianni Versace purchased in 1993 for $3.7 million. This is now a luxury boutique hotel. Nearby, behind the Art Deco Welcome Center, the Beach Patrol Station is a classic Nautical Moderne building, characterized by a maritime influence, with ship's railings along

> **It is effectively a catwalk for a constant procession of beautiful people and avant-garde outfits; even the street cleaners look cool.**

the top and porthole windows; it still functions as the base for local lifeguards. The Waldorf Towers Hotel is another fantastic example of this type of architecture, and led to the coining of the phrase "Nautical Moderne." Its ornamental lighthouse is one of the most evocative examples of Ocean Drive's "architecture for the seashore." There is little to lure visitors south of 6th Street, but from the tip of South Pointe Park you can watch cruise liners entering Government Cut.

900

The number of
preserved properties
in and around
Ocean Drive.

↑ Ocean Drive thoroughfare lined
with Art Deco buildings and
palm trees illuminated at night

CASA CASUARINA

Also known as the
Versace Mansion, this
iconic home on Ocean
Drive was owned by
the legendary fashion
designer from 1992
until 1997, when he
was shot on its front
steps and subsequently
killed. The mansion
was built in Mediter-
ranean Revival style
(p72) and Versace
added grand touches to
it, including 24-karat
gold tiles by the pool.
It opened as a luxury
hotel in 2015, and offers
a fantastic restaurant,
Gianni's, and 10
splendid suites to
choose from.

1 "Eyebrows" – flat overhangs
above the windows at the
Waldorf Towers Hotel – are
ideal for providing shade.

2 The giant planters found
outside Casa Casuarina feature
the Versace Medusa motif.

3 Miami Beach Patrol
Headquarters is a fine example
of the Nautical Moderne style.

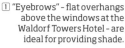

OCEAN DRIVE: DECO STYLE

The cream of South Beach's world-renowned Art Deco District, is found on Ocean Drive. Its splendid array of buildings illustrates Miami's unique interpretation of the Art Deco style, which took the world by storm in the 1920s and 1930s. Florida's version, often called Tropical Deco, is fun and jaunty. Ocean Drive is an evocative neighborhood with an aesthetic that you won't find in many other American cities.

STYLISH ARCHITECTURE

Using inexpensive materials, architects managed to create an impression of stylishness for what were, in fact, very modest hotels. Hotels were often made to look like ocean liners (Nautical Moderne) or given the iconography of speed (Streamline Moderne).

COMMON MOTIFS

Motifs such as flamingos and sunbursts are common, and South Beach's seaside location inspired features more befitting an ocean liner than the hotels of a busy urban center. Bas-relief friezes are also a recurrent decorative element on facades.

↑ Bright facades of Art Deco hotels lining the colorful Ocean Drive

Windows are often continuous around corners.

White, blue, and green were popular colors in the 1930s and 1940s; they echo Miami's tropical vegetation and the ocean.

Circles as windows were inspired by portholes used in ship design.

The lobby of the Majestic has splendid brass elevator doors.

Neon was used to outline architectural elements.

Ocean Drive

The Celino (1937)

Henry Hohauser, the most famous architect to work in Miami, designed this hotel. It has fine etched windows.

Imperial (1939)

The design of the Imperial echoes that of the earlier nautical themed Park Central next door.

Majestic (1940)

This hotel was the work of Albert Anis, the architect responsible for designing a vast collection of hotels on Ocean Drive including the nearby Avalon and Waldorf.

ART DECO: FROM PARIS TO MIAMI

The Art Deco style emerged following the 1925 Exposition Internationale des Arts Décoratifs et Industriels Modernes in Paris. Traditional Art Deco combined influences from Art Nouveau's flowery forms and Egyptian imagery, to the geometric patterns of Cubism. In 1930s America, Art Deco buildings reflected the belief that technology was the way forward, absorbing features that embodied the Machine Age and the fantasies of science fiction. Art Deco evolved into a style called Streamline Moderne, which dominates Ocean Drive. South Beach's buildings showcase a unique mix of classic Art Deco details with creative tropical motifs.

1 The neon sign of the Colony Hotel.

2 A geometric top facade of a hotel.

3 Ornate Tropical Deco design found on Ocean Drive.

4 Tall palm trees running parallel to pretty pastel hotels.

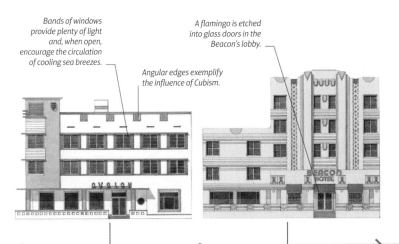

Bands of windows provide plenty of light and, when open, encourage the circulation of cooling sea breezes.

A flamingo is etched into glass doors in the Beacon's lobby.

Angular edges exemplify the influence of Cubism.

Avalon (1941)

The Avalon is a fine example of Streamline Moderne. The lack of ornamentation and the asymmetrical design are typical, as is the emphasis on horizontal as opposed to vertical lines. The Avalon comprimises two hotels on opposite corners of 7th Street.

Beacon (1936)

The traditional abstract decoration above the ground floor windows of the Beacon has been brightened by a contemporary color scheme, an example of Leonard Horowitz's Deco Dazzle. The Beacon was architect Henry O. Nelson's only creation on Ocean Drive.

DIFFERENTIATING THE ART DECO STYLES

Three principal styles exist in South Beach: traditional Art Deco, the more futuristic Streamline Moderne, and Mediterranean Revival, which is derived from French, Italian, and Spanish architecture. The unusual injection of Mediterranean Revival influences along Ocean Drive is noticeable mainly between 9th and 13th streets. It is here that visitors will find some of South Beach's best-known Art Deco buildings, so it's worth taking the time to wander down these streets. Even a short walk proves highly rewarding as you will pass by the various features that define each style, including chic, evocative signs, windows, and friezes.

> **You will pass by the various features that define each style, including chic, evocative signs.**

↑ Hotel Breakwater's Nautical-themed tower soaring above the palm trees

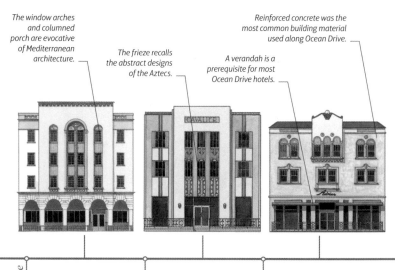

The window arches and columned porch are evocative of Mediterranean architecture.

The frieze recalls the abstract designs of the Aztecs.

A verandah is a prerequisite for most Ocean Drive hotels.

Reinforced concrete was the most common building material used along Ocean Drive.

Ocean Drive

Edison (1935)

Hohauser (p70) experimented here with Mediterranean Revivalism, although he was preceded by the architect of the nearby Adrian, Henry Moloney.

Cavalier (1936)

With its sharp edges and variety of colors, this traditional Art Deco hotel provides quite a contrast to the rounded lines of the Cardozo next door.

Adrian (1934)

With its subdued colors, intricate stucco work, and chiefly Mediterranean inspiration, the Adrian stands out among neighboring buildings.

PRESERVING SOUTH BEACH

The campaign to save the Art Deco architecture of South Beach began in 1976, when Barbara Capitman (1920–90) set up the Miami Design Preservation League – at a time when much of the area was destined to disappear under a sea of high-rises. Three years later, 1 sq m (2.5 sq km) of South Beach became the first 20th-century district in the country's National Register of Historic Places. Battles still raged against developers throughout the 1980s and 1990s, when candlelit vigils helped to save some buildings.

Did You Know?
___

The Art Deco renaissance on Ocean Drive happened after a destructive hurricane in 1926.

Flat roofs are the norm along Ocean Drive, but these are often interrupted by a tower or other vertical projection.

The central tower imitates both a ship's funnel and the totems of Native American culture.

Colored strips, or "racing stripes," invoke a feeling of speed and motion.

The railings edging the roof imitate those on a ship's deck.

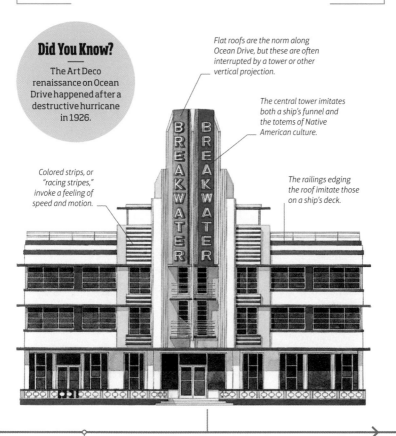

Breakwater (1939)

The Breakwater, by Croatian-born architect Anton Skislewicz, is a classic Streamline Moderne hotel with its racing stripes and a striking central tower. It features a Ziggurat parapet roofline, stucco walls, and terrazzo floor designs. A multimillion-dollar renovation in 2011 saw the hotel restored to its original splendor.

EXPERIENCE MORE

Española Way

E2 **W** visitespanola
way.com

Between Washington and
Drexel avenues, Española
Way is a tiny, tree-lined
enclave of Mediterranean
Revival buildings, where
ornate arches, capitals, and
balconies adorn salmon-
colored, stuccoed frontages.
Built in 1922–5, it is said
to have been the inspiration
for Addison Mizner's Worth
Avenue in Palm Beach (p112).
Española Way was
originally an artists' colony
but gradually became an
infamous red-light district.

Did You Know?

A multimillion-dollar
makeover in 2017
revitalized the charm
of pedestrian-only
Española Way.

In recent decades, however,
its intended use has been
resurrected as it now houses
several boutiques and offbeat
art galleries.

The Beach

F1–F5 **W** miamiand
beaches.com

Much of the sand flanking
Miami Beach was imported
a few decades ago, and it
continues to be replenished
to counter coastal erosion.
The vast stretches of sand
are still impressive and
people flock to them.
Up to 5th Street the beach
is popular with surfers. The
immense beach beyond is an
extension of SoBe's persona,
with colorful lifeguard huts
and hordes of posing bathers.
Alongside runs Lummus
Park. The beach around 12th
Street is particularly popular
with the LGBT+ community.
This gentrified area was
added to the Register of
Historic Districts in 2006.

> **CHANGING COLORS
> IN SOUTH BEACH**
>
> Art Deco buildings
> were originally white,
> with only the trim in
> bright colors. In the
> 1980s, designer
> Leonard Horowitz
> smothered some
> 150 buildings in color.
> Purists express dismay
> at this reinvention
> of the classic look of
> South Beach, but
> advocates argue that
> the Deco details are
> better highlighted.

Collins and
Washington Avenues

E3 & F3 **ℹ** 1920 Meridian
Avenue (Miami Beach
Visitor Center); www.
miamibeachchamber.com

These two streets lack the
polish of the neighboring
Ocean Drive, but renovations
are underway to rejuvenate
both boulevards. Some of

Surfers wading into the water at South Beach, with the Miami Beach skyline in the background

South Beach's top clubs are here, and there is also an abundance of modest Art Deco buildings worth seeing. The Marlin Hotel, at 1200 Collins Avenue, is one of the district's best known and finest Streamline buildings. It used to be owned by Christopher Blackwell, founder of Island Records. Behind, at 1300 Washington Avenue, Miami Beach Post Office is one of SoBe's starker Deco creations; three murals inside depict early Spanish and American encounters with Florida's Indigenous peoples.

Farther north up Collins Avenue, past Lincoln Road, the buildings are interesting rather than beautiful. High-rise 1940s hotels such as the Delano and Ritz Plaza still bear Art Deco traits, particularly in their towers, inspired by the futuristic fantasies of comic strips such as *Buck Rogers* and *Flash Gordon*. The strikingly non-Deco interior of the luxury Delano Hotel on South Beach is well worth seeing, with its billowing white drapes and original works by Gaudí, Dalí, and Man Ray.

5

Jewish Museum of Florida

🔵 E4 🏠 301 Washington Ave 🕐 Times vary, check website 🗓 Jewish and national hols 🌐 jmof.fiu.edu

Built in 1936, Miami Beach's first synagogue reopened in 1995 as a museum and research center of Jewish life in Florida. Colorful stained-glass windows and other Art Deco features make it almost as memorable as the exhibitions that are staged here.

6

The Wolfsonian-Florida International University

🔵 E3 🏠 1001 Washington Ave 🕐 Times vary, check website 🌐 wolfsonian.org

The museum at this university, set in a 1920s building which used to be the Washington Storage Company, where Miami's wealthy stored their valuables while traveling north, now holds a remarkable collection of decorative and fine arts from the period 1850–1950, primarily from North America and Europe. The museum's collection of 200,000 objects includes books, posters, furniture, and sculpture, and focuses on the aesthetic, political, and social significance of design around the turn of the century.

↑ Viewers at an exhibition at The Wolfsonian-Florida International University

7 Holocaust Memorial

📍E1 🏛1933–45 Meridian Ave 🕐9am–9pm daily 🌐holocaustmemorial miamibeach.org

Miami Beach has one of the largest populations of Holocaust survivors in the world, hence the great appropriateness of Kenneth Treister's gut-wrenching memorial, finished in 1990. The centerpiece is an enormous bronze arm and hand stretching skyward, representing the final grasp of a dying person. It is stamped with a number from Auschwitz and covered with nearly 100 life-size bronze statues of men, women, and children in the throes of unbearable grief. Around this central plaza is a tunnel lined with the names of Europe's concentration camps, a graphic pictorial history of the Holocaust, and a granite wall inscribed with the names of thousands of victims.

8 Lincoln Road Mall

📍E2 🕐10am–10pm daily, (to 11pm Thu–Sun) 🌐lincolnroadmall.com

Developer Carl Fisher envisaged this street as the "Fifth Avenue of the South" when it was planned in the 1920s. Four decades later, Morris Lapidus (designer of the Fontainebleau Hotel) turned the street into one of the country's first pedestrian malls, but this did not prevent its decline in the 1970s.

The street's revival was initiated by the establishment of the ArtCenter South Florida here in 1984, which changed the mall from just a shopping destination into a cultural hub. Between Lenox and Meridian Avenues there are three exhibition areas and several studios, as well as other independent galleries.

The galleries are usually open in the evenings. This is when the mall comes alive, when theater-goers frequent the Art Deco Lincoln and Colony theaters nearby. Those searching for a less intense alternative to Ocean Drive hang out in the voguish restaurants and cafes, such as Paul bakery at No. 450 – Lincoln Road's outpost of the French cafe chain. At night, the Streamline Moderne Sterling Building at No. 927 looks terrific – its glass blocks emanating a blue glow.

9 The Bass

📍F1 🏛2100 Collins Ave 🕐Noon–5pm Wed–Sun 🌐thebass.org

This Mayan-influenced Deco building was erected in 1930

as the city's library and art center. As a museum, it came of age in 1964 when philanthropists John and Johanna Bass donated their art collection.

The gallery space houses permanent and temporary exhibitions, the former displaying more than 2,800 pieces of sculpture, graphic art, and photography. Highlights include Renaissance works, paintings from the northern

SHOOTING FASHION IN MIAMI BEACH

With its Deco buildings, palm trees, beach, and warm climate, South Beach is one of the world's most popular places for fashion shoots. The season runs from October through to March, when the weather in Europe and northern America is too cold for outdoor modeling. Stroll around SoBe in the early morning, and you will spot teams of photographers, make-up artists, and models. Ocean Drive is the top spot for shoots.

← The imposing four-story-high sculpture at the center of the Holocaust Memorial

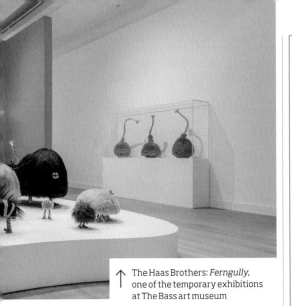

↑ The Haas Brothers: *Ferngully*, one of the temporary exhibitions at The Bass art museum

European schools, and 16th-century Flemish tapestries. There are also exhibits on contemporary architecture.

 Central Miami Beach

📍F1 🌐miamiand beaches.com

Miami Beach north of 23rd Street, sometimes called Central Miami Beach, is a largely unprepossessing sight. The most eye-catching building in the area is the curvaceous Fontainebleau hotel.

Completed in 1954, the Fontainebleau was designed by architect Morris Lapidus (b.1903) for his client, hotelier Ben Novack. The hotel's dated grandeur still impresses, particularly the pool with waterfall, and the lobby with Lapidus's signature bow ties on the tiles. The hotel was an ideal setting for the James Bond film *Goldfinger* in the 1960s. Star guests have included Frank Sinatra, Elvis Presley, and the Obamas. Today the lobby is still one of the best places to spot celebrities in Central Miami Beach.

↑ The iconic Fontainebleau hotel, designed by the architect Morris Lapidus in the 1950s

EAT

Stiltsville Fish Bar
A whimsical restaurant specializing in local fish and cocktails inspired by Hemingway's Key West lifestyle. There are great sunset views from the bar.

📍D2 🏠1787 Purdy Ave
🌐stiltsvillefishbar.com

 ⑤⑤⑤

Joe's Stone Crab
Opened in 1913, this SoBe legend still retains its tablecloths, smartly dressed waiters, and chandeliers. Try the black claws of the local stone crab.

📍E5 🏠11 Washington Ave ⏰Oct–May
🌐joesstonecrab.com

⑤⑤⑤

Sushi Garage
In a former auto-body shop near Maurice Gibb Memorial Park, this diner offers Japanese and South American fusion dishes while colorful artificial fish float overhead.

📍D2 🏠1784 West Ave
⏰Dinner only
🌐sushigarage.com

⑤⑤⑤

Villa Azur
Dine under the stars at this elegant restaurant while savoring French and Mediterranean dishes, such as butter-flied branzino and chateaubriand steak. Book for the Thursday night dinner party.

📍F1 🏠309 23rd St
🌐villaazurmiami.com

⑤⑤⑤

A SHORT WALK
SOUTH BEACH

Distance 1.5 miles (2 km) **Time** 25 minutes

The district of South Beach, which runs from 6th to 23rd streets between Lenox Avenue and Ocean Drive, has been a romantic and buzzy area since the 1980s. Helped by the interest shown by celebrities such as Gloria Estefan and Jennifer Lopez, the area has become one of the trendiest places in the States. For many visitors the Art Deco buildings serve merely as a backdrop for a hedonistic playground, where days are for sleeping, lying on the beach, or long workouts at the gym, and evenings are for dancing into the early hours. Whether your passions are social or architectural, this route can be enjoyed both during the day and night – when a sea of neon enhances the party atmosphere.

↑ The colorful Old City Hall, which towers above the surrounding streets

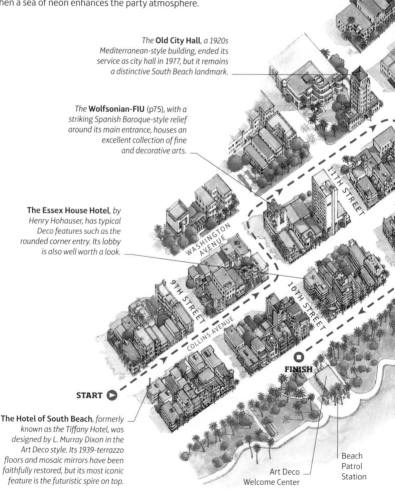

The **Old City Hall**, *a 1920s Mediterranean-style building, ended its service as city hall in 1977, but it remains a distinctive South Beach landmark.*

The **Wolfsonian-FIU** *(p75), with a striking Spanish Baroque-style relief around its main entrance, houses an excellent collection of fine and decorative arts.*

The **Essex House Hotel,** *by Henry Hohauser, has typical Deco features such as the rounded corner entry. Its lobby is also well worth a look.*

11TH STREET

WASHINGTON AVENUE

9TH STREET

10TH STREET

COLLINS AVENUE

FINISH

START ▶

The **Hotel of South Beach,** *formerly known as the Tiffany Hotel, was designed by L. Murray Dixon in the Art Deco style. Its 1939-terrazzo floors and mosaic mirrors have been faithfully restored, but its most iconic feature is the futuristic spire on top.*

Art Deco Welcome Center

Beach Patrol Station

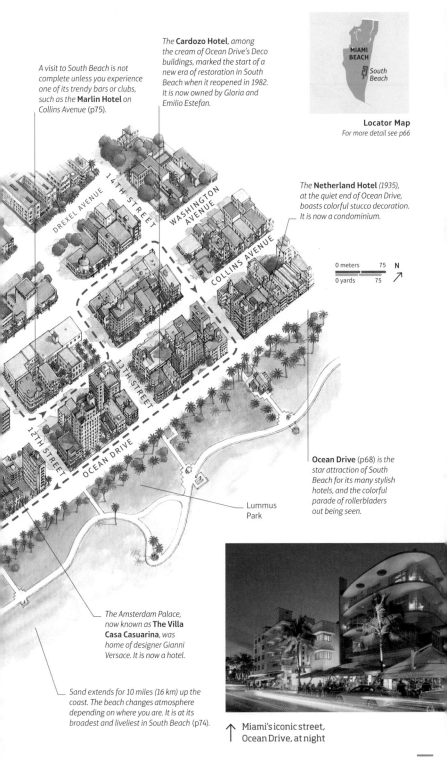

A visit to South Beach is not complete unless you experience one of its trendy bars or clubs, such as the **Marlin Hotel** on Collins Avenue (p75).

The **Cardozo Hotel**, among the cream of Ocean Drive's Deco buildings, marked the start of a new era of restoration in South Beach when it reopened in 1982. It is now owned by Gloria and Emilio Estefan.

MIAMI BEACH

South Beach

Locator Map
For more detail see p66

The **Netherland Hotel** (1935), at the quiet end of Ocean Drive, boasts colorful stucco decoration. It is now a condominium.

DREXEL AVENUE

14TH STREET

WASHINGTON AVENUE

COLLINS AVENUE

13TH STREET

12TH STREET

OCEAN DRIVE

0 meters 75
0 yards 75
N

Ocean Drive (p68) is the star attraction of South Beach for its many stylish hotels, and the colorful parade of rollerbladers out being seen.

Lummus Park

The Amsterdam Palace, now known as **The Villa Casa Casuarina**, was home of designer Gianni Versace. It is now a hotel.

Sand extends for 10 miles (16 km) up the coast. The beach changes atmosphere depending on where you are. It is at its broadest and liveliest in South Beach (p74).

↑ Miami's iconic street, Ocean Drive, at night

79

DOWNTOWN AND CORAL GABLES

The early city of Miami existed on 1 sq mile (2.5 sq km) on the banks of the Miami River. Even after World War II, Miami was still little more than a seaside or sleepy resort, and it wasn't until the arrival of Cuban exiles from 1959 onward that Miami grew into a true metropolis. The effect of this Cuban influx is visible most clearly in Little Havana. The area of the original city is now the hub of Miami's financial district – Brickell – which developed thanks to a banking boom in the 1980s. Its futuristic skyscrapers, bathed nightly in neon, demonstrate the city's status as a major financial and trade center. A little further north, Downtown is made up of soaring condos – home to the city's financiers.

Coral Gables, one of the country's richest neighborhoods, is (and feels like) a separate city within Greater Miami. Aptly named the City Beautiful, its elegant homes line winding avenues shaded by banyans and live oaks. They back up to hidden canals and many have their own jetties. Regulations ensure that new buildings use the same architectural vocabulary advocated by George Merrick when he planned Coral Gables in the 1920s.

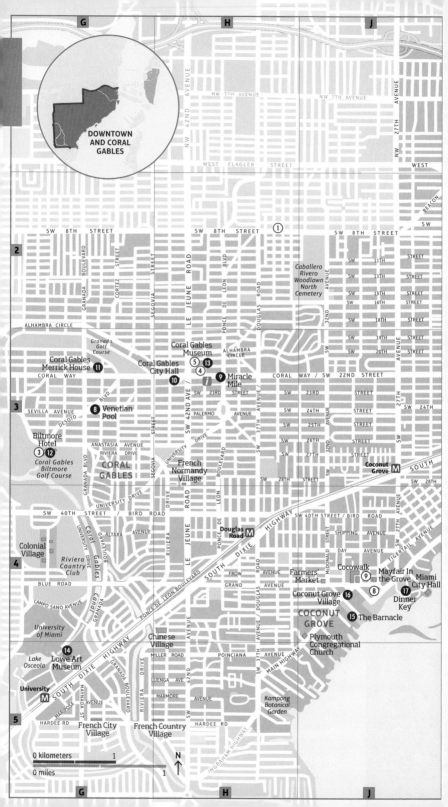

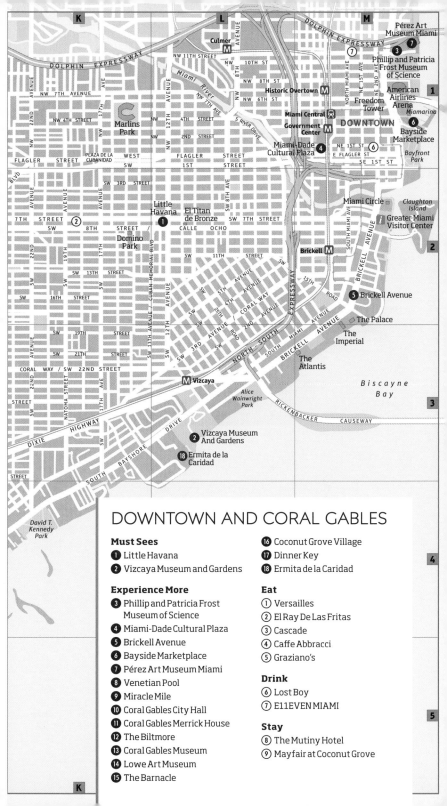

DOWNTOWN AND CORAL GABLES

Must Sees
1 Little Havana
2 Vizcaya Museum and Gardens

Experience More
3 Phillip and Patricia Frost Museum of Science
4 Miami-Dade Cultural Plaza
5 Brickell Avenue
6 Bayside Marketplace
7 Pérez Art Museum Miami
8 Venetian Pool
9 Miracle Mile
10 Coral Gables City Hall
11 Coral Gables Merrick House
12 The Biltmore
13 Coral Gables Museum
14 Lowe Art Museum
15 The Barnacle
16 Coconut Grove Village
17 Dinner Key
18 Ermita de la Caridad

Eat
1 Versailles
2 El Ray De Las Fritas
3 Cascade
4 Caffe Abbracci
5 Graziano's

Drink
6 Lost Boy
7 E11EVEN MIAMI

Stay
8 The Mutiny Hotel
9 Mayfair at Coconut Grove

PICTURE PERFECT
The Latin Walk of Fame

Have your camera at the ready at intervals along Calle Ocho between 12th and 17th Avenues, where Latin celebrities such as Julio Iglesias and Gloria Estefan are honored with stars on the pavement in Little Havana's version of Hollywood's Walk of Fame.

LITTLE HAVANA

◉ L2

Cubans live all over Greater Miami, but the 3.5 sq miles (9 sq km) of Little Havana has been a surrogate homeland to thousands of immigrants since the 1960s. Time here is best spent out in the streets, where the bustling workday atmosphere is vibrant. A salsa beat emanates from every other shop; *bodegas* (canteens) sell Cuban specialties; and locals knock back thimblefuls of *cafe cubano*.

Calle Ocho

Little Havana's principal commercial thoroughfare and sentimental heart is Southwest 8th Street, better known as Calle Ocho. Its liveliest stretch, between 11th and 17th Avenues, is best enjoyed on foot, but other points of interest are more easily explored by car.

The compact **Little Havana Welcome Center** offers information about attractions and events in the neighborhood, while further along, the **Little Havana Visitors Center** is more of a gift shop with all sorts of

souvenirs, a small coffee bar, and a room of Coca-Cola memorabilia.

Recalling the spirit of Havana cigar factories, **El Titan de Bronze**, on Calle Ocho, is family-owned, and all the cigars are made by "Level 9" masters. Visitors are welcome to watch the handful of cigar rollers at work. The leaves are grown in Nicaragua – reputedly from Cuban tobacco seeds, the world's best. A few blocks to the west of the cigar factory, you'll find the **Cubaocho Museum & Performing Arts Center**, a museum, bar and

EAT

Versailles
This is a cultural bastion of Miami's Cuban community and is possibly the best place for classic Cuban cuisine outside Cuba. The Cuban sandwich is a specialty.

📍H3 🏠3555 Southwest 8th St 🌐versailles restaurant.com

$(§)$(§)$(§)$

El Rey De Las Fritas
A popular busy diner justly famous for its *fritas* (Cuban hamburger) and *frita a caballo* (burger with cheese and a fried egg on top).

📍H3 🏠1821 SW 8th St 🌐elreydelasfritas.com

$(§)$(§)$(§)$

↑ The mural on Calle Ocho welcoming visitors to Little Havana

community center in one. It celebrates Cuban culture through various exhibitions and events. It also provides a venue for retirees to meet, smoke cigars, and play dominoes. Also found on 8th Street are several spiritual stores dedicated to the practice of the Afro-Cuban religion Santería.

North of Calle Ocho at West Flagler Street and Southwest 17th Avenue, Plaza de la Cubanidad has a map of Cuba sculpted in bronze. José Martí's enigmatic words alongside translate as "the palm trees are sweethearts that wait." The monument is in part a memorial to the victims of the "Tugboat '13 de Marzo' massacre," who were trying to escape Cuba in 1994.

Little Havana Welcome Center
🏠1442 SW 8th St 📞(305) 643-5500
🕐Times vary

Little Havana Visitors Center
♿ 📍K2 🏠1600 SW 8th St
🕐10am–6pm daily

El Titan de Bronze
🏠1071 W 8th St 📞(305) 860-1412
🕐9am–5pm Mon–Fri; 8am–4pm Sat

Cubaocho Museum & Performing Arts Center
🏠1465 SW 8th St 🕐10am–midnight Mon–Fri, 11am–3am Sat & Sun 🌐cubaocho.com

Cuban Memorial Boulevard
Southwest 13th Avenue is the site of the Brigade 2506 Memorial, which remembers the Cubans who died in the Bay of Pigs invasion of Cuba in 1961. People gather here on April 17 to remember the attempt to overthrow Fidel Castro's regime.

↑ Little Havana's Memorial Boulevard, the district's nationalistic focal point

2 ⃝ ⃝ ⃝ ⃝ ⃝

VIZCAYA MUSEUM AND GARDENS

🅰 L3 🏠 3251 S Miami Ave Ⓜ Vizcaya 🕐 9:30am– 4:30pm Thu–Mon
(book in advance) 🌐 vizcaya.org

This opulent former private residence is a chance to experience a variety of grand architectural styles and a wealth of interesting artifacts, as well as one of the city's most impressive gardens.

Florida's grandest residence was completed in 1916 as the winter retreat for millionaire industrialist James Deering. His vision was to replicate a 16th-century Italian estate, but one that had been altered by succeeding generations. Hence, Vizcaya and its opulent rooms are a blend of styles from Renaissance to Neo-Classical. The formal gardens combine the features of Italian and French gardens with Florida's tropical foliage.

In 1952, it was bought by Miami-Dade County, and opened to the public soon after.

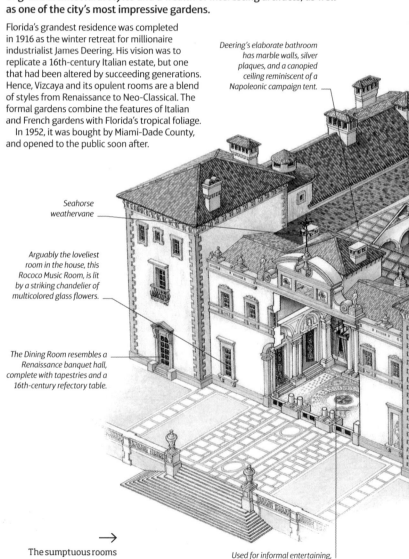

Deering's elaborate bathroom has marble walls, silver plaques, and a canopied ceiling reminiscent of a Napoleonic campaign tent.

Seahorse weathervane

Arguably the loveliest room in the house, this Rococo Music Room, is lit by a striking chandelier of multicolored glass flowers.

The Dining Room resembles a Renaissance banquet hall, complete with tapestries and a 16th-century refectory table.

→

The sumptuous rooms and their various styles at Vizcaya

Used for informal entertaining, the East Loggia contains a model caravel, a favorite Deering motif.

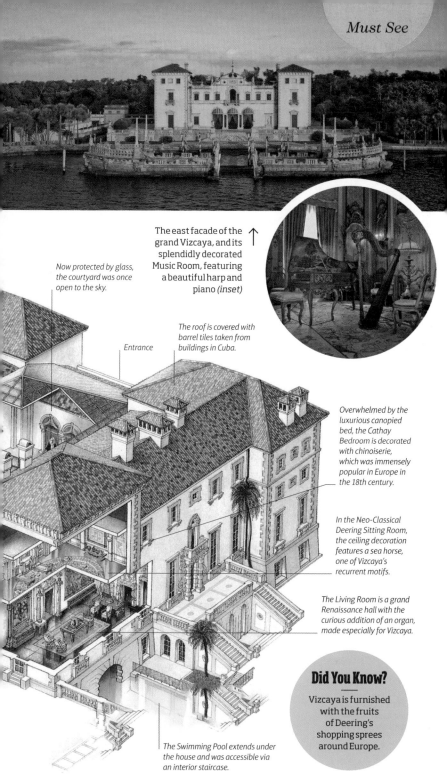

The east facade of the grand Vizcaya, and its splendidly decorated Music Room, featuring a beautiful harp and piano *(inset)*

Now protected by glass, the courtyard was once open to the sky.

The roof is covered with barrel tiles taken from buildings in Cuba.

Entrance

Overwhelmed by the luxurious canopied bed, the Cathay Bedroom is decorated with chinoiserie, which was immensely popular in Europe in the 18th century.

In the Neo-Classical Deering Sitting Room, the ceiling decoration features a sea horse, one of Vizcaya's recurrent motifs.

The Living Room is a grand Renaissance hall with the curious addition of an organ, made especially for Vizcaya.

Did You Know?

Vizcaya is furnished with the fruits of Deering's shopping sprees around Europe.

The Swimming Pool extends under the house and was accessible via an interior staircase.

EXPERIENCE MORE

Phillip and Patricia Frost Museum of Science

📍 M1 🏛 1101 Biscayne Blvd 🚇 Museum Park
🕐 9:30am–6pm daily
🌐 frostscience.org

The aim of this striking museum, in the bayfront area called Museum Park, is to help visitors explore the power of science. It has interactive exhibits on the human body and engineering, as well as a planetarium and an expansive aquarium.

Miami-Dade Cultural Plaza

📍 M1 🏛 101 West Flagler St 🚇 Government Center 🕐 Times vary, check website
🌐 historymiami.org

Designed by the celebrated American architect Philip Johnson in 1982, the Miami-Dade Cultural Plaza houses a splendid history museum and a library, which contains four million books.

HistoryMiami concentrates on pre-1945 Miami. There are informative displays on the Spanish colonization and Seminole culture among other topics, but it is the old photographs that really bring Miami's history to life. These photographs explore the hardships endured by the early pioneers as well as the fun and games of the Roaring Twenties.

Brickell Avenue

📍 M2 🚇 Brickell, Government Center 🚉 Various stations 🛈 701 Brickell Ave, Suite 2700; www.miamiandbeaches.com

In the early 20th century, the building of palatial mansions along Brickell Avenue earned it the name Millionaires' Row. Today, its northern section is Miami's palm-lined version of New York's Wall Street – its

---

BISCAYNE BAY BOAT TRIPS

"Estates of the Rich and Famous" boat tours provide a leisurely view of Biscayne Bay between Downtown and Miami Beach. Tours begin by sailing past the world's busiest cruise port, situated on Dodge and Lummus islands. Near the eastern end of MacArthur Causeway, they pass unbridged Fisher Island, a highly exclusive residential enclave, with homes rarely costing less than $500,000. The tour continues north around man-made Star, Palm, and Hibiscus islands. Mansions in every possible architectural style lurk beneath the tropical foliage, among them the former homes of Frank Sinatra and Al Capone, as well as the abodes of celebrities such as Matt Damon and Julio Iglesias.

The impressive three-level aquarium at the Frost Museum of Science

international banks enclosed in modern, glass blocks. South of the bend at Southwest 15th Road is a series of startling apartment houses glimpsed in the opening credits of TV series *Miami Vice* (p48). Designed in the early 1980s by an iconoclastic firm of Postmodernist architects called Arquitectonica, the buildings – now condos – are still very impressive.

The most memorable is the Atlantis (at No. 2025), for its "skycourt" – a hole high up in its facade containing a palm tree and Jacuzzi. The punched-out hole reappears as an identically sized cube in the grounds below. Arquitectonica also designed the Palace, at No. 1541, and the Imperial, at No. 1627. Described as "architecture for 55 mph" (that is, best seen when passing in a car), these exclusive residences and high-rise office buildings were designed to be admired from a distance.

Bayside Marketplace

📍M1 🏠401 Biscayne Blvd 🚇College/Bayside ⏰10am-10pm Mon-Sat (to 11pm Fri & Sat), 11am-9pm Sun 🌐baysidemarketplace.com

By far the most popular spot Downtown among tourists (and the best place to park in the area), Bayside Market-place is an undeniably fun complex. It curves around Miamarina, where a plethora of boats lie docked. Some are private, but others can be booked for trips around the stunning Biscayne Bay. With its numerous bars and restaurants, Bayside is a good place to eat as well as to shop. The food court on

the first floor is fine for a fast-food meal. Bands often play on the waterfront esplanade.

Pérez Art Museum Miami

📍M1 🏠1075 Biscayne Blvd 🚇Museum Park ⏰Times vary, check website 🌐pamm.org

Named after its benefactor, real-estate developer Jorge Pérez, the Pérez Art Museum Miami (PAMM) houses a collection of 20th- and 21st-century international art. Its stylish galleries feature exhibits of contemporary works in a variety of mediums, including photography and sculpture. Set in lush gardens, the museum occupies an impressive building designed by Swiss architects Herzog and de Meuron.

Did You Know?

The Pérez Art Museum Miami hosts regular film screenings and concerts.

DRINK

Lost Boy

Downtown Miami mainstay with an airy interior, red brick walls, plush bar stools, and a Victorian saloon theme. Serves classic cocktails, decent beers on draught, and a menu of charcuterie, sandwiches and pot pies.

📍M1 🏠157 E Flagler St ⏰Noon-midnight daily 🌐lostboydrygoods.com

E11EVEN MIAMI

This is part cabaret and part nightclub, with trapeze dancers, a roof-top lounge, and a restaurant. Not a cheap evening, but this venue is fast becoming a Florida institution.

📍M1 🏠29 NE 11th St 🌐11miami.com

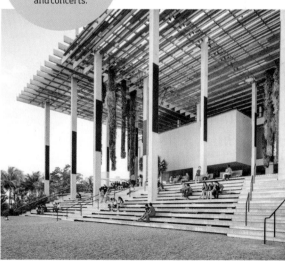

↑ Visitors relaxing on the steps at the back of the Pérez Art Museum Miami

STAY

The Mutiny Hotel

This hotel is famous as the Mafia headquarters that inspired the 1983 version of *Scarface*. Its poolside restaurant offers a modern take on classic Latin American dishes.

📍J4 🏠2951 S Bayshore Dr 🌐providentresorts.com/the-mutiny-hotel-miami

⑤⑤⑤

The Mayfair at Coconut Grove

The Mayfair offers many comforts such as Japanese soaking tubs in most rooms. There's also a heated outdoor pool with cabanas.

📍J4 🏠3000 Florida Ave 🌐mayfairhotel miami.com

⑤⑤⑤

8

Venetian Pool

📍G3 🏠2701 De Soto Blvd Ⓜ️Douglas Rd, Vizcaya 🕐Times vary, check website 🌐coral gables.com/venetianpool

Arguably one of the most beautiful swimming pools in the world, the Venetian Pool was fashioned from a coral rock quarry in 1923 by the artist Denman Fink and the architect Phineas Paist. Decorative elements – including pink stucco towers and loggias, candy-cane Venetian poles, a cobble-stone bridge, caves, and waterfalls – surround the clear, spring-fed waters. It also features two lookout towers. The pool was originally one of the most fashionable social spots in Coral Gables: see the photographs in the lobby of beauty pageants staged here during the 1920s.

9

Miracle Mile

📍H3 🏠Coral Way between Douglas and Le Jeune roads Ⓜ️Douglas Rd, Vizcaya 🌐experiencecoralgables.com

In 1940, a developer hyped Coral Gables' main shopping street by naming it Miracle Mile. Colorful canopies adorn shops as prim and proper as their clientele.

The Colonnade Building, at No. 169, was built in 1926 by George Merrick as the sales headquarters for his real-estate business. Its superb rotunda is now a lobby for the deceptively modern and very impressive Colonnade Hotel. Caffe Abbracci offers Italian food and celebrity-viewing opportunities. Nearby, at Salzedo Street and Aragon Avenue, the Old Police and Fire Station Building, built in 1939, houses the Coral Gables Museum (*p93*).

The crystal-clear waters of the beautiful, palm-fringed Venetian Pool

that illustrates Coral Gables' early days, *Landmarks of the Twenties*, was the work of the artist John St. John in the 1950s; he artificially aged it by chain-smoking and exhaling onto the paint as it dried.

Coral Gables Merrick House

G3 **907 Coral Way**
1–4pm Wed & Sun
coralgables.com/coral-gables-merrick-house

When Reverend Solomon Merrick brought his family to Florida from New England in 1899, they settled in a wooden cabin south of the growing city of Miami. They later added a much larger extension and named the house Coral Gables, thinking the local oolitic limestone used to build it was coral because of the fossilized marine life it contained. The city of Coral Gables took its name from this house.

The house has now been turned into a museum, with the emphasis firmly on the family – particularly

Coral Gables City Hall

H3 **405 Biltmore Way** **Douglas Rd**
Closed due to COVID-19
coralgables.com

Constructed in 1928, Coral Gables City Hall epitomizes the Spanish Renaissance style favored by George Merrick and his colleagues. Its semicircular facade even has a Spanish-style coat of arms, which was designed for the new city of Coral Gables by Denman Fink, George Merrick's uncle. Fink was also responsible for the mural of the four seasons that decorates the dome of the bell tower. Above the stairs, a mural

→

The Coral Gables Merrick House, former home of George Merrick

GEORGE MERRICK'S DREAM CITY

With the help of Denman Fink as artistic advisor, Frank Button as land-scaper, and Phineas Paist as architectural director, George Merrick conjured up a city that he planned as an aesthetic wonderland. The dream spawned the biggest real-estate venture of the 1920s. The 1926 hurricane and the Wall Street crash left Merrick's Coral Gables incomplete, but what remains is a great testament to his imagination.

Solomon's famous son, George Merrick, a real-estate developer. Some of the furniture on display was owned by the Merricks, and there are family portraits and paintings by George's mother and his uncle. The grounds have been reduced in size, but the small garden is awash with tropical trees and plants. Guided tours of the house are compulsory and take place at 1, 2 and 3pm.

Seeing the family home gives visitors a chance to appreciate the comparatively modest background of Coral Gables' ambitious and imaginative creator.

The Biltmore

🅖 G3 🏠 1200 Anastasia Ave Ⓜ Douglas Rd Ⓦ biltmorehotel.com

One of Coral Gables' most outstanding single buildings, The Biltmore hotel was completed in 1926. In its heyday, when it hosted celebrities such as the infamous Al Capone (who had a speakeasy here), actress Judy Garland, and the Duke and Duchess of Windsor, guests were punted along canals in gondolas. It served as a military hospital during

Did You Know?

The Biltmore is said to be haunted, due to a gangster murder and its time as a military hospital.

FACT MEETS FICTION

In the 1980s, the public perception of Miami was as the drug and crime capital of the entire country. Ironically, the popular TV series *Miami Vice (p48)* played on this reputation, glamorizing both the city and the violence. The best novels about Miami in the 1990s have also emanated from its seedier side. Its two most renowned crime writers are Edna Buchanan, winner of a Pulitzer prize for news reporting at the *Miami Herald*, and Carl Hiaasen, a columnist for the same newspaper. However fanciful his plots might seem (a celebrity bass fisherman, or talk-show hosts having plastic surgery on the air), Carl Hiaasen claims the ideas come straight from the *Herald*'s news pages. *Striptease* was the first of his novels to be made into a movie.

World War II, when its marble floors were covered in linoleum, and it remained a veterans' hospital until 1968. The hotel went bankrupt in 1990, but then opened its doors to visitors again two years later.

A 315-ft (96-m) near replica of Seville Cathedral's Giralda tower, which was also the model for Miami's Freedom Tower, rises from the hotel's imposing facade. Inside, Herculean pillars line the grand lobby, while the terrace offers views of one of the largest hotel swimming pools in the US. The Biltmore's famous swimming instructor Johnny Weismuller, known for his role as Tarzan in the franchise films of the 1930s and 1940s, set

a world record here. Sunday tours of the hotel depart from the desk.

---

  13 🗡️ 🎨 🛍️

Coral Gables Museum

📍 H3 🏛️ 285 Aragon Ave
Ⓜ️ Douglas Rd 🕐 10am-5pm Mon-Fri, 10am-6pm Sat & Sun 🌐 coralgablesmuseum.org

Housed primarily in the Old Police and Fire Station building, this local museum offers a wide variety of exhibitions about Coral Gables and the surrounding area. Along with the main building, the museum complex includes beautiful outdoor spaces and the Fewell Gallery. Permanent exhibits at the complex include a show of large-format images by photographer Clyde Butcher which focus on the natural beauty of the Tamiami Trail, while a separate

exhibition of the history of the trail that does not shy away from describing its devastating impact on the Everglades.

Coral Gables' founder and developer George Merrick (p91) is the focus of another exhibition, showing how he was inspired to build a place where "your castles in Spain are made real." The museum is also the City of Coral Gables official visitor center and a great starting point for a wide variety of tours.

---

14 🗡️

Lowe Art Museum

📍 G5 🏛️ 1301 Stanford Dr
Ⓜ️ University 🕐 10am-4pm Tue-Sat, noon-4pm Sun 🌐 lowemuseum.org

Located in the middle of the campus of the University of Miami in Coral Gables, this museum was founded in 1950 thanks to a donation from philanthropists Joe and Emily Lowe. First named the Lowe Art Gallery, it was renamed Lowe Art Museum in 1968. More than 19,000 objects are in the museum's collection, which showcases many of the world's most important artistic traditions spanning over 5,000 years of human history. Visitors will find impressive Renaissance and Baroque works, in addition to an excellent series of Native American art. There is also an Egyptian collection, some fine works in the 17th-century and contemporary European and American collections, Afro-Cuban lore, 20th-century photography and historical memorabilia. Ancient art from Latin America and Asia is also well represented.

↑ Sculpture in Lowe Art Museum's Ancient Americas collection

EAT

Cascade
The Biltmore's al fresco restaurant, Cascade overlooks the hotel's famous swimming pool.

📍 G3 🏛️ 1200 Anastasia Ave 🌐 biltmorehotel.com

💲💲💲

Caffe Abbracci
This beloved Italian restaurant in Coral Gables serves classics such as black lobster and risotto.

📍 H3 🏛️ 318 Aragon Ave 🌐 caffeabbracci.com

💲💲💲

Graziano's
Contemporary Argentinian restaurant featuring a fire pit and two large grills. Find classic steaks, lamb, and fish dishes here.

📍 H3 🏛️ 394 Giralda Ave 🌐 grazianosgroup.com

💲💲💲

 ←

The palm tree lined monumental facade of the historic Biltmore Hotel

↑ The Barnacle, built in the late 19th century and the oldest home in Dade County

The Barnacle

📍J4 🏠 3485 Main Hwy, Coconut Grove ⏰ Times vary, check website 🌐 floridastateparks.org

Hidden from Main Highway by tropical hardwood trees, the Barnacle is the oldest home in Dade County. It was designed and occupied by Ralph Munroe, a Renaissance man who made his living from boat building and wrecking. A botanist and photographer, Munroe was also an avid environmentalist with a strong belief in self-sufficiency.

The house is named for the little crustacean because of the conical shape of its roof. In 1891, when it was first constructed, the house was a bungalow, built of wood salvaged from wrecks and laid out to allow air to circulate (essential in those pre-air-conditioning times). Then, in 1908, Munroe raised the building and added a new ground floor to accommodate his growing family. Inside the two-story house visitors can explore rooms filled with old family heirlooms and wonderful, dated practical appliances, such as an early refrigerator. The hour-long tours of the property also take in Munroe's clapboard boathouse, full of his tools and workbenches. Along-side, you can see the rail track that Munroe used to winch boats out of the bay, plus replicas of two of his sailboats.

The Barnacle is also a good birdwatching site, its tropical forest providing shelter for woodpeckers and nightjars, as well as kingfishers, pelicans, and cormorants.

Coconut Grove Village

📍J4 Ⓜ Coconut Grove, Douglas Rd 🌐 coconut grovevc.org

A fabled hippy hangout in the 1960s, these days the focal point of Coconut Grove cultivates a more salubrious air. Well-groomed young couples wining and dining beneath beautiful old-fashioned street lamps now typify what is often known simply as "the village." Only the odd snake charmer and neck masseur, plus a few New Age shops, offer glimpses of alternative lifestyles. It is worth visiting at night or on the weekend to see the lively Grove at its best.

The village's nerve center is at the intersection of Grand Avenue, McFarlane Avenue, and Main Highway, where visitors will find the lively CocoWalk. This outdoor mall is one of the most popular destinations here. Its courtyard is full of brilliant cafes and souvenir stands, while on upper floors a band often plays. In addition to many clothing shops, there are also family restaurants, a movie theater, and a night-club. It was extensively renovated in 2020.

A short distance east along Grand Avenue, a stylish shopping area called Mayfair in the Grove is worth visiting as much for its striking ensemble of Spanish tiles, waterfalls, and foliage, as for its shops. But in order to better appreciate Coconut Grove's relaxed cafe lifestyle, head along the sidestreets of Commodore Plaza and Fuller Street. For a different

> The Barnacle is also a good birdwatching site: its tropical forest providing shelter for woodpeckers and nightjars.

atmosphere, browse the food stands of the colorful Farmers' Market, held on Saturdays at Margaret Street and Grand Avenue. This area "is also the center of Miami's Bahamian-American community, the largest of any city in the US. The neighborhood comes alive during Coconut Grove's exuberant Goombay Festival every July.

A five-minute stroll south along Main Highway will pass through a shady, affluent neighborhood where palms, bougainvillea, and hibiscus conceal elegant clapboard villas. At 3400 Devon Road stands the picturesque Plymouth Congregational Church, which looks as though it was built much longer ago than 1916. It is usually locked, but the ivy-covered facade and setting are the main attraction.

Dinner Key

⊞ J4 🏠 3400 Pan American Dr Ⓜ Coconut Grove

The name is thought to derive from the early days when settlers had picnics here. In the 1930s, Pan American Airways transformed the area of Dinner Key into the busiest seaplane base in the US. It was also the point of departure for Amelia Earhart's doomed round-the-world flight in 1937. Visitors can still see the airline's sleek Streamline Moderne-style terminal which houses Miami City Hall – the hangars where seaplanes were once harbored are now boatyards where visitors can join a boat tour along Miami's coastline. To see how some people enjoy their leisure time, walk among the luxurious yachts moored in Miami's most prestigious marina.

The conical church of Ermita de la Caridad and the mural *(inset)* by Teok Carrasco above the altar

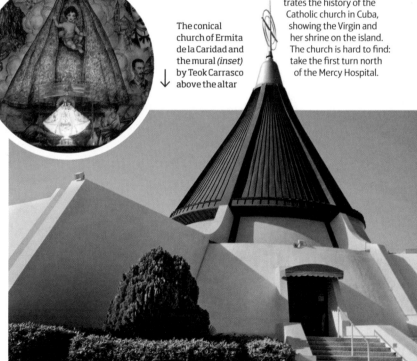

INSIDER TIP
Coconut Grove Arts Festival

In mid-February, hundreds of artists showcase their work at the three-day Coconut Grove Arts Festival *(www.cgaf. com)*, which also offers food events and music.

Ermita de la Caridad

⊞ L3 🏠 3609 S Miami Ave Ⓒ (305) 854-2404 Ⓜ Vizcaya Ⓞ Noon–8pm daily

This conical church, erected in 1966, is a very holy place for Miami's Cuban residents – a shrine to their patron saint, the Virgin of Charity. A mural above the altar (which faces Cuba rather than being oriented eastward), illustrates the history of the Catholic church in Cuba, showing the Virgin and her shrine on the island. The church is hard to find: take the first turn north of the Mercy Hospital.

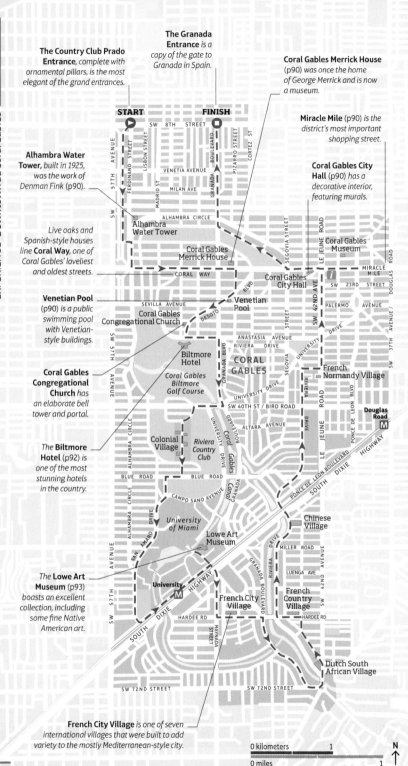

The Country Club Prado Entrance, complete with ornamental pillars, is the most elegant of the grand entrances.

The Granada Entrance is a copy of the gate to Granada in Spain.

Coral Gables Merrick House (p90) was once the home of George Merrick and is now a museum.

Miracle Mile (p90) is the district's most important shopping street.

Alhambra Water Tower, built in 1925, was the work of Denman Fink (p90).

Coral Gables City Hall (p90) has a decorative interior, featuring murals.

Live oaks and Spanish-style houses line **Coral Way**, one of Coral Gables' loveliest and oldest streets.

Venetian Pool (p90) is a public swimming pool with Venetian-style buildings.

Coral Gables Congregational Church has an elaborate bell tower and portal.

The **Biltmore Hotel** (p92) is one of the most stunning hotels in the country.

The **Lowe Art Museum** (p93) boasts an excellent collection, including some fine Native American art.

French City Village is one of seven international villages that were built to add variety to the mostly Mediterranean-style city.

START

FINISH

SW 8TH STREET

VENETIA AVENUE

MILAN AVE

ALHAMBRA CIRCLE

Alhambra Water Tower

CORAL WAY

SEVILLA AVENUE

Coral Gables Congregational Church

Coral Gables Merrick House

Venetian Pool

Coral Gables City Hall

Coral Gables Museum

MIRACLE MILE

SW 23RD STREET

PALERMO AVENUE

Biltmore Hotel

Coral Gables Biltmore Golf Course

ANASTASIA AVENUE

RIVIERA DRIVE

CORAL GABLES

French Normandy Village

UNIVERSITY DRIVE

SW 40TH ST / BIRD ROAD

ALTARA AVENUE

Colonial Village

Riviera Country Club

Douglas Road M

BLUE ROAD

BLUE ROAD

CAMPO SANO AVENUE

PONCE DE LEON BOULEVARD

SOUTH DIXIE HIGHWAY

University of Miami

Lowe Art Museum

Chinese Village

MILLER ROAD

LUENGA AVE

University M

SOUTH DIXIE HIGHWAY

French City Village

French Country Village

HARDEE RD

HARDEE RD

Dutch South African Village

SW 72ND STREET

SW 72ND STREET

0 kilometers 1

0 miles 1

N

57TH AVENUE
FERDINAND STREET
LISBON STREET
MADRID ST
GRANADA BLVD
PIZARRO STREET
CORTEZ ST
SEGOVIA STREET
LE JEUNE ROAD
SW 42ND AVE
DOUGLAS ROAD
SW 37TH AVENUE
DESOTO
SW 57TH AVENUE
GRANADA BOULEVARD
CORAL GABLES CANAL
ALHAMBRA CIRCLE
ALHAMBRA CIRCLE
SW ALHAMBRA DRIVE
UNIVERSITY DRIVE
RIVIERA DRIVE
LE JEUNE ROAD
GRANADA BOULEVARD
RIVIERA DRIVE
SW 42ND AVENUE
MAYNADA STREET

A DRIVING TOUR
CORAL GABLES

Locator Map
For more detail see p82

Length 14 miles (23 km) **Starting point** Anywhere, but the route is best made in a counterclockwise direction
Stopping-off point Miracle Mile

This driving tour wends its way along Coral Gables' lush and peaceful lanes, connecting the major landmarks of George Merrick's 1920s dream city *(pp86–7)*. As well as much-admired public buildings such as the Biltmore Hotel, it takes in two of the original four grand entrances and six of Merrick's unique international "villages."

It is possible to visit all the sights on the tour in one busy day. Allow time to get lost; Coral Gables is confusing for a planned city. Signs for streets, named after Spanish places, are often hard to spot, lurking on white stone blocks in the grass. Wednesdays and Sundays are the best days to visit because of the opening hours of the Coral Gables Merrick House and the Lowe Art Museum.

Did You Know?

Merrick marketed Coral Gables as a "Spanish city," with street names taken from a book of tales.

The stunning turquoise water at the Venetian Pool, surrounded by an abundance of flora ↑

BEYOND THE CENTER

In the late 19th century the area around Miami River was largely undeveloped. It was business-woman Julia Tuttle who won the area its first major investment, encouraging Henry Flagler to bring the Florida East Coast Railroad to the region in 1896. Over the next few decades the Miami metropolitan area expanded drastically with the arrival of workers and investors keen to profit from the thriving city. The Great Depression slowed investment for a while, but Miami's growth picked up during World War II and the postwar years.

Greater Miami isn't as famous as the central hub of Miami Beach and Downtown, but there are still some places well worth exploring for the cool art scenes, historic sights, and great beaches.

Must See

❶ The Ancient Spanish Monastery

Experience More

❷ North Beaches

❸ Fairchild Tropical Botanic Garden

❹ Key Biscayne

❺ Wynwood Arts District

❻ Little Haiti

❼ Coral Castle

❽ Institute of Contemporary Art

❾ Gold Coast Railroad Museum

❿ Wings Over Miami

⓫ Charles Deering Estate

①

THE ANCIENT SPANISH MONASTERY

🏠16711 W Dixie Hwy, N Miami Beach 🚌3, 93 🕐Check website for details
🌐spanishmonastery.com

Originally built in Spain in the 12th century, this beautiful building has been painstakingly reconstructed in North Miami Beach, surrounded by landscaped gardens to create a scene of serene elegance.

Now a working church, the stunning and peaceful cloisters of this complex have an unusual history. Built between 1133–41 in Spain, the monastery became a granary in the mid-19th century. In 1925 it was bought by newspaper tycoon William Randolph Hearst, and the cloisters' 35,000 stones were packed into crates and shipped to the US. When the crates were opened during a security check the stones were repacked incorrectly, and remained in New York until 1952, when it was decided to piece together "the world's largest and most expensive jigsaw puzzle." These cloisters resemble the original, but there is still a pile of unidentified stones in the gardens.

Statue of Alphonso VII, patron of the monastery

→
The Ancient Spanish Monastery and its grounds

←
An archway made from the original 12th-century stones from Spain

Chapterhouse

The Chapel, at one time the dining hall, is still used for worship.

The cloister entrance is a carved, early Gothic arch.

The quiet gardens are a popular spot for wedding photos.

→

Statue of Alfonso VII of Castile and León, founder of the monastery

EXPERIENCE MORE

❷ North Beaches

🏠 Collins Ave 🚌 E (105), G (107), H (108), S (119), 120 Beach MAX 🌐 miami beaches.com

The barrier islands north of Miami Beach are occupied mainly by smart residential areas and a few oceanfront resorts along Collins Avenue. The North Beach areas are quieter than South Beach, but the hotels are right on the sands, and are less expensive.

A strip of sand between 79th and 87th Streets separates Miami Beach from Surfside, a seaside community popular with French Canadians. At 96th Street, Surfside merges with Bal Harbour, a stylish enclave with some flashy hotels and a swanky mall. Northward is Haulover Park, with dune-backed sands facing the ocean.

Did You Know?

North Shore Open Space Park, filled with fun playgrounds, is found in the North Beach areas.

❸ Fairchild Tropical Botanic Garden

🏠 10901 Old Cutler Rd 🚌 57, 136 (then a short walk) 🕐 Times vary, check website 🌐 fairchildgarden.org

This huge tropical garden, established in 1938, doubles as a major botanical research institution. Around a series of artificial lakes stands one of the largest collections of palm trees in the world and an impressive array of cycads – relatives of palms and ferns bearing giant red cones.

During 40-minute trolley tours, guides describe how plants are used in the manufacture of medicines and perfumes (the flowers of the ylang-ylang tree, for example, are used in Chanel No. 5). Allow another two hours to explore independently.

Next to the Fairchild Tropical Botanic Garden is the waterfront **Matheson Hammock Park**, with walking and cycling trails through mangrove swamps. Most popular is its Atoll Pool, an artificial salt-water swimming pool, encircled by sand and palm trees alongside Biscayne Bay. There is also a marina with a sailing school, and a firstrate beachfront restaurant.

Matheson Hammock Park

 🏠 9610 Old Cutler Rd, Coral Gables ☎ (305) 665-5475 🕐 Sunrise-sunset daily

❹ Key Biscayne

🏠 Rickenbacker Causeway Hwy-913 🚌 B (102)

Key Biscayne has some of the city's best beaches. One of the most impressive is the beach in **Crandon Park**, which is 3 miles (5 km) long with palm trees and an offshore sandbar. The view of Downtown from Rickenbacker Causeway, linking the mainland to Virginia Key and Key Biscayne, is one of Miami's best. A fenced beachfront picnic area can harbor up to 2,000 people. At the key's southern end, **Bill Baggs Cape Florida State Park** has a shorter beach joined to more picnic areas by boardwalks across dunes. The lighthouse near the tip is South Florida's oldest building.

Crandon Park

🏠 6747 Crandon Blvd 🕐 Daily 🌐 miamidade.gov

Bill Baggs Cape Florida State Park

🏠 1200 Crandon Blvd 🕐 Daily 🌐 florida stateparks.org

→ Colorful street art decorating a building, part of the Wynwood Walls project

Wynwood Arts District

 NE 20th to 29th sts, E of I-95 🚌2 🌐wynwood miami.com

A vibrant arts district in what was once the manufacturing area of Greater Miami, Wynwood is known for its outdoor arts scene, where sombre blocks of gray industrial buildings have seen a rebirth through colorful murals and graffiti. The gathering of brilliant artists creating works here in turn promoted the opening of galleries and performing arts spaces. Restaurants and cafes followed, bringing more creative businesses. Today Wynwood is one of the top spots for hip culture, featuring food tours, art walks, retail shops, design companies, office space for entrepreneurs, and much more. At its heart and soul is the project that started it all – The Wynwood Walls. The late Tony Goldman's creative spotlight turned to the street art in the area and transformed the community.

⑥ Little Haiti

🏠 46th to 79th sts, E of I-95 🚌2, 202 Little Haiti Connection

Since the 1980s, many Haitian refugees have settled in this part of Miami. The **Little Haiti Cultural Complex** is the heart of the community. Its main building is the Caribbean Marketplace, with ironwork modeled after the Iron Market in Port-au-Prince in Haiti. Every Saturday, a Caribbean market is held here, while on the third Friday of every month the free Sounds of Little Haiti music event takes place. The **Libreri Mapou** bookstore sells Haitian literature and souvenirs. The Toussaint Louverture Memorial Statue stands at North Miami Avenue and the **Haitian Heritage Museum** is a little further south in the Design District. Haitian music blares out of local shops; some of which stock herbal potions and saints' ephemera.

Little Haiti Cultural Complex
🏠 250 NE 59th Terrace
🕐 10am-9pm Fri, 10am-4pm Sat 🌐 miamigov.com/LHCC

← Cape Florida Lighthouse at the tip of Bill Baggs Cape Florida State Park

Libreri Mapou
🏠 5919 NE 2nd Avenue
🌐 mapoubooks.com

Haitian Heritage Museum
🏠 4141 NE 2 Ave
🕐 10am-5pm Tue-Fri
🌐 haitianheritage museum.org

EAT

Phuc Yea
The decor at this Cajun-Vietnamese fusion restaurant has echoes of Raffles Long Bar.

🏠 7100 Biscayne Blvd 🕐 Tue
🌐 phucyea.com

$$$

Malibu Farm Miami Beach
Oceanfront dining in the trendy MidBeach area. The house specialty is Sundowners, shareable plates served nightly (5-7pm).

🏠 4525 Collins Ave
🌐 edenroc hotel miami.com

$$$

Error

  103

↑ Crescent shapes sculpted into coral rock by Edward Leedskalnin at Coral Castle

7

Coral Castle

28655 S Dixie Hwy, Homestead Dadeland South then bus Busway Max 38, 70 9am-6pm daily coralcastle.com

From 1920 to 1940, a Latvian immigrant named Edward Leedskalnin single-handedly built this series of giant castle-like sculptures out of coral rock, using tools assembled from automobile parts. He sculpted most of the stones 10 miles (16 km) away in Florida City, moving them again on his own to their present site. Some, such as a working telescope, represent their creator's great passion for astronomy. Others, such as the heart-shaped table, remember his Latvian fiancée Agnes, who canceled their wedding just the day before it was due to take place.

8

Institute of Contemporary Art

61 NE 41st St Metrobus 9 Times vary, check website icamiami.org

Miami's Institute of Contemporary Art moved to its current location in the Design District in 2017. From the roadside, the building appears as a dramatic metal-clad, geometric structure containing vast amounts of display space over three floors. To the rear, however, Spanish architects Aranguren and Gallegos have created a wall of glass with a dual function: ushering in daylight and offering visitors a view of the gallery's charming sculpture garden.

Founded by Miami-based billionaires Norman and Irma Braman, the gallery is dedicated to promoting continuous experimentation

INSIDER TIP
First Fridays

On the first Friday of each month, the Institute of Contemporary Art hosts free events promoting talent from the Miami Design District. Check the gallery's calendar online for events.

in contemporary art. The institute has its own permanent collection of works by contemporary European and American artists, from Tracey Emin and Louise Bourgeois to Chris Ofili and Julian Schnabel, as well as local talent like Hernan Bas and Mark Handforth. The temporary exhibitions often aim for provokingly didactic comparisons, yoking together well-known artists like Picasso and Lichtenstein with lesser-known Miami-based talents.

Admission is free, but visitors should still book tickets in advance to reserve entry to the museum.

> **Founded by Miami-based billionaires Norman and Irma Braman, the Institute of Contemporary Art is dedicated to promoting continuous experimentation.**

Gold Coast Railroad Museum

 12450 SW 152nd St
Ⓜ Dadeland North then Zoo
Bus 🚌 252 🕙 10am–4pm
Mon, Wed & Fri, 11am–4pm
Sat & Sun 🅦 goldcoastrail
roadmuseum.org

This unusual museum is a must for railroad enthusiasts. Highlights include the presidential railroad car "Ferdinand Magellan," two California Zephyr cars, and three old Florida East Coast Railway steam locomotives. Children can ride a two-foot gauge railroad on weekends.

⑩ Wings Over Miami

🏠 14710 SW 128th St
🚌 136, 137 (both require a walk) ☎ (305)-233-5197
🕙 10am–5pm Wed–Sun

This museum is dedicated to the preservation of old aircraft. Its hangars contain a superb collection of finely preserved examples of operating aircraft, including a 1943 AT-6D Texan "Old Timer," a Douglas B-23 Dragon, and a British Provost jet, as well as other exhibits such as a machine-gun turret.

All these planes take to the sky during the Memorial Day weekend celebration. In January or February they are sometimes joined by B-17 and B-24 bombers in the Wings of Freedom event.

⑪ Charles Deering Estate

🏠 16701 SW 72nd Ave
🕙 10am–5pm daily
🅦 deeringestate.com

While his brother James enjoyed the splendor of Vizcaya (p86), famous business-man and philanthropist Charles Deering had his own stylish winter retreat on Biscayne Bay. The 444 acre (180 ha) estate – including a stunning mansion in the Mediterranean Revival style – was acquired by the state in 1985, and offers public access to Biscayne Bay.

Among the Charles Deering Estate's buildings are the main house and a 19th-century inn called Richmond Cottage which, when it was built, was the southernmost hotel on the US mainland.

The grounds are another attraction, with mangrove and rockland pine forests, a saltmarsh, and what is apparently the largest virgin coastal tropical hardwood hammock on the US mainland. There is an extensive fossil site on the grounds, and youth camps, conservation programs, and canoe tours on the weekend.

↑ Restored AT-6D Texan in the vast hangar at the Wings Over Miami aircraft museum

↑ Mediterranean Revival architecture at the Charles Deering Estate

DRINK

Broken Shaker at Freehand Miami

Freehand Miami is a boho hostel with a pool in the garden, a scattering of eclectic furniture, and the award-winning Broken Shaker bar, which offers some of the best cocktails in Miami.

🏠 2727 Indian
Creek Dr 🅦 thefree
hand.com

Brick

A colorful open-air shack and beer garden renowned for its craft brews and bourbons, Brick is also one of the liveliest places in town for late-night DJs and dancing.

🏠 187 NW 28th St
🅖 brickmia.com

El Patio

This shabby-chic Latin venue serves cocktails and burgers but majors on live music. The dance floor is often packed.

🏠 167 NW 23rd St
🅖 elpatiowyn
wood.com

EXPERIENCE FLORIDA

Kayaking on the waters of Silver Springs

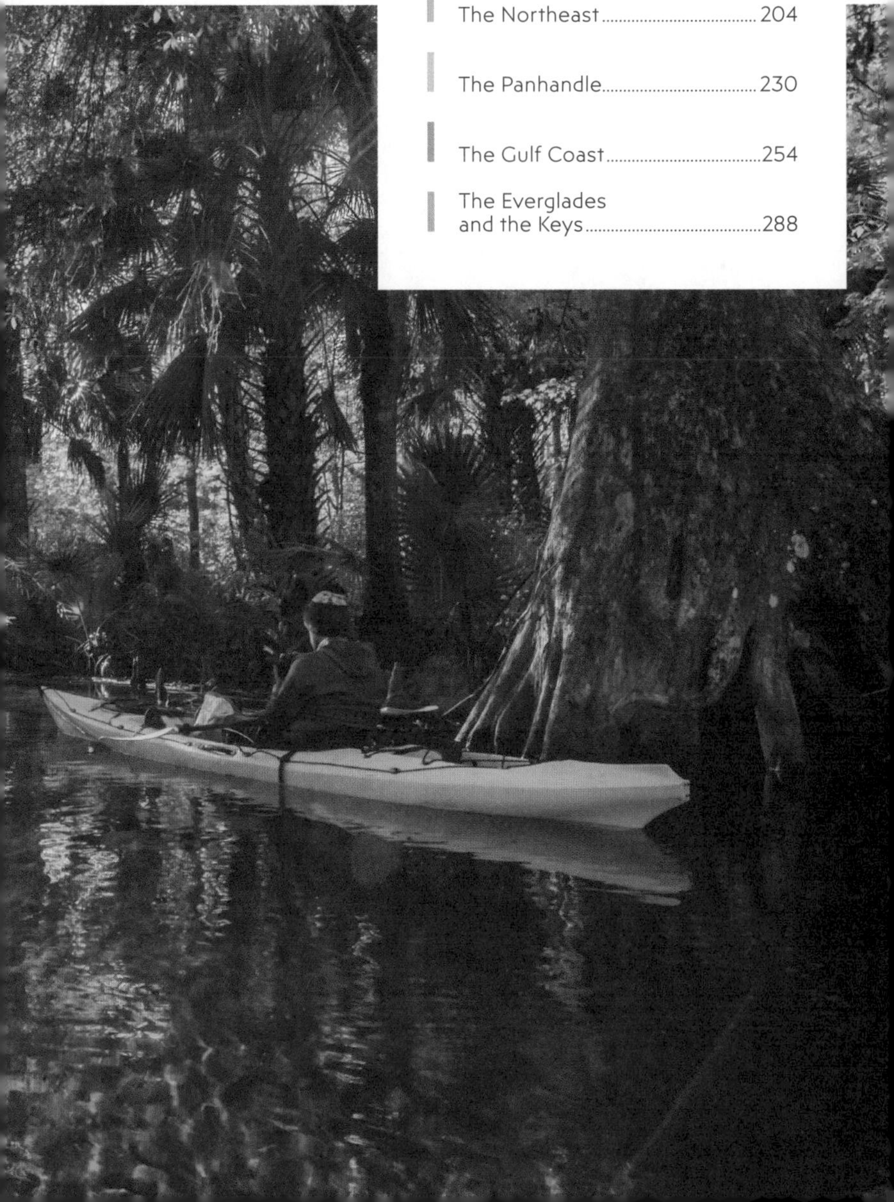

THE GOLD AND TREASURE COASTS

Named for the booty found in Spanish galleons wrecked along their shores, the Gold and Treasure coasts today are two of the state's wealthiest regions. The promise of winter sunshine once lured only the well-to-do, but now it entices millions of visitors every year. Vacations center on the pencil-thin barrier islands that extend right along the coast, squeezed between prime beaches and the Intracoastal Waterway.

The Treasure Coast to the north – stretching from Sebastian Inlet down to Jupiter Inlet – is relatively undeveloped, with great sweeps of wild, sandy beaches and affluent but understated communities. To the south, the 60-mile (97-km) Gold Coast extends from just north of West Palm Beach down to Miami. Before being opened up by Flagler's East Coast Railroad in the late 19th century, this part of Florida was a wilderness populated by Seminoles and the occasional settler. Today, except for golf courses and scattered parks, it is unremittingly built up.

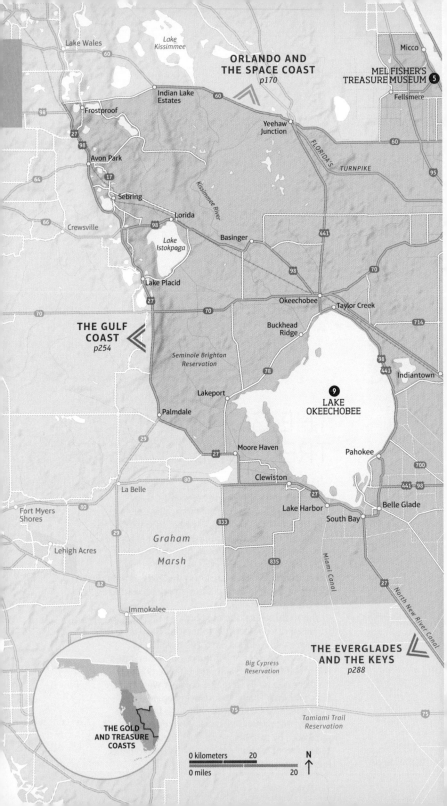

THE GOLD AND TREASURE COASTS

Must Sees
1. Palm Beach
2. Boca Raton
3. Fort Lauderdale

Experience More
4. Sebastian Inlet
5. Mel Fisher's Treasure Museum
6. Fort Pierce
7. West Palm Beach
8. Lake Worth Beach
9. Lake Okeechobee
10. Delray Beach
11. Butterfly World
12. Stuart
13. Jupiter
14. Hutchinson Island
15. Jupiter Island
16. Hollywood
17. Flamingo Gardens
18. Dania Beach
19. Seminole Casinos
20. Arthur R. Marshall Loxahatchee National Wildlife Refuge
21. Vero Beach
22. Davie
23. Juno Beach

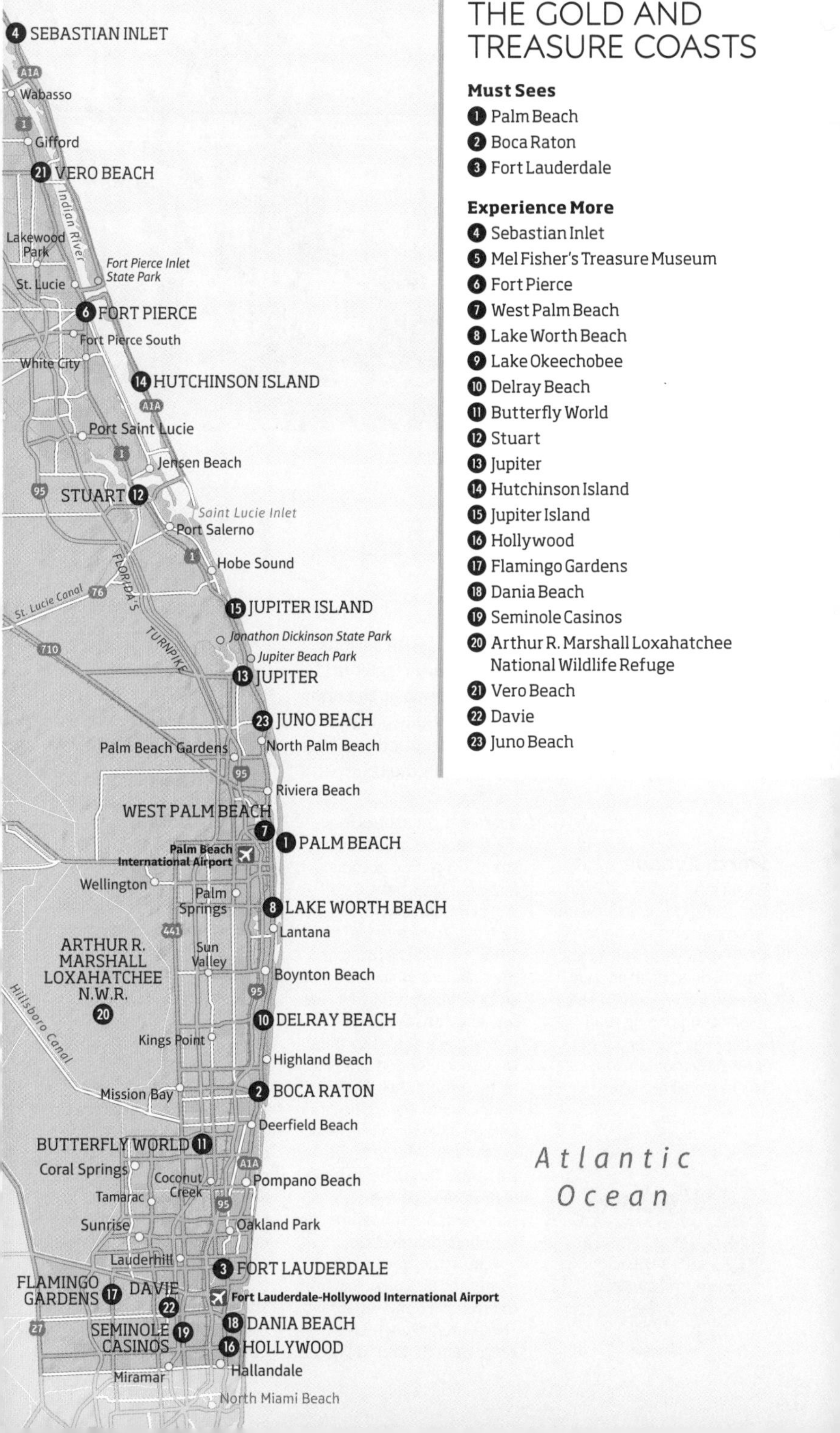

❶

PALM BEACH

🅰 G5 ✈🚋🚌 🅦 thepalmbeaches.com

Palm Beach has long been synonymous with serious American wealth. Pioneer developer Henry Flagler (p114), created this winter playground for the rich at the end of the 19th century. Though still essentially a winter resort, Palm Beach is now open all year round and lays claim to being one of the richest towns in the US.

①

Worth Avenue

For an insight into the Palm Beach lifestyle, Worth Avenue is compulsory viewing. While their employers toy over an Armani dress or an antique Russian icon, chauffeurs keep the air conditioning running in the Rolls Royces outside. Stretching four fabulous blocks from Lake Worth

Did You Know?

Winter temperatures in Palm Beach County average 74°F (23°C).

Beach to the Atlantic Ocean, it is the town's best known street, which first became fashionable with the construction of the exclusive Everglades Club at the western end in 1918. This was the result of the collaboration between the architect Addison Mizner *(see box)* and Paris Singer, heir to the sewing machine fortune. Originally intended as a hospital for officers shellshocked during World War I, it never housed a single patient, and instead became the town's social hub. Today, the building's loggias and Spanish-style courtyards are still an upscale, members-only enclave.

Across the street are Via Mizner and Via Parigi, lined with colorful shops and restaurants. These interlinking pedestrian alleys were created by Mizner

MIZNER'S SPANISH FANTASY

Addison Mizner (1872–1933) came to Palm Beach from New York in 1918. He soon began to design houses here, ultimately changing the face of both Palm Beach and Florida. By adapting the design of old Spanish buildings to suit his environment, Mizner created a new style of architecture. He became a multi-millionaire, but the collapse of the Florida land boom in the late 1920s hit him hard, and Mizner ended his life dependent on friends.

in the 1920s, and are Worth Avenue's aesthetic highlights. Inspired by the back streets of Spanish villages, the lanes are a riot of arches, twisting flights of steps, fountains, and pretty courtyards. At the mouth of the alleys are the office tower and villa that Mizner designed for himself, connected by a walkway that forms the entrance to Via Mizner's shopping area. The other vias off Worth Avenue are more modern but nonetheless charming.

A pretty, palm-lined stretch of Worth Avenue

② Society of the Four Arts

🏛 2 Four Arts Plaza
🕐 Times vary, check
website 🌐 fourarts.org

Founded in 1936, the Society of the Four Arts incorporates two libraries and an auditorium for lectures, concerts, and films. The latter was originally part of a private club designed by Mizner, but Maurice Fatio's Italianate library building is more striking. The grounds include modern sculptures.

③ The Breakers

🏛 1 South County Rd
🌐 thebreakers.com

Rising above Florida's oldest golf course, this mammoth Italian Renaissance structure is the third hotel on the site, miraculously built in less than a year. The hotel has always been a focal point for the town's social life, and is refreshingly welcoming to nonresidents, who can visit the restaurants, spa, and golf course, or just peruse the boutique stores on site. South of the hotel are three 19th-century wooden mansions, which were originally rented out to Palm Beach's wealthier winter visitors.

④ Palm Beach Suburbs

Palm Beach's high society usually hides away behind appropriately high hedges in multimillion-dollar mansions. Some of these were built by Addison Mizner and his imitators in the 1920s, but since then hundreds of others have sprung up in various architectural styles.

The most easily visible accommodation can be seen along South Ocean Boulevard, nicknamed "Mansion Row." Mar-a-Lago (No. 1100) is Palm Beach's grandest residence, with 58 bedrooms and three bomb shelters. Built by Joseph Urban and Marion Wyeth in 1927, it was bought in 1985 by Donald Trump, who converted it into a private club. The homes in the northern suburbs are more secluded. No. 1095 North Ocean Boulevard was used as a winter retreat by the Kennedy family until 1995. Glimpsing how the other half lives is widely discouraged by the minimum speed limit of 25 mph (40 km/h). Cycling is therefore an attractive option.

SHOP

Worth Avenue offers the quintessential Palm Beach luxury shopping experience. Jewelry stores abound, including those specializing in high-quality imitations. Visitors will also find fancy gift shops, high-end designer boutiques, and luxury department stores.

Saks Fifth Avenue
🏛 172 Worth Ave
🌐 saksfifthavenue.com

Tiffany & Co.
🏛 259 Worth Ave
🌐 tiffany.com

Giorgio's of Palm Beach
🏛 230 Worth Ave
🌐 giorgiosof palmbeachcom

Richter's of Palm Beach
🏛 224 Worth Ave
🌐 worth-avenue.com/ business/richters-of- palm-beach

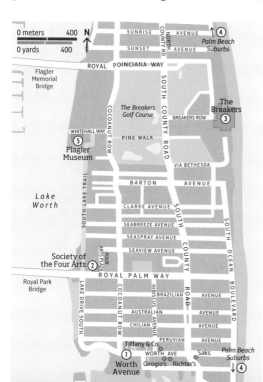

⑤ 🗝 🏍 🖥 🛍

FLAGLER MUSEUM

🅰 Coconut Row & Whitehall Way 🕙 10am–5pm Tue–Sat, noon–5pm Sun
🆆 flaglermuseum.us

One of Palm Beach's most distinctive and alluring buildings, this museum was once home to the Flagler family, who famously brought the railroad to Florida. It's now a museum where visitors can experience the Flagler's luxurious lifestyle.

This mansion– known as Whitehall – was built in 1902 by the famous oil and railroad tycoon Henry Flagler. He gave the home to his third wife, Mary Lily Kenan, as a wedding present. It was intended only as a winter residence, when the Flaglers would travel down to Palm Beach every year in one of their private railroad cars. Railcar No. 91, which was constructed to resemble a Gilded Age railway palace, is now on display in the Flagler Kenan Pavilion at the southern end of the grounds.

In 1925, 12 years after Flagler's death, a ten-story tower was added to the rear, and Whitehall became a hotel. Jean Flagler Matthews bought her grandfather's mansion in 1959 and, after costly restoration, turned it into an art museum and a key cultural venue for Palm Beach.

The Yellow Roses Room had matching wallpaper and furnishings – an innovation for its time.

Billiard room

FLAGLER'S LEGACY

Flagler and many other tycoons of the Gilded Age built much of their empires through convict leasing - a practice that disproportionately impacted the African-American community. Flagler was also able to use debt peonage - where convicts who had finished their sentences kept working to pay off debts - to complete the Florida East Coast Railway.

The Flaglers' private bathroom has a gorgeous double washstand made of onyx.

The master bedroom is furnished in yellow silk damask, a copy of the original Rococo-style fabric.

Lined with leather-bound books and filled with ornate objects, this wood-paneled library has a somewhat intimate feel.

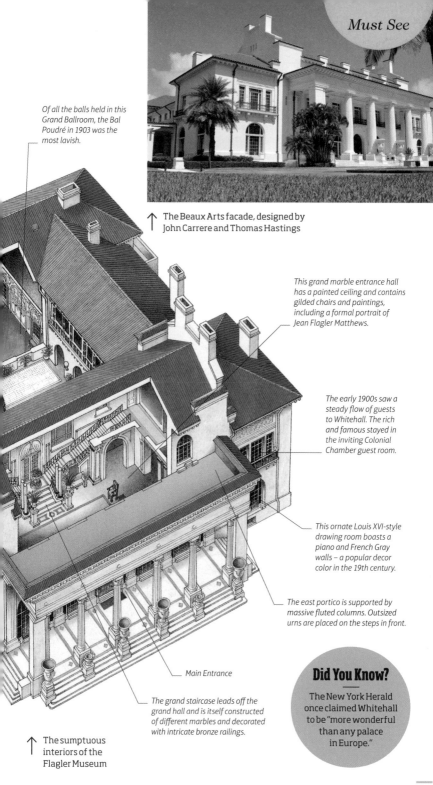

Of all the balls held in this Grand Ballroom, the Bal Poudré in 1903 was the most lavish.

↑ The Beaux Arts facade, designed by John Carrere and Thomas Hastings

This grand marble entrance hall has a painted ceiling and contains gilded chairs and paintings, including a formal portrait of Jean Flagler Matthews.

The early 1900s saw a steady flow of guests to Whitehall. The rich and famous stayed in the inviting Colonial Chamber guest room.

This ornate Louis XVI-style drawing room boasts a piano and French Gray walls – a popular decor color in the 19th century.

The east portico is supported by massive fluted columns. Outsized urns are placed on the steps in front.

Main Entrance

The grand staircase leads off the grand hall and is itself constructed of different marbles and decorated with intricate bronze railings.

↑ The sumptuous interiors of the Flagler Museum

Did You Know?

The New York Herald once claimed Whitehall to be "more wonderful than any palace in Europe."

A DRIVING TOUR
PALM BEACH

Length 4 miles (7 km) **Starting point** The tour is best followed in a clockwise direction since Worth Avenue is one way **Stopping-off point** Green's Pharmacy

Circled by the main thoroughfares of South County Road and Cocoanut Row, this tour links all the major sights of central Palm Beach, including Henry Flagler's impressive home, Whitehall. The section of the tour along Lake Drive South forms part of the scenic Palm Beach bicycle trail, which flanks Lake Worth Beach and extends into the suburbs. Although the tour is intended to be made by car, parts (or all) could equally be made by bicycle, on foot, or even on skates. These alternatives avoid the problem of Palm Beach's zealous traffic cops who patrol the streets in motorized golf carts. The Palm Beach Bicycle Trail Shop *(www.palmbeachbicycle.com)*, is a good starting point if you want to rent a bicycle, tandem, or skates to explore the area.

THE GOLD AND TREASURE COASTS

Palm Beach ●

Locator Map
For more detail see p110

Did You Know?

Palm Beach got its name after a shipwreck in 1878 caused a cargo of coconuts to be strewn along the beach.

↑ Items on display in one of the stunning rooms at the Flagler Museum, also known as Whitehall

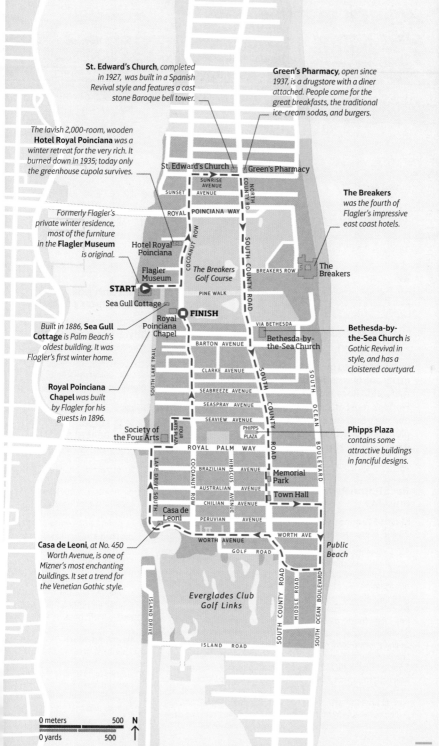

St. Edward's Church, *completed in 1927, was built in a Spanish Revival style and features a cast stone Baroque bell tower.*

Green's Pharmacy, *open since 1937, is a drugstore with a diner attached. People come for the great breakfasts, the traditional ice-cream sodas, and burgers.*

The lavish 2,000-room, wooden **Hotel Royal Poinciana** *was a winter retreat for the very rich. It burned down in 1935; today only the greenhouse cupola survives.*

St. Edward's Church

Green's Pharmacy

The Breakers *was the fourth of Flagler's impressive east coast hotels.*

SUNRISE AVENUE

SUNSET AVENUE

NORTH COUNTY RD.

ROYAL POINCIANA WAY

Formerly Flagler's private winter residence, most of the furniture in the **Flagler Museum** *is original.*

Hotel Royal Poinciana

COCONUT ROW

SOUTH COUNTY ROAD

The Breakers Golf Course

BREAKERS ROW

The Breakers

Flagler Museum

PINE WALK

START

Sea Gull Cottage

FINISH

Royal Poinciana Chapel

VIA BETHESDA

Built in 1886, **Sea Gull Cottage** *is Palm Beach's oldest building. It was Flagler's first winter home.*

Bethesda-by-the-Sea Church

Bethesda-by-the-Sea Church *is Gothic Revival in style, and has a cloistered courtyard.*

BARTON AVENUE

CLARKE AVENUE

Royal Poinciana Chapel *was built by Flagler for his guests in 1896.*

SOUTH LAKE TRAIL

SEABREEZE AVENUE

SEASPRAY AVENUE

SEAVIEW AVENUE

SOUTH COUNTY ROAD

SOUTH OCEAN BOULEVARD

Society of the Four Arts

FOUR ARTS PLAZA

PHIPPS PLAZA

Phipps Plaza *contains some attractive buildings in fanciful designs.*

ROYAL PALM WAY

LAKE DRIVE SOUTH

COCONUT ROW

BRAZILIAN AVENUE

HIBISCUS AVENUE

Memorial Park

AUSTRALIAN AVENUE

Town Hall

CHILIAN AVENUE

Casa de Leoni

PERUVIAN AVENUE

WORTH AVENUE

WORTH AVE

Casa de Leoni, *at No. 450 Worth Avenue, is one of Mizner's most enchanting buildings. It set a trend for the Venetian Gothic style.*

GOLF ROAD

Public Beach

ISLAND DRIVE

Everglades Club Golf Links

SOUTH COUNTY ROAD

MIDDLE ROAD

SOUTH OCEAN BOULEVARD

ISLAND ROAD

0 meters 500

0 yards 500

N

↑ The sprawling, water-front location of Boca Raton Resort and Club

❷

BOCA RATON

G5 🚗🚌 ℹ️1555 Palm Beach Lakes Blvd; www.myboca.us

First envisioned by the architect Addison Mizner (p112) and once advertised as "the greatest resort in the world," Boca Raton has today become one of Florida's most affluent cities. Corporate headquarters and high-tech companies sit alongside country clubs, plush shopping malls, and gorgeous homes inspired, if not built, by Mizner.

①

Boca Raton Resort and Club

📍2501 E Camino Real, 33432 🌐bocaresort.com

After initiating the early-20th-century development of Palm Beach, Addison Mizner turned his attention to a pineapple-growing settlement in the south. However, instead of his envisaged masterpiece of city planning, only a handful of buildings were completed by the time Florida's property bubble burst in 1926. Boca, as it is often called today, remained little more than a hamlet until the late 1940s.

The nucleus of Mizner's vision was the ultra-luxurious Cloister Inn, finished in 1926 with his trademark Spanish details. It stands off the eastern end of Camino Real, which was intended as the city's main thoroughfare, and is now part of the greatly expanded and exclusive Boca Raton Resort and Club. Non-residents can visit only on a weekly tour arranged by the Boca Raton Historical Society, which is based at the Town Hall on Palmetto Park Road. A few rooms here have simple displays regarding local history.

Just opposite, built in a style that epitomizes Mizner's work, is the open-air Mizner Park. This is perhaps the most impressive of Boca's dazzling malls that illustrate the city's rarefied lifestyle.

②

Lynn University Conservatory of Music

📍3601 N Military Trail 🌐lynn.edu/academics/colleges/conservatory

The Conservatory of Music at Lynn University admits a highly select group of gifted

LOCAL BEACHES

Spanish River Park
An attractive beach with pleasant shady picnic areas. Its loveliest spot is a lagoon on the Intracoastal Waterway.

Red Reef Park
Head here to stroll along the boardwalk criss-crossing the top of the dunes, enjoy uncrowded sands, and snorkel around an artificial reef just offshore.

Deerfield Beach
This is the area's most inviting community, thanks to its fishing pier and fine beach backed by a palm-lined promenade.

music students from all over the world to train for a career in solo, chamber, and orchestral music performance – many ultimately achieving worldwide acclaim. As a center for the celebration of music, the Conservatory attracts thousands of music lovers who attend around 100 student, faculty, and guest artist performances, as well as master classes and lectures each year.

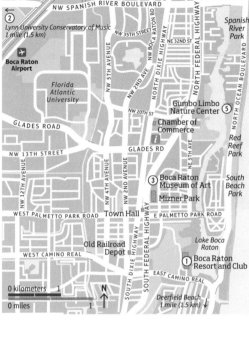

Boca Raton Museum of Art

⬛ 501 Plaza Real, Mizner Park ⏰ 11am-7pm Wed-Sun 🌐 bocamuseum.org

Located in a spectacular setting within beautiful Mizner Park in downtown Boca Raton, this museum contains 44,000 sq ft (4,088 sq m) of space for world class exhibitions, and an impressive display of contemporary art.

Sports Immortals Museum

⬛ 6830 N Federal Hwy ⏰ 10am-6pm Mon-Fri, 11am-5pm Sat & Sun 🌐 sportsimmortals.com

A must-visit for sports fans in Boca, this museum is home to the largest and most diverse collection of sporting memorabilia in the world. Among the staggering 10,000 sports mementos are Babe Ruth's baseball bat, Pelé's soccer uniform, and Muhammad Ali's boxing robes. Perhaps the most prized item in the collection is a rare cigarette card worth an astonishing $1,000,000; the card was withdrawn when the baseball player depicted objected to any association with tobacco.

↑ Visitors examining an Andy Warhol exhibition within the Boca Raton Museum of Art

Gumbo Limbo Nature Center

⬛ 1801 North Ocean Blvd ⏰ 9am-4pm Mon-Sat, noon-4pm Sun 🌐 gumbolimbo.org

Founded in 1984, this first-rate, highly informative center lies next to the Intracoastal, within Red Reef Park. A number of hikes through the site are especially popular. There is a wooden boardwalk that winds through mangroves and a tropical hardwood hammock to a tower, which offers sensational panoramic views of the surrounding area.

Another highlight of the center is the sea turtle rehabilitation program, which focuses on monitoring nests and rescuing sick or injured turtles within a 5-mile (8 km) span of beaches in Boca.

Other attractions at this lush site include a butterfly garden and an aquarium populated with thousands of tropical fish.

❸

FORT LAUDERDALE

 G5 🚗🚆🚌🚕 ℹ️ 100 East Broward Blvd; www.sunny.org

During the second Seminole War (p45), Fort Lauderdale consisted of little more than three forts, but by 1900, it had become a busy trading post on the New River. Today, Greater Fort Lauderdale wears many hats: it is at once an important business and cultural center, a popular beach resort, and a giant cruise port. However, it is still the city's myriad waterways that define its unique character.

①

History Fort Lauderdale

📍 219 SW 2nd Ave ⏰ 10am-4pm daily 🌐 historyfort lauderdale.org

The New River Inn – Broward County's oldest hotel – was built in 1905. Today it houses a museum, which contains various fascinating exhibits that chart the area's history and the growth of the city up to the 1940s. A small theater shows amusing silent movies that were made during the 1920s heyday of south Florida's movie industry. You can also attend workshops and lectures.

②

NSU Museum of Art

📍 1 E Las Olas Blvd ⏰ 11am-5pm Mon-Sat; noon-5pm Sun 🌐 nsuartmuseum.org

This fine art museum, housed in an impressive postmodern building, is best known for its large assemblage of works of CoBrA art. The name CoBrA derives from the initial letters of Copenhagen, Brussels, and Amsterdam, the capitals of the home countries of a group of Expressionist painters who worked from 1948–51. The museum displays works by Karel Appel, Pierre Alechinsky, and Asger Jorn, who were the

movement's leading exponents. The William Glackens Wing features works by the American Impressionist after whom it is named.

---

③

Museum of Discovery and Science

📍 401 SW 2nd St ⏰ 10am-5pm Tue-Sat, noon-5pm Sun 🌐 mods.org

This is one of the largest and best museums of its kind in Florida. Here, a multitude of creatures, including alligators and snakes, appear in re-created Florida "ecoscapes." In the AutoNation® IMAX® theater, movies are projected onto a huge 60-ft (18-m) screen. This is also one of the few places in the world to show 3-D IMAX movies, where the audience uses personal headsets for 360-degree sound. The latest

Did You Know?

The vanished flights that sparked the lore of the Bermuda Triangle took off from this city in 1945.

← The skyline and waterways of Fort Lauderdale, lit up as dusk falls

addition to the museum, the EcoDiscovery Center, offers an array of interactive exhibits, including an otter habitat.

④

Stranahan House

🏠 335 SE 6th Ave ⏰ For tours only; 1, 2 & 3pm daily 🚫 Public hols 🌐 stranahan house.org

The city's oldest surviving house, a pine and oak building built by the pioneer Frank Stranahan in 1901, became the center of Fort Lauderdale's community, serving as a trading post, meeting hall, post office, and bank. The photos of Stranahan trading with the local Seminoles are more evocative of the early days than the furnishings

inside. Goods such as alligator hides and egret plumes were brought by the Seminoles from the nearby Everglades in their dugout canoes.

⑤

Las Olas Boulevard

Despite a constant stream of traffic, the section of Las Olas Boulevard between 6th and 11th Avenues is the city's most picturesque and busiest street. A winning mix of formal, casual, and chic boutiques and eateries line this thoroughfare, where it is possible to buy anything from a fur coat to Haitian art. Those who are not serious shoppers should visit in the evenings, when the sidewalks overflow with drinkers and diners, and the palm trees are outlined with twinkling lights.

Heading toward the beach, the boulevard passes a canal-lined area from which there is a closer look at a more lavish Fort Lauderdale lifestyle.

TOP 3 WAYS TO EXPLORE THE WATERWAYS

Jungle Queen Riverboat

🌐 junglequeen.com

This old-fashioned riverboat takes visitors up the New River on an exciting half-day trip.

Carrie B Riverboat

🌐 carriebcruises.com

The 90-minute tours depart from the Riverwalk, and pass mansions and manatees en route.

Water Taxis

🌐 watertaxi.com

Operating much like shared land taxis, this fleet of boats travel up New River to Downtown and anywhere from the port north to Oakland Park Boulevard.

↑ Palms lining the edge of Fort Lauderdale's beach, as it meets the promenade

The Beach

Until the mid-1980s, when the local authorities began to discourage them, students by the thousand would descend on Fort Lauderdale for Spring Break. Today, the excellent beach is still the liveliest along the Gold Coast – especially at the end of Las Olas Boulevard, where in-line skaters cruise, and strollers enjoy the beach-front promenade. Beachside Fort Lauderdale also offers plenty of activities to suit active family vacations.

Hugh Taylor Birch State Park

🏠 3109 E Sunrise Blvd
📞 (954) 564-4521
🕐 8am–6pm daily

This park is 180 acres (73 ha), part of 3 miles (5 km) of barrier island, which Chicago lawyer Hugh Taylor Birch bought in 1894. It amounts to one of the Gold Coast's few undeveloped oases of greenery. Visitors come here to rent canoes on the freshwater lagoon, wander along a trail through a tropical hammock, and, above all, to take their daily exercise along a scenic circular road.

International Swimming Hall of Fame

🏠 1 Hall of Fame Dr 🕐 9am–5pm Mon–Fri 🌐 ishof.org

If you ever wanted to know about the history of Oman's aquatic sports, or the evolution of diving positions, this is the place. The museum contains a fascinating collection of aquatic memorabilia; including ancient wooly bathing suits; amusing mannequins of stars, such as Johnny "Tarzan" Weismuller, holder of 57 world swimming records; and a collection of over 20 Olympic medals won in aquatic sports since 1896.

EXPLORING DOWNTOWN FORT LAUDERDALE

Downtown Fort Lauderdale, with its modern, sleek, glass-sided office buildings, presents the city's business face. A hop-on, hop-off trolley tour provides an easy way to get to explore the heart of the city, linking the downtown area and the beach. Alternatively, the city's Riverwalk follows a 1.5-mile (2.4-km) stretch of the New River's north bank and passes most of the historical landmarks. This promenade starts near Stranahan House (p121), goes through a strip of parkland, and ends up by the Broward Center for the Performing Arts.

Old Fort Lauderdale extends along Southwest 2nd Avenue, and is comprised of an attractive group of early 1900s buildings The King-Cromartie House, built in 1907 on the south bank of the river, was transported by barge to its present site in 1971. Its modest furnishings reflect the basic living conditions of Florida's early settlers. Behind the home is a replica of the city's first schoolhouse, which opened in 1899.

Until the mid-1980s, when the local authorities began to discourage them, students by the thousand would descend on Fort Lauderdale for Spring Break.

SHOP

(9) (img) (img)

Bonnet House Museum and Gardens

📍 900 N Birch Rd 🕐 9am-4pm Tue-Sun 🌐 bonnet house.org

This unusually furnished house is by far the most enjoyable piece of old Fort Lauderdale. It stands amid idyllic tropical grounds, where the bonnet water lily, from which the house took its name, once grew. Originally purchased by lawyer Hugh Taylor Birch in 1895, the property has witnessed more than 4,000 years of Florida history.

Artist Frederic Bartlett, who was married to Birch's daughter Helen, built this cozy, plantation-style winter home himself in 1920, and examples of his work, especially murals, are everywhere.

Swans and monkeys inhabit the grounds, which are also home to one of the largest orchid collections in southeast US. Guided tours are available and several concerts and classes are held for adults throughout the year. There is also an annual orchid festival where plant lovers can buy varieties of exotic plants, view pretty displays and enjoy delectable food.

Sawgrass Mills Mall

Florida's second largest mall houses over 300 retail outlets. The Colonnade Outlets promise discounted designer names across 70 stores.

📍 12801 W Sunrise Blvd 🌐 simon.com/mall/sawgrass-mills

Swap Shop of Fort Lauderdale

The American version of a bazaar, this place has whole rows devoted to jewelry, sunglasses, and other trinkets. Visitors are also lured by the fresh produce sold here and the delightful nursery.

📍 3291 W Sunrise Blvd 🕐 9am-5pm Mon-Wed & Fri, 8am-5pm Thu, 7:30am-5:30pm Sat & Sun 🌐 floridaswapshop.com

A sun-dappled passage outside the Bonnet House, and its water lily-dotted grounds *(inset)*

EXPERIENCE MORE

4

Sebastian Inlet

G4 · 700 Main St, Sebastian; www.sebastian chamber.com · Sebastian

At Sebastian Inlet, the Atlantic Ocean mingles with the brackish waters of the Indian River section of the Intracoastal Waterway. The **Sebastian Inlet State Park** spans this channel and, with its 3 miles (5 km) of pristine beaches, is one of the most popular state parks in Florida.

A tranquil cove on the northern side of the inlet is an ideal place to swim – avoiding the waves that make the southern shores (on Orchid Island) one of the best surfing spots on Florida's east coast. Competitions take place on many weekends, and there are boards for rent. The park is also famous for its fishing, and the inlet's mouth is invariably crowded with fishing boats. The two jetties on either side are also crammed with anglers, while more lines dangle in the Indian River.

Did You Know?

Atlantic bottlenose dolphins inhabit the waters surrounding the Sebastian Inlet State Park.

At the southern end of the park, the **McLarty Treasure Museum** takes a detailed look at the history surrounding the loss of the Spanish Plate Fleet in 1715. On July 31 a hurricane wrecked 11 galleons on the shallow reefs off the coast between Sebastian Inlet and Fort Pierce. The ships were en route from Havana back to Spain, laden with booty from Spain's American colonies. About a third of the 2,100 sailors lost their lives, while the survivors set up a camp where the McLarty Treasure Museum now stands.

Immediately following this tragedy, some 80 percent of the cargo was salvaged by the survivors, helped by local Ais people. The fleet then lay undisturbed until 1928, when one of the wrecks was rediscovered. Salvaging resumed in the early 1960s; since then, millions of dollars worth of treasures have been recovered. Finds on display include gold and silver coins but most are domestic items.

Sebastian Inlet State Park

 9700 S Hwy A1A, Melbourne Beach · 24 hours daily · floridastateparks.com

McLarty Treasure Museum

13180 N Hwy A1A · (772) 589-2147 · 10am–4pm daily

5

Mel Fisher's Treasure Museum

G4 · 1322 US Hwy 1, Sebastian · Sebastian · 10am–5pm Mon–Sat, noon–5pm Sun · Sep · melfisher.com/Sebastian

An intriguing rags-to-riches story is presented at this

→ The fishing pier at Sebastian Inlet State Park, stretching into the Atlantic Ocean

The historic and educational National Navy UDT-SEAL Museum, north of Fort Pierce

museum. "The World's Greatest Treasure Hunter," Mel Fisher died in 1998, but his treasure-hunting team of divers carry on his legacy.

The museum contains treasures from different wrecks, including the 1715 fleet (which his team has been salvaging for decades), and the Atocha. There are jewels, a gold bar, and more everyday items. In the Bounty Room, visitors can buy original Spanish reales, or copies of historic jewelry. The Mel Fisher Maritime Museum *(p300)* in Key West is also worth a visit.

❻ Fort Pierce

🅰G4 ✈🚌 ℹ 2300 Virginia Ave; www.cityoffort pierce.com

Fort Pierce's biggest draw is its barrier islands, reached by crossing two causeways that sweep across the Intracoastal Waterway.

Take the North Beach Causeway to reach North Hutchinson Island. Its southern tip is occupied by the **Fort Pierce Inlet State Park**, which includes the town's best beach. Just to the north is the **National Navy UDT-SEAL Museum**. From 1943 to 1946, more than 3,000 US Navy frogmen of the Underwater Demolition Teams (UDTs) trained here. By the 1960s, they had become an elite advance fighting force known as SEALs (Sea, Air, Land commandos). The museum explains the frogmen's roles in World War II, Korea, Vietnam, and in the present.

Half a mile (1 km) away is Jack Island – actually a peninsula. This mangrove-covered preserve teems with birdlife and is crossed by a short trail leading to an observation tower. On the southern causeway linking Fort Pierce to Hutchinson Island is the **St. Lucie County Historical**

Museum. Its displays include finds from the 1715 wrecks in the Galleon Room, and reconstructions of a Seminole camp. Visitors can also explore the adjacent "Cracker" style home *(p32)*.

Back on the mainland, literature buffs can follow the **Zora Neale Hurston Dust Tracks Heritage Trail**, dedicated to the writer's final years.

Fort Pierce Inlet State Park

⊛ 🅰905 Shorewinds Dr, N Hutchinson Island ⏰8am–sunset daily 🔗floridastateparks.org

National Navy UDT-SEAL Museum

⊛🅰🅰3300 N Hwy A1A ⏰10am–4pm Tue–Sat, noon–4pm Sun 🔗navy sealmuseum.com

St. Lucie County Historical Museum

⊛ 🅰414 Seaway Dr ⏰10am–4pm Tue–Sat; noon–4pm Sun 🔗stlucieco.gov

Zora Neale Hurston Dust Tracks Heritage Trail

🅰Garden of Heavenly Rest Cemetery, Avenue S and 17th St 🔗cityoffortpierce.com

7

West Palm Beach

G5 1555 Palm Beach Lakes Blvd; www.palmbeachfl.com

At the end of the 1800s, Henry Flagler *(p114)* decided to move the unsightly homes of Palm Beach's workers to the mainland, out of sight of the tourists. He thus created West Palm Beach, which has been the commercial center of Palm Beach County ever since.

The Downtown Waterfront Commons on Clematis Street is alive with visitors enjoying the picturesque Lake Worth Beach, and is home to an extensive calendar of events. Just north of Downtown West Palm Beach, Northwood Village is also worth a visit for its restaurants, antique shops, and vintage boutiques.

Aimed at children, the **South Florida Science Center and Aquarium** offers great hands-on exhibits on subjects such as light, sound, color, and the weather. You can attempt to create your own clouds, and even touch a mini-tornado.

The **Norton Museum of Art** was established in 1941 with about 100 canvases belonging to Ralph Norton, a Chicago steel magnate who had retired to West Palm Beach. The French Impressionist and Post-Impressionist collection includes works by Cézanne, Braque, Picasso, Matisse, and Gauguin, whose moving *Agony in the Garden* is the museum's most famous painting. *Night Mist* (1945) by Jackson Pollock forms part of the Norton's impressive store of 20th-century American art. This gallery also features some fine works by Winslow Homer, Georgia O'Keeffe, Edward Hopper, and Andy Warhol. The third main collection comprises an array of artifacts from China, including ceramic figures of animals and courtiers from the Tang Dynasty (4th–11th centuries AD). There are also more modern sculptures by Brancusi, Degas, and Rodin.

Just north of downtown, the **Richard and Pat Johnson Palm Beach County History Museum** occupies the 1916 Neo-Classical courthouse, which operated until 1995 and was restored before reopening as a museum in 2008. Permanent exhibits chronicle Palm Beach history, with maps and special displays on city founders such as Addison Mizner. Short-term exhibits rotate year-round in the Courtroom Gallery.

Across the inlet, Singer Island and Palm Beach Shores are relaxing, slow-paced communities with a splendid wide beach. Boating and fishing are popular activities here, and there are plenty of options for those who want to charter sport-fishing boats or book a cruise to explore the waterways.

At the north end of Singer Island is **John D. MacArthur Beach State Park**. Here, a dramatic boardwalk bridge meanders across a mangrove-lined inlet of Lake Worth Beach to a hardwood hammock and a lovely beach. In the summer, visitors can see nesting loggerhead turtles while on

Visitors admiring 20th-century art *(inset)* at Norton Museum of Art ↓

↑ A wooden walkway bordered by plants and palm trees, Singer Island

a guided walk. For those who enjoy shopping, the Gardens Mall, 2 miles (3 km) inland in Palm Beach Gardens, has fragrant walkways and glass elevators that link approximately 200 stores.

South Florida Science Center and Aquarium
◈ 🏠 4801 Dreher Trail N 🕙 9am–5pm Mon–Fri, 10am–6pm Sat & Sun 🌐 sfsciencecenter.org

Norton Museum of Art
◈◈◐☺◐ 🏠 1451 South Olive Ave 🕙 Times vary, check website 🌐 norton.org

Richard and Pat Johnson Palm Beach County History Museum
◉ 🏠 300 North Dixie Highway 🕙 10am–4pm Tue–Sat 🌐 pbchistory.org

John D. MacArthur Beach State Park
◈◉ 🏠 A1A, 2 miles (3 km) N of Riviera Bridge 🕙 8am–5pm daily 🌐 macarthurbeach.org

---

8

Lake Worth Beach
🅰 G5 🚌 ℹ️ 501 Lake Ave; lakeworthbeachfl.gov

Lake Worth Beach is an unpretentious community. On its barrier island side there is a jolly public beach scene; on the mainland, antique shops set the tone along Lake and Lucerne avenues. Visitors will find an Art Deco movie theater converted into an space for art exhibitions, live music clubs, coffeehouses, art galleries, antique malls, retail stores, and restaurants. The community has worked hard to retain its old Florida flavor, with rules in place that protect the town from insensitive development.

STAY

The Colony Hotel
Colonial-style hotel with a pool in the shape of Florida.

🅰 G5 🏠 155 Hammon Ave, Palm Beach 🌐 thecolonypalmbeach.com

$$$

The Brazilian Court Hotel
Suites offer whirlpool baths and patios.

🅰 G5 🏠 301 Australian Ave, Palm Beach 🌐 thebraziliancourt.com

$$$

The Chesterfield Palm Beach
One of the city's best hotels. Enjoy fine dining alongside live music.

🅰 G5 🏠 363 Cocoanut Row, Palm Beach 🌐 chesterfieldpb.com

$$$

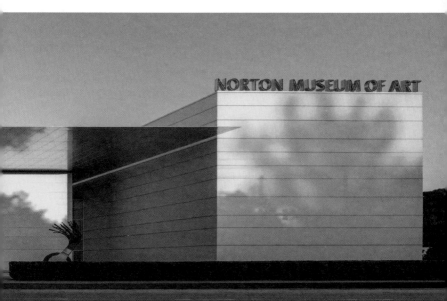

NORTON MUSEUM OF ART

↑ Fisherman throwing his net into Lake Okeechobee, also known as the "Big O"

9

Lake Okeechobee

⚑F5 🛈115 E Main St, Pahokee 🚌Palm Trans bus to Pahokee 🌐okeechobee. uslakes.info

Meaning "big water" in the Seminole language, Okeechobee is the largest lake in Florida and one of the biggest in the US. The "Big O," as the lake is often called, is famous for its abundance of fish, particularly largemouth bass. **Roland Martin Marina,** or any of the many marinas, will rent visitors a boat, tackle, bait, picnic food, or a guide and chartered boat. Nearby Clewiston offers the best facilities, with three marinas and a choice of decent motels.

For those who are not anglers, time in Florida is better spent elsewhere. The birdlife is rich along the shore, but the lake is too big to be scenic, and a high encircling dike, which protects the countryside from floods, prevents views from the road. Pahokee is one of the few places to offer easy lakeside access, and it boasts possibly the best sunsets in Florida, after the Gulf Coast.

Did You Know?

Lake Okeechobee covers 750 sq miles (1,942 sq km).

The communities at the lake's southern end are dependent on sugar for their prosperity. Half the sugarcane in the country is grown in the plains around local cities of Belle Glade and Clewiston ("America's Sweetest Town"), where the rich soil is even darker than chocolate.

A one-time federal plan to buy the sugarcane land south of Lake Okeechobee and return it to marshland, in order to cleanse the water draining into the Everglades, has hit some stumbling blocks. Meanwhile, Big Sugar continues to produce its sweet product near the Big Water.

Roland Martin Marina
🏠920 E Del Monte Ave, Clewiston ⏰5:30am–5pm daily 🌐rolandmartin marina.com

10

Delray Beach

⚑G5 🚉🚌 🛈2 South Ocean Blvd; www.visitdelray beach.org

Arguably the most welcoming place between Palm Beach and Boca Raton, Delray Beach exudes an upscale but friendly air. The town is justifiably proud of the national awards for "civic-mindness" and being the "Most Fun Small Town in America" that it received in 1993, 2001, and 2017.

The long stretch of sedate beach here is magnificent, and makes for a great day spent on the sand or in the water. Between November and April, **Delray Yacht Cruises** runs daily paddleboat trips along the Intracoastal Waterway. Drift fishing boats also offer rides.

Delray's heart lies inland, along Atlantic Avenue – an inviting street softly lit at night by old-fashioned lamps and lined with palm trees, chic cafes, antique shops, and art galleries. Alongside lies Old School Square, with a cluster of attractive 1920s buildings and assorted performance venues. Nearby, snug **Cason Cottage Museum** has been meticulously restored to the way it might have looked originally, around 1915.

Morikami Museum and Japanese Gardens is one of the few museums in the US devoted exclusively to Japanese culture. The museum complex is located on land donated by a farmer named George Morikami; he was one of a group of Japanese pioneers who established the Yamato Colony (named after ancient Japan) on the northern edge of Boca Raton (p118) in 1905. With the help of money from a development company owned by Henry Flagler (p114), Morikami and his associates hoped to grow rice, tea, and silk. The project never took off, however, and the colony gradually petered out.

On a small island in a lake, the Yamato-kan villa provides displays that tell the settlers' story and also delve into past and present Japanese culture. There are interesting reconstructions of a bathroom, a modern bedroom, and eel-and-sake restaurants.

Six historic garden sites surround the villa, and paths lead into serene pinewoods.

A building across the lake holds exhibitions on all matters Japanese, a cafe serving Japanese food, and a traditional teahouse where tea ceremonies are performed once a month. The museum also hosts regular events, from traditional craft and cooking workshops to film series and lectures. A particular highlight of the museum's calendar are the authentic seasonal festivals such as Hinamatsuri.

Delray Yacht Cruises
🅰 801 East Atlantic Ave
🅦 delraybeachcruises.com

Cason Cottage Museum
♿ 🅐 🕐 🅰 5 NE 1st St 🅞 For tours only; Nov-Apr: 11am-3pm Thu-Sat 🅦 delraybeach history.org/cason_cottage

Morikami Museum and Japanese Gardens
♿ 🙂 🕐 🅰 4000 Morikami Park Rd 🅞 10am-5pm Tue-Sun 🅦 morikami.org

↑ A couple of colorful winged residents at Butterfly World

⑪

Butterfly World

🅰 G5 🅰 3600 W Sample Rd, Coconut Creek 🅡 Deerfield Beach (Amtrak & Tri-Rail) 🚌 Pompano Beach 🅞 9am-5pm Mon-Sat, 11am-5pm Sun 🅦 butterflyworld.com

Within giant walk-through aviaries brimming with tropical flowers, thousands of dazzling butterflies from all over the world flit about, often landing on visitors' shoulders. Since the aviaries are effectively solar powered, the butterflies are most active on warm, sunny days, so it is worth planning a visit accordingly. There are also cabinets of emerging pupae and a fascinating collection of mounted insects – including morpho butterflies, with their incredible metallic blue wings, and beetles and grasshoppers the size of an adult hand. Outside, enjoy a wander around the extensive and peaceful gardens no matter the weather.

← Strolling by a tranquil pond at the Morikami Museum and Japanese Gardens

The distinctive Jupiter Inlet Lighthouse and its serene grounds ↑

⑫ Stuart

🅰 G4 🛈 101 SW Flagler Ave, Stuart, Martin County; www.discover martin.com

The magnificent causeway across the island-speckled Indian River from Hutchinson Island offers a fine approach to Martin County's main town. Ringed by affluent waterfront enclaves and residential golf developments, Stuart has a fetching, rejuvenated downtown area, which is by-passed by the busy coastal highways. South of Roosevelt Bridge, along Flagler Avenue and Osceola Street, is a short riverside boardwalk, a smattering of 1920s brick and stucco buildings, and a number of art galleries. In the evenings, live music emanates from buzzing restaurants and bars.

⑬ Jupiter

🅰 G5 🛈 800 N US Hwy 1, Palm Beach County; www.jupiter.fl.us

This small town is best known for its fine beaches and spring-training

camps of the Miami Marlins and St. Louis Cardinals baseball teams.

Close by, on the south side of Jupiter Inlet, Jupiter Beach Park is easily accessible and has a superb beach of golden sand, complete with lifeguards – it is also a mecca for anglers and pelicans. There are picnic pavilions, tables, a children's play area, restrooms, and a fishing jetty. Visitors can enjoy a good view across to scenic **Jupiter Inlet Lighthouse**, dating from 1860 and the oldest structure in the county, which can be climbed for a wider perspective. The old oil house at its base is now a small museum. On the other side of the Jupiter Inlet, the

FLORIDA'S SEA TURTLES

From May to September, female turtles lumber up the beaches of Florida's central east coast at night to lay their eggs in the sand. Two months later the hatchlings emerge and dash for the ocean, again at night. Sea turtles are threatened partly because hatchlings are disoriented by lights from buildings. To join an organized turtle watch, call local chambers of commerce, such as the one in Juno Beach.

DuBois Pioneer Home – built in 1898 – is a fine example of a pioneer home. Nearby, the huge **Carlin Park** has playing fields, picnic areas, tennis courts, and a guarded beach.

Jupiter Inlet Lighthouse

⊘ 🅰 500 Captain Armour's Way 🕐 Times vary, check website 🅦 jupiterlight house.org

DuBois Pioneer Home

⊘ 🅰 19075 DuBois Rd 🕐 10am–1pm Tue–Thu (by guided tour only)

Carlin Park

🅰 400 South State Rd A1A 📞 (561) 966-6600 🕐 Sunrise to sunset daily (lifeguards on duty 9am–5:20pm)

⑭ Hutchinson Island

🅰 G4 🛈 1900 Ricou Jensen Beach, St Lucie County/ Martin County; www. jensenbeachflorida.info

Extending for more than 20 miles (32 km), this barrier island is most memorable for its breathtaking beaches. In the south, sun-worshipers

→

Watching the waves and playing in the sand on one of Jupiter Island's beaches

was for the early caretakers, who often stayed only a year. A replica of an 1840s "surf boat" used on rescue missions sits outside. Beyond the refuge is Bathtub Beach, the best on the island. The natural pool formed by a sandstone reef offshore provides a safe, popular swimming spot.

Elliott Museum
⊛ 🏠 825 NE Ocean Blvd
🕐 10am–5pm daily
🔤 hsmc-fl.com

House of Refuge Museum at Gilbert's Bar
⊛ 🏠 301 SE MacArthur Blvd 🕐 10am–4pm Mon-Sat; 1–4pm Sun 🔤 hsmc-fl.com/house-of-refuge

---

⑮

Jupiter Island

🅰 G5 🏷 800 N US Hwy 1, Martin County; www.townofjupiterisland.com

Much of this long, thin island is a well-to-do residential neighborhood, but there are also several excellent public beaches.

Toward Jupiter Island's northern end, **Hobe Sound National Wildlife Refuge** beckons with more than 3 miles (5 km) of beach, mangroves, and magnificent unspoiled dunes. The other half of the refuge, a strip of

head for Sea Turtle Beach and the adjacent Jensen Beach Park, close to the junction of routes 707 and A1A. Stuart Beach, at the head of the causeway across the Indian River from Stuart, is well frequented, too.

Near Stuart Beach is the **Elliott Museum**, created in 1961 in honor of inventor Sterling Elliott, some of whose quirky contraptions are on show. Focusing on art, history, technology, and innovation, the museum was completely rebuilt in 2013.

Continuing south for about a mile (1.5 km), you will reach the **House of Refuge Museum at Gilbert's Bar**. Erected in 1875, it is one of ten such shelters along the east coast, established by the Lifesaving Service (predecessors of the US Coast Guard) for shipwreck victims. The stark rooms in the charming clapboard house show how hard life

pine scrub flanking the Intracoastal Waterway, is a haven for birds, including the Florida scrub jay. There is a nature center by the junction of US 1 and A1A.

Blowing Rocks Preserve, a short distance south, has a fine beach. During storms, holes in the shoreline's limestone escarpment shoot water skyward – hence the name.

Hobe Sound National Wildlife Refuge
⊛ 🏠 13640 SE Federal Hwy 📞 (772) 546-6141 🕐 Nature Center: 9am–3pm Mon-Fri 🔤 fws.gov/refuge/hobe_sound

---

EAT

Jetty's Waterfront Restaurant
Savor fresh seafood on a terrace overlooking the Jupiter Inlet Lighthouse. Highlights include Jetty's crab cakes and conch fritters.

🅰 G5 🏠 1075 Hwy A1A, Jupiter 🔤 jettysjupiter.com

Hutchinson Island, a barrier island with beautiful beaches

EAT & DRINK

Le Tub Saloon

Legendary brews, burgers and delicious Key lime pie in a quirky 1950s gas station setting.

G6 ⌂1100 N Ocean Dr, Hollywood Ⓦtheletub.com

Ⓢ Ⓢ Ⓢ

Jaxson's

Jaxson's serves fine lunches but its delicious ice creams are the big draw here.

G5 ⌂128 S Federal Hwy, Dania Beach Ⓦjaxsonsicecream.com

Ⓢ Ⓢ Ⓢ

Las Vegas Cuban Cuisine

This is just one venue from a local chain that offers tasty Cuban fare.

Ⓐ G6 ⌂810 Stirling Rd, Hollywood Ⓦlasvegas cubancuisine.com

Ⓢ Ⓢ Ⓢ

Hollywood

Ⓐ G6 Ⓡ Ⓔ ⓘ 330 N Federal Hwy, Broward County; www.hollywood chamber.org

In 1920 a Californian named Joseph Young arrived in the south of Florida with the intention of building his dream city. His vision came to life in Hollywood, and despite great damage during a hurricane in 1926, the city is now a large and laid-back resort city. It's especially popular with those from colder climes who migrate to the greater Fort Lauderdale area every winter to enjoy the lovely city and warm weather.

In the historic arts district around Young Circle, the **Art and Culture Center of Hollywood** holds art exhibitions, theater, music, and dance performances.

Visit the Hollywood Beach Broadwalk, a 2.5-mile (4-km) cycling and walking path along the beach, dotted with live music venues and family-friendly restaurants and live music venues. The sandy city beach itself is also a lovely spot for families to just sit back and relax.

The **Anne Kolb Nature Center** includes a five-level observation fishing pier, two nature trails, outdoor amphitheater, and exhibit hall. The **Topeekeegee Yugnee Park** offers picnic and playground areas, a water park, paved pathways for walking and biking, and basketball and tennis courts.

Art and Culture Center of Hollywood

Ⓐ ⌂1650 Harrison St Ⓒ10am–5pm Mon-Sat, noon–4pm Sun Ⓦartand culturecenter.org

Anne Kolb Nature Center

⌂751 Sheridan St Ⓒ8am–7:30pm daily Ⓦbroward. org/Parks

Topeekeegee Yugnee Park

⌂3300 N Park Rd Ⓒ9am–5pm daily Ⓦbroward.org

Flamingo Gardens

Ⓐ F4 ⌂3750 S Flamingo Rd, Davie, Broward County Ⓡ Ⓔ Fort Lauderdale Ⓒ9:30am–5pm daily Ⓦflamingogardens.org

These beautiful gardens started out in 1927 as a weekend retreat for the Wrays, a citrus-farming family. You can tour the Wrays' 1930s home, furnished in period style, but the gardens are

Beachgoers heading to a vintage-style food truck at Hollywood Beach

the main attraction. When you need a break from the region's big cities, they offer a much-needed haven of peace and quiet. Trolley tours pass groves of lemon and kumquat trees, live oaks, banyans, and other beautiful and exotic vegetation. The gardens are also home to many Florida birds, including the bald eagle and pink flamingos. Several species of duck, gulls, doves, and waders – including the roseate spoonbill – inhabit a walk-through aviary split into habitats such as cypress forest and mangrove swamp. Popular Wildlife Encounter shows are held here in the afternoons.

90

The number of native wildlife species living in the Flamingo Gardens.

 Pink flamingos by a pond at the aptly named Flamingo Gardens

18 Dania Beach

🅰 G5 🚉🚌 ℹ 1500 SW 2nd Ave, Dania Beach, Broward County; www.daniabeachfl.gov

The city of Dania Beach blends seamlessly into the coastal conurbation. Some locals visit just to watch a game of jai alai, but the other main attraction in town is the **Dr. Von D. Mizell-Eula Johnson State Park**. To the south of the park stretches one of the Gold Coast's loveliest beaches: more than 2 miles (3 km) in length and backed by pine trees. Canoes can be rented to explore the scenic, mangrove-lined creek that runs through the heart of the park. The **Dania Beach Pier** will appeal to those who enjoy strolling by the ocean or sea fishing. The magnificent views of the coastline from the pier are well worth the small entrance fee.

Dr. Von D. Mizell-Eula Johnson State Park
♿ 🏠 6503 N Ocean Dr 📞 (954) 923-2833 🕐 8am–6pm daily

JAI ALAI – A MERRY SPORT

This curious game originated some 300 years ago in the Basque Country (jai alai means "merry festival" in Basque), and was brought to the US in the early 1900s via Cuba. Florida has several arenas, or "frontons" – particularly in the south. Watching a game of jai alai makes for a cheap but lively night out. People yell and cheer loudly during the points, since many will have put money on the outcome.

Dania Beach Pier
♿ 🏠 300 N Beach Rd 🕐 6am–midnight daily

19 🛍️

Seminole Casinos

🅰 G4

At the crossroads of State Road 7/441 and Route 848/Stirling Road, on the western edge of Hollywood, is the Seminole Tribe of Florida Hollywood Reservation, home of the tribal headquarters.

Gambling is legal on the reservations, and here the **Seminole Classic Casino** offers poker, bingo, and other classic gaming. The main attraction, however, is the **Seminole Hard Rock Hotel and Casino**, which also features tropical pool area and Hard Rock Live.

Seminole Classic Casino
🏠 4150 N State Rd 7 🕐 24 hours daily 🌐 seminole classiccasino.com

Seminole Hard Rock Hotel and Casino
🏠 1 Seminole Way 🕐 24 hours daily 🌐 seminole hardrockhollywood.com

20

Arthur R. Marshall Loxahatchee National Wildlife Refuge

⚑F4 🚊Boynton Beach
🚌Delray Beach ⏰5am-
10pm daily ℹ️10216
Lee Rd, Boynton Beach
🌐fws.gov/loxahatchee

This 221-sq mile (572-sq km) refuge, which contains the most northerly remaining part of the Everglades, shelters a superb and abundant range of wildlife. The best time to visit is early or late in the day, and ideally in winter, when many migrating birds make temporary homes here.

The Visitor Center, situated off Route 441 on the refuge's eastern side, 10 miles (16 km) west of Delray Beach, has a good information center explaining the ecology of the Everglades; it also provides the starting point for two memorable trails that are worth exploring.

Walking in Loxahatchee National Wildlife Refuge, and a red-shouldered hawk (inset) ↑

The half-mile (1 km) Cypress Swamp Boardwalk enters a magical natural world, with guava and wax myrtle trees and many epiphytes growing beneath the canopy. The longer Marsh Trail passes by marshland, whose water levels are manipulated to produce the best possible environment for waders and waterfowl. On a winter afternoon this trail is a bird-watcher's paradise, with a cacophony of sound from heron, grebe, ibis, and many other birds. There is also a great lookout platform. Eagle-eyed visitors may also spot turtles and alligators.

Those with their own canoes can embark on the 6-mile (10-km) canoe trail. In addition, there is an extensive program of guided nature walks.

> On a winter afternoon the Longer Marsh Trail is a bird-watcher's paradise, with a cacophony of sound from herons, grebe, ibis, and many other birds.

21

Vero Beach

⚑F3 🚌 ℹ️1216 21st St, Indian River County; https://visitindianriver county.com

The main town of Indian River County, Vero Beach, and in particular its resort community on Orchid Island (North Hutchinson Island), is a beautiful place. Mature live oaks line the residential streets, and buildings are restricted to four stories. Pretty clapboard houses along Ocean Drive contain galleries, boutiques, and antiques shops.

The **Vero Beach Museum of Art** in Riverside Park on Orchid Island shows high-profile exhibitions, displaying state, regional, and national works of art. It also hosts seminars, workshops, and performances, and even has a sculpture

garden. However, the town is most famous for its beaches and two hotels. The Driftwood Resort, in the heart of ocean-front Vero Beach, began life in 1935 as a beach house. It was created out of reclaimed wood and driftwood by a local eccentric, Waldo E. Sexton, and filled with an amazing array of bric-a-brac, still present today. Seven miles (11 km) north at Wabasso Beach, one of the best of the superb shell-strewn sands on Orchid Island, is the Vero Beach Resort – Disney's first Florida hotel outside Orlando.

The **Indian River Citrus Museum**, on the mainland, is dedicated to the area's chief crop. All kinds of artifacts relevant to the citrus industry are displayed, including some old photographs, harvesting equipment, and brand labels.

Vero Beach Museum of Art
 3001 Riverside Park Dr 10am–4:30pm Mon–Sat, 1–4:30pm Sun)
vbmuseum.org

Indian River Citrus Museum
2140 14th Ave
10am–4pm Tue–Fri
veroheritage.com

 INSIDER TIP
Dress Like a Davie Cowboy

Immerse yourself in cowboy town and stock up on saddles, cowboy hats, and boots at Grif's Western Wear, a cow-boy supermarket in Davie at 6211 South West 45th St.

22
Davie
F4 4185 Davie Rd, Broward County; www. davie-coopercity.org

Centered on Orange Drive and Davie Road, and surrounded by paddocks and stables, the town of Davie reflects Florida's long cowboy history, with cacti growing outside the town hall's wooden huts. Davie's real character is most clearly reflected in the popular events held at the **Bergeron Rodeo Grounds**, home to the Davie Rodeo Association. Whatever your opinion is of rodeo, the arena is interesting and it also hosts many events, including brilliant concerts, and car, monster truck, horse, and even airboat shows.

Bergeron Rodeo Grounds
4271 Davie Rd
davie-fl.gov

23
Juno Beach
 F4 2195 Southern Blvd, West Palm Beach; www.thepalm beaches.com

The pristine sands by Juno Beach, a small community that stretches north to Jupiter Inlet, are one of the world's most productive nesting sites for loggerhead turtles. In Loggerhead Park, nestled between US 1 and Route A1A, the fascinating **Loggerhead Marinelife Center** is an eco-science center and nature trail. Injured turtles recuperate in tanks. A path leads to the beach where turtles nest in the summer. Reservations are a must.

Loggerhead Marinelife Center
14200 US 1 10am–5pm Mon–Sat, 11am–5pm Sun marinelife.org

↑ Dusk falling on Juno Beach's scenic fishing pier, stretching into the ocean

WALT DISNEY WORLD® RESORT

Since opening in 1971, Walt Disney World® Resort has exploded from a single theme park to become a fun-filled destination and cultural rite of passage, welcoming around 60 million visitors every year. Despite its size, the resort has managed to retain its nostalgic charm while simultaneously expanding and adding innovative new experiences and attractions every year.

The Magic Kingdom® remains the heart of the city-sized expanse, with its fairy-tale enchantments and iconic 189-ft- (58-m-) tall Cinderella Castle. But there's much more beyond this famous park, and most visitors opt for longer stays in order to explore Disney's three additional attractions—Epcot®, Disney's Animal Kingdom®, and Disney's Hollywood Studios®. Each one is worth at least a day, so allow plenty of time to take in an African safari, enjoy world-class thrill rides, or celebrate cinematic triumphs. The resort also offers plenty to see outside the parks, with two water parks, four golf courses, a campground, and the newly revitalized Disney Springs® providing unexpected culinary splendor, boutique shopping, and a lively downtown district ideal for date night.

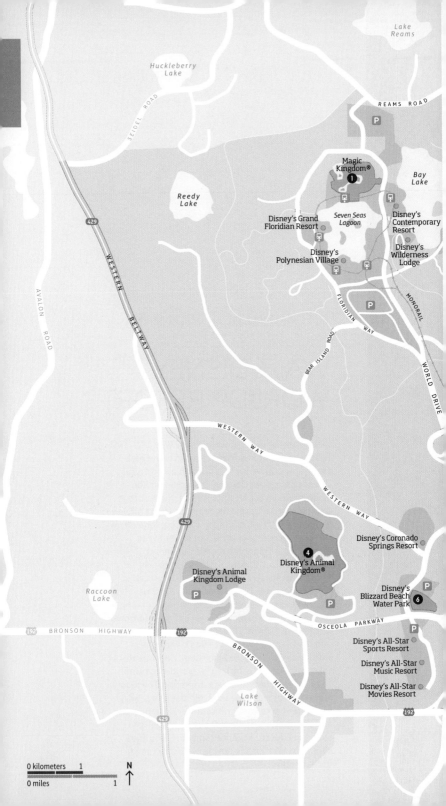

Huckleberry
Lake

Lake
Reams

REAMS ROAD

SEIDEL ROAD

Reedy
Lake

Magic
Kingdom® ❶

Bay
Lake

Disney's Grand
Floridian Resort

Seven Seas
Lagoon

Disney's
Contemporary
Resort

Disney's
Polynesian Village

Disney's
Wilderness
Lodge

WESTERN BELTWAY

429

AVALON ROAD

FLORIDIAN WAY

BEAR ISLAND ROAD

MONORAIL

WORLD DRIVE

WESTERN WAY

WESTERN WAY

429

Disney's Coronado
Springs Resort

Disney's Animal
Kingdom® ❹

Raccoon
Lake

Disney's Animal
Kingdom Lodge

Disney's
Blizzard Beach
Water Park ❻

192 BRONSON HIGHWAY

192

OSCEOLA PARKWAY

BRONSON HIGHWAY

Disney's All-Star
Sports Resort

Disney's All-Star
Music Resort

Disney's All-Star
Movies Resort

Lake
Wilson

192

429

0 kilometers   1

0 miles   1

N ↑

WALT DISNEY WORLD® RESORT

Must Sees

1. Magic Kingdom®
2. Disney's Hollywood Studios®
3. Epcot®
4. Disney's Animal Kingdom®

Experience More

5. Disney Springs®
6. Disney's Blizzard Beach Water Park
7. Disney's Typhoon Lagoon Water Park

WINTER GARDEN VINELAND ROAD

Lake Mabel

535

Disney's Fort Wilderness

Four Seasons Resort

WINTER

GARDEN

VINELAND ROAD

VISTA BOULEVARD

BUENA VISTA DRIVE

535

EPCOT CENTER DRIVE

BONNET CREEK PKWY

PALM PKWY

4

Disney's Port Orleans Resort

Hyatt Regency Grand Cypress

Disney's Saratoga Springs Resort

Disney's Old Key West Resort

Disney Springs®

535

Disney's Beach Club Resort

Cirque du Soleil®

Epcot®

World Showcase

Disney's BoardWalk

BUENA VISTA DRIVE

Disney's Typhoon Lagoon Water Park

Lake Bryan

APOPKA VINELAND ROAD

EPCOT CENTER DRIVE

Disney's Riviera Resort

Fantasia Gardens Miniature Golf

Disney's Caribbean Beach Resort

Disney's Hollywood Studios®

Waldorf Astoria

Disney's Pop Century Resort

536

INTERNATIONAL DRIVE

DRIVE

Disney's Art of Animation Resort

417

OSCEOLA PARKWAY

OSCEOLA PARKWAY

WORLD

ESPN Wide World of Sports

4

IRLO BRONSON MEMORIAL HWY

192

417

WALT DISNEY WORLD® RESORT

7 DAYS
at Walt Disney World® Resort

There are many ways to approach a Disney vacation, but this week-long family break is an ideal mix of must-see attractions, extravagant shows, and character interactions children will remember for a lifetime.

Day 1

Arrive early at the Magic Kingdom® *(p148)* to beat the crowds and tackle the popular attractions, like Seven Dwarfs Mine Train and Peter Pan's Flight. Use mobile ordering for an on-the-go lunch without waiting, and see the eye-popping floats of the Disney Festival of Fantasy Parade. When the sun is hottest, head indoors for family shows like Mickey's PhilharMagic. Later, dine at the Be Our Guest Restaurant *(p152)* then stay for Happily Ever After, Disney's best fireworks show.

Day 2

Head first to Hollywood Studios® *(p154)* and its larger-than-life Toy Story Land *(p159)* for Slinky Dog Dash and Toy Story Mania!®, breaking for a morning bite at Woody's Lunch Box. Tackle thrill rides like

The Twilight Zone Tower of Terror™ and the Rock 'N' Roller Coaster® Starring Aerosmith, before a cinematic lunch at Sci-Fi Dine-In Theater Restaurant. Escape late afternoon heat with Indiana Jones – Epic Stunt Spectacular and a trip on Mickey and Minnie's Runaway Railway. Dine at the 50's Prime Time Café and end the evening with the majestic Fantasmic show.

Day 3

Take a leisurely morning breakfast with your favorite characters at 1900 Park Fare, inside Disney's Grand Floridian Resort & Spa. Hop on the monorail to Epcot® *(p160)* for classic rides like Soarin'™ and Test Track®. Spend the afternoon in Future World, making sure to stop at Turtle Talk with Crush for an interactive

1 A Magic Kingdom® parade.
2 The Slinky Dog Dash.
3 The Bibbidi Bobbidi Boutique (© Disney).
4 A Mickey pretzel snack.
5 Tree of Life, at Animal Kingdom®.

show with characters from Finding Nemo. Then head to World Showcase *(p162)* – Epcot's famous collection of country-themed pavilions – for shopping, dining, and entertainment. Stay until closing for another spectacular fireworks show.

Day 4

The earlier you arrive at Disney's Animal Kingdom®, the shorter the line for its most popular ride: AVATAR Flight of Passage. Have a quick sit-down lunch at Harambe Market and then ride the exciting Kilimanjaro Safaris® later in the afternoon, when the animals are more active. Dine at Yak & Yeti™ before taking a late-night ride on Expedition Everest – Legend of the Forbidden Mountain™, then spend some time admiring the nighttime projections on the Tree of Life®.

Day 5

Take the day off to relax by your hotel pool or head to one of Walt Disney World®'s two water parks *(p168)*. In the late afternoon, shop and snack your way across Disney Springs® *(p168)*, the resort's

downtown district, and make a stop at the Bibbidi Bobbidi Boutique to get a royal makeover. Book Hoop-Dee-Doo Musical Revue for dinner, a raucous live show with delectable food.

Day 6

Dedicate a whole day to Star Wars: Galaxy's Edge *(p157)* at Hollywood Studios®. Opened in late 2019, this attracts extra visitors, so expect crowds and lines. Head back to Disney Springs for one of the can't-miss dinner experiences, like Morimoto Asia.

Day 7

Spend your last day once again enjoying the charm of the Magic Kingdom *(p145)*. Enjoy a slower-paced morning by booking a character breakfast at The Crystal Palace. Spend the rest of the day riding any classics you may have missed on your first visit, like Pirates of the Caribbean®. Have a Thanksgiving-style feast at Liberty Tree Tavern, and skip the evening fireworks in favor of a ride on Big Thunder Mountain Railroad.

Exquisite Entertainment

Bask in the bliss of joyous performances that little ones will adore, with your favorite Disney characters at the helm. Walt Disney World® Resort's stunning stage shows can include brand new songs you're sure to adore, like Finding Nemo – The Musical, which features original songs from the music team behind *Frozen*. Movies come to life with unique experiences like For The First Time In Forever: A Frozen Sing-Along Celebration, and Turtle Talk With Crush, an interactive experience with *Finding Nemo* and *Finding Dory* characters. And be sure to catch at least one parade – these magical moving shows will be sure to leave you with a smile on your face and a spring in your step.

→
Mickey and Minnie Mouse on a parade float on Main Street, U.S.A.®

WALT DISNEY WORLD® RESORT FOR
FAMILIES

There's no better place for families than Walt Disney World® Resort, where beloved characters from the silver screen and TV screen come to life, and the whole family can share in extravagant shows for long-lasting memories.

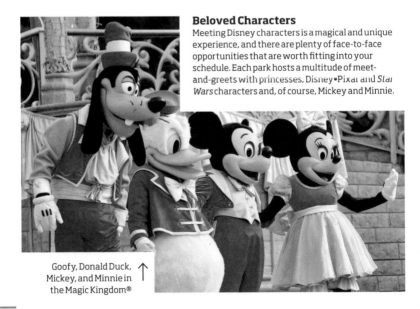

Beloved Characters

Meeting Disney characters is a magical and unique experience, and there are plenty of face-to-face opportunities that are worth fitting into your schedule. Each park hosts a multitude of meet-and-greets with princesses, Disney•Pixar and *Star Wars* characters and, of course, Mickey and Minnie.

Goofy, Donald Duck, Mickey, and Minnie in the Magic Kingdom® ↑

TOP 5 CHARACTER ENCOUNTERS

Mickey Mouse
at Magic Kingdom®
Town Square Theater.

Anna and Elsa
at Epcot® Norway
Pavilion.

Donald Duck
at Epcot® Mexico
Pavilion.

**Mickey and Minnie
Mouse and Goofy**
at Epcot® Character Spot.

Disney Princesses
at Magic Kingdom's
Fairy Tale Hall.

Delicious Disney

Mickey Mouse-shaped pretzels and ice cream treats are everywhere and you can have a meal with princesses in Cinderella's Castle or the Norway pavilion of Epcot®, or eat with Winnie The Pooh, Minnie Mouse, or Chip 'n' Dale at lunch, while Be Our Guest *(p152)* at Disney's Magic Kingdom® offers French fare in the spectacular Beast's Castle.

← A cheery, thirst-quenching Minnie Mouse popsicle

Awesome Attractions

The fun at this resort isn't just limited to normal rides like rollercoasters: there are unique and memorable experiences around every turn, like taking a safari in Disney's Animal Kingdom, or a flight over the globe at Epcot. Fantasyland *(p152)* in the Magic Kingdom is the best place for families, with lots of rides for the little ones.

↑ The Big Thunder Mountain Railroad rollercoaster

Fine Dining

Disney Springs® *(p168)* has celebrity chefs José Andrés and Masaharu Morimoto, and other upscale dining includes Tiffins at Disney's Animal Kingdom® *(p164)* and Victoria & Albert's at Walt Disney World Resort® *(p168)*; for cakes, head to Amorette's Patisserie.

Fantastic table spreads at one of the resort's many restaurants (© Disney) ↑

WALT DISNEY WORLD® RESORT FOR
GROWN-UPS

Walt Disney World® Resort may have a reputation for perfect family vacations, but there's plenty for kid-free adults too: inspiring cuisine, exceptional nightlife, and a refined and relaxing experience.

Lively Nightlife

Disney's sublime theming extends to its hotel bars, and locales such as AbracadaBar, a magician's watering hole featuring cocktails with mystical ingredients, and Trader Sam's Grog Grotto add special gusto to a night out. A gaggle of adult-oriented experiences await at Disney Springs® *(p168)*, from The Edison's late-night burlesque-inspired entertainment to STK's DJ-fueled nights. For the best live music, swing by Raglan Road or the House of Blues, or visit Disney's Boardwalk for some rousing piano melodies at Jellyrolls.

→

The Indiana Jones themed Jock Lindsey's Hangar Bar at Disney Springs® (© Disney)

Taking a Break

Though vacationing families permeate the resort, there are plenty of opportunities for adults to enjoy a relaxing getaway. Make a reservation at the renowned Senses – A Disney Spa at Disney's Grand Floridian Resort, or try one of the special experiences, like a horse-drawn carriage ride at Disney's Port Orleans Resort – Riverside, for a scenic break from the standard theme park fare.

$\rightarrow$

Treatment at Senses - A Disney Spa in the Grand Floridian Resort (© Disney)

Attractions and Events

Single-rider lines are a fast track to rides like Rock 'n' Roller Coaster® Starring Aerosmith. The World Showcase at Epcot® *(p162)* offers cocktails and food in its 11 national pavilions, all in a gorgeous waterfront setting. Disney After Hours events at Magic Kingdom®, Disney's Animal Kingdom®, and Disney's Hollywood Studios® offer late-night access to near-empty parks on a separate ticket.

$\leftarrow$

Outside the Rock 'n' Roller Coaster® Starring Aerosmith

EPCOT®

Epcot® has four annual food festivals, with world cuisine tastings and entertainment, wine pairing dinners, cooking demonstrations and ticketed tastings. Epcot® International Festival of the Arts is usually mid-January through mid-February; Epcot® International Flower & Garden Festival March through early June; Epcot® International Food & Wine Festival late August through November; and Epcot® International Festival of the Holidays mid-November to year-end.

① ⚡ Ⓜ 🍴 🖥 🛍

MAGIC KINGDOM®

🅰A6 🏠1180 Seven Seas Dr., Lake Buena Vista
🕐Times vary, check website Ⓦdisneyworld.disney

Serving as the epicenter of Walt Disney World®
Resort, all six lands in this flagship park are packed
with attractions that bring fairy tales and familiar
films to life. Between Cinderella Castle and the
nightly fireworks show, it proves there's magic
in the everyday.

① MAIN STREET, U.S.A.®

A nostalgic vision of turn-of-the-century America, Main Street, U.S.A.® is the ideal fantasy of a small town. Classic show tunes play overhead as the real steam-powered Walt Disney World® Railroad train, which loops around the park, slows to a halt at Main Street station. Here, guests can meet Mickey Mouse or Tinker Bell at Town Square Theater, catch a ride aboard an antique jitney, or shop for souvenirs.

Guests are allowed inside Main Street, U.S.A.® before the rest of the park each morning, time for a cup of coffee from Starbucks® (inside Main Street Bakery) or an indulgence at Main Street Confectionery while waiting for "rope drop" to ceremoniously mark the day's official opening. At night, the area assumes an even more magical ambience when thousands of lights bring a warm glow to the street.

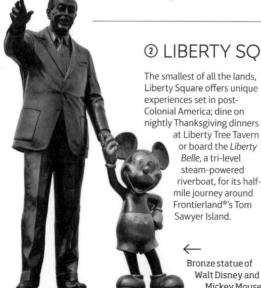

② LIBERTY SQUARE

The smallest of all the lands, Liberty Square offers unique experiences set in post-Colonial America; dine on nightly Thanksgiving dinners at Liberty Tree Tavern or board the *Liberty Belle*, a tri-level steam-powered riverboat, for its half-mile journey around Frontierland®'s Tom Sawyer Island.

← Bronze statue of Walt Disney and Mickey Mouse on Main Street

Honoring each of the nation's former leaders is the Hall of Presidents, where a multimedia show of all 45 US presidents is hosted by Audio-Animatronics®. For a more lighthearted lesson, The Muppets Present…Great Moments In American History, sees Kermit the Frog, Miss Piggy, and other Muppets recite hilarious renditions of key events in US history.

The Haunted Mansion®, a slow-moving spooky favorite, sits at the end of Liberty Square. Passengers board "Doom Buggies" through a haunted house full of thrills, yet not too scary for kids.

↑ The hustle and bustle on picturesque Main Street, U.S.A.®

HOLIDAY SEASON AT MAGIC KINGDOM®

From August through October, the park transforms itself for Halloween. Mickey's Not-So-Scary Halloween Party–a ticketed event offered on select nights–celebrates with a wonderful Boo-To-You Halloween parade. Come November, a 65-foot tree is the perfect setting for the ticketed Mickey's Very Merry Christmas Party, which brings festive treats to the park.

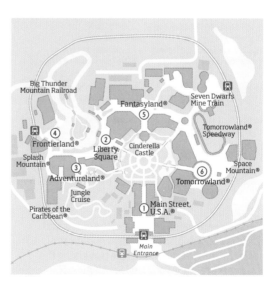

Big Thunder Mountain Railroad

Fantasyland®

Seven Dwarfs Mine Train

⑤

Tomorrowland® Speedway

④ Frontierland®

② Liberty Square

Cinderella Castle

Splash Mountain®

③ Adventureland®

⑥ Tomorrowland®

Space Mountain®

Jungle Cruise

Pirates of the Caribbean®

① Main Street, U.S.A.®

Main Entrance

③ ADVENTURELAND®

As an entertaining fusion of the exotic and tropical, this lush land is best epitomized by its Jungle Cruise boat ride traversing the rivers of Asia, Africa, and South America, made iconic with wacky jokes from onboard "skippers" helming each boat. The cruise has proved so popular that an entire restaurant, Jungle Navigation Co. LTD Skipper Canteen, serves up cuisines from the tributaries highlighted within the attraction; stop in for *shu mai* (Chinese dumplings), *cachapas* (Venezuelan corn pancakes), and other delectable fare.

With plenty of sing-along opportunities, Captain Jack Sparrow and his buccaneer crew lead you through a foggy battle and burning city on the much-loved Pirates of the Caribbean® attraction. A firm favorite with park visitors, this ride passes through underground prisons, fighting galleons of the 16th century, and past scenes of Disneyfied mayhem. The marketplace gift shop at the end of the voyage offers a plethora of worthy treasure and pirate-themed accessories for fans of the movie franchise to get lost in, including swords, hats, plastic hooks, and pirate treasure.

The land is also home to The Magic Carpets of Aladdin spinning ride, which takes visitors over the magical Adventureland®. If you're lucky enough to ride in the front row, you can even control the height of your flying carpet, with access to an onboard lever.

To break away from the crowds and the heat, Walt Disney's Enchanted Tiki Room is another amusing indoor attraction. A blast from the past featuring a chorus of Audio-Animatronic® birds and varied flora in an air-conditioned Polynesian escape, visitors can sing along to a variety of upbeat songs, including "The Tiki, Tiki, Tiki Room," written by the Sherman brothers, who also wrote for films from *Mary Poppins* to the *Jungle Book*.

↑ The Magic Carpets of Aladdin ride; Captain Jack Sparrow ready to lead a voyage *(inset)*

> **INSIDER TIP**
> **Frozen Treats**
>
> Adventureland® is home to two popular chilled treats, each with a legion of fans. Try both and pick your favorite: Dole Whip (pineapple soft-serve ice cream) or Orange Swirl, (vanilla soft-serve swirled with orange soft-serve).

> **As an entertaining fusion of the exotic and tropical, this lush land is best epitomized by its Jungle Cruise boat ride traversing the rivers of Asia, Africa, and South America.**

GETTING AROUND THE PARK

Walking is the best way to get around the Magic Kingdom ® - especially if you're on a tight schedule. But if you're not in a rush there are a few other ways to travel in style. Take a trip down Main Street, U.S.A.® in a horse-drawn trolley, or board the riverboat at Liberty Square for a tour around Tom Sawyer Island. Most iconic is the steam train which circles the park, calling at Main Street, U.S.A., Fantasyland®, and Frontierland®.

④ FRONTIERLAND®

This idealized version of the Wild West hosts two of Disney's most adventurous attractions. Set amidst the caves and caverns of an abandoned mining town, Big Thunder Mountain Railroad remains one of the most enduring attractions at The Magic Kingdom®. This roller-coaster sees an off-kilter train go askew through mine shafts, past intricate rocks, and alongside a dinosaur skeleton for an uproarious and delightfully unpredictable jaunt. For a slightly wilder experience, try to secure a car at the rear of the ride.

Splash Mountain®, a fun flume ride with a progression of small drops culminating in a thrilling five-story plummet, offers a rousing encore of a hundred Audio-Animatronic® figures celebrating in unison at the end. If you choose to sit at the front, be prepared to get wet along the way, with many drops and dips. For children too small for this ride, the Laughin' Place, near the exit of Splash Mountain, is an enjoyable play area and a good alternative.

With its ethos of the past, Frontierland is also home to bygone amusements that are particularly popular with young visitors, like Country Bear Jamboree, in which animatronic bears in concert put on a gleefully nostalgic display, and Tom Sawyer Island. Only reachable by raft, this exciting island functions as a child's dream adventure play-ground with a fort, swinging bridges, waterfalls, and tunnels surrounded by Rivers of America.

The red, craggy rocks of the Big Thunder Mountain Railroad roller-coaster ↑

⑤ FANTASYLAND®

An idyllic wonderland of fairy tale castles and magical adventures, Fantasyland® boasts the highest concentration of rides, most of which are ideal for younger children. To make the day easier on little ones, use FastPass+ to avoid standing in the long lines at the most in-demand experiences: the family-friendly roller-coaster Seven Dwarfs Mine Train, and a ride in a magic pirate ship on Peter Pan's Flight.

The must-see stop on any tour of the Magic Kingdom® is the Cinderella Castle: the symbolic heart of the entire Walt Disney World® Resort. Out front, a stage hosts the Mickey's Royal Friendship Faire show throughout the day, and the castle becomes a backdrop for Happily Ever After, the spectacular multimedia fireworks display performed nightly. It's easy to get caught up snapping pictures of the exterior, but head inside to admire the stained glass windows depicting this classic rags-to-riches fairy-tale. The castle is also home to the Bibbidi Bobbidi Boutique, which offers glitzy royal makeovers for boys and girls. Book in advance and you can even eat here at Cinderella's Royal Table, which offers princess meet-and-greets and prix-fixe dining.

An expansion brought two, smaller castles to Fantasyland: one inspired by the *Little Mermaid*, and another based on *Beauty and the Beast*. Other highlights include a boat ride through the charming utopia envisioned by "it's a small world"®, Mickey's PhilharMagic 3-D movie, royal meet-and-greets at Princess Fairytale Hall, and the Storybook Circus mini-land, where you'll find the classic Dumbo the Flying Elephant attraction.

EAT

Be Our Guest Resturant

Book 180 days in advance to eat at this French restaurant inside Beast's Castle. There are three themed rooms, and at dinner-time guests can meet the towering figure of the Beast himself.

🏠 **Fantasyland®**

$$$

← Crowds admiring the spectacular Cinderella Castle, on the border of Fantasyland®

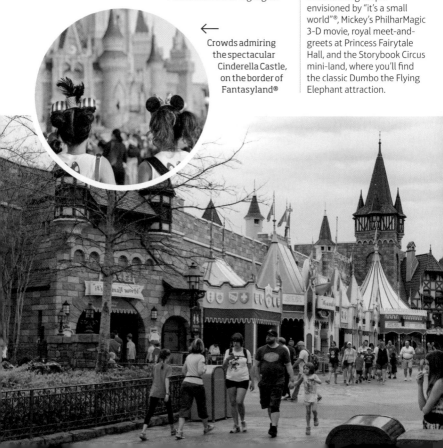

⑥ TOMORROWLAND®

With a retro, yet futuristic feel, a walk around Tomorrowland® feels like stepping into a future as imagined by American movie-makers in the 1950s. It's such a popular and iconic land in the world of Disney parks that it has even inspired its own film.

This area of the Magic Kingdom® has the energy of a mini metropolis, and bursts with kinetic attractions like the Astro Orbiter spin ride and the TRON roller-coaster opening in 2022, based on a similar ride at Shanghai Disney Resort. The white, ridged structure at the heart of Tomorrowland® is the Space Mountain® roller-coaster, which seems to launch you beyond the atmosphere for a journey of sharp turns, soaring heights, and plummeting drops

↑ Crowds crossing the bridge from the Central Plaza toward the bright lights of Tomorrowland®

through outer space. Needless to say, this ride is a must for adults and older children.

Two Pixar-inspired attractions provide offerings for the whole family. Face off with a partner on Buzz Lightyear's Space Ranger Spin, a superb and highly addictive adventure that sets you in a two-seater car fitted with laser cannons, electronic scoreboards, and a control that allows you to rotate the car rapidly for a better aim. This has become one of the few rides that children tear their parents away from, such is its popularity. And if you need a break from the rides, drop into the Monsters, Inc. Laugh Floor, an interactive comedy club event led by one-eyed hero Mike Wazowski and friends, which provides belly laughs for young and old alike.

Another attraction that provides a nice break from rides is the rotating theater of Walt Disney's Carousel of

Progress. This 21-minute Audio-Animatronics show charts the evolution of technology in 20th- and 21st-century America, providing a nostalgic look at bygone eras, and features yet another Sherman brothers hit with "There's a Great Big Beautiful Tomorrow."

A lot of visitors miss out on the Tomorrowland® Transit Authority PeopleMover, but this serene yet interesting 10-minute ride provides some of the best views in the park and an opportunity to relax after a great deal of walking. Board the PeopleMover near the Astro Orbiter for a journey through Space Mountain and a peek inside several other attractions, as well.

Did You Know?

Fantasyland® is said to have been Walt Disney's favorite themed land in the whole resort.

← Visitors wandering down a street in Fantasyland®, Magic Kingdom®

📷 PICTURE PERFECT
Purple Wall

Made famous by Instagram, this simple purple backdrop is located on the walkway between Tomorrowland Terrace and the land's main entrance. Other decorative walls can be found around the resort.

DISNEY'S HOLLYWOOD STUDIOS®

AA7 **⌂**351 S Studio Dr., Lake Buena Vista **⏱**Times vary, check website
Wdisneyworld.disney.go.com

With the addition of Toy Story Land and the immersive, intergalactic *Star Wars*: Galaxy's Edge opening in fall 2019, this park is undergoing a transformation to become the place to experience Disney-helmed films in person, while long-held favorites, like Fantasmic, still enthrall.

① HOLLYWOOD BOULEVARD

Delightful Art Deco–styled buildings vie with a replica of Grauman's Chinese Theater to present an idealized image of Hollywood. Shop for high-quality souvenirs at the many boutiques lining the park's entrance and you might even encounter the overzealous Citizens of Hollywood who enact pop-up scenes throughout the day. Mickey & Minnie's Runaway Railway, the first-ever Mickey Mouse ride, opened in the former spot of The Great Movie Ride late in 2019 and promises to make you the star of your very own Mickey cartoon short. The Wonderful World of Animation, a cinematic nighttime projection show featuring state-of-the-art technology, takes visitors on a journey through over 90 years of Disney animation, including *Sleeping Beauty* and many more.

Rock 'n' Roller Coaster® Starring Aerosmith

Twilight Zone Tower of Terror™

Beauty and the Beast- Live on Stage

Sunset Boulevard ②

Main Entrance

Animation Courtyard ⑦

① Hollywood Boulevard

③ Echo Lake

⑧ Toy Story Land

Commissary Lane ④

Indiana Jones™ Epic Stunt Spectacular!

⑥ Grand Avenue

Star Tours® – The Adventures Continue

⑤

Star Wars: Galaxy's Edge

② SUNSET BOULEVARD

Muster your bravery, as this path dead-ends at two intense thrill rides. Turn left to reach Rock 'n' Roller Coaster® Starring Aerosmith, a wild indoor ride with a nearly 60mph (100 km/h) launch that plays the band's hits at random and contains Walt Disney World®'s only upside-down inversion. From here head right for the unmissable lightning-ravaged and decrepit Hollywood Tower Hotel beholding Orlando's scariest ride – The Twilight Zone Tower of Terror™. It plummets riders 13 stories down in a supernatural Fifth Dimension-breaching attraction based on the 1950s television show.

Beauty and the Beast— Live on Stage, a Broadway-style rendition of the popular 1991 animated classic, and Lightning McQueen's Racing Academy, featuring Tow Mater, Cruz Ramirez, and other heroes from the Cars film franchise, fulfill a cinematic ethos, while at night, a stunning waterfront theatre seating 10,000 fills with attendees for Fantasmic. Combining delicately staged choreography and special effects set to electrifying music, it is a one-stop shop for the best of Disney entertainment.

EAT

Whether you choose an elegant eatery modeled after a Hollywood institution, an indoor drive-in theater, or a replica 1950s diner, it's definitely worth making a reservation at one of the full-service restaurants at Disney's Hollywood Studios®. It's also possible to book ahead for dining events with great views of nighttime shows. You can reserve a table by phone (407) 939-3463) or online (www.disney world.disney.go.com).

50's Prime Time Café
🅰 Echo Lake

⑤⑤⑤

The Hollywood Brown Derby
🅰 Hollywood Boulevard

⑤⑤⑤

Sci-Fi Dine-In Theater Restaurant
🅰 Commissary Lane

⑤⑤⑤

Mama Melrose's Ristorante Italiano
🅰 Grand Avenue

⑤⑤⑤

Fantasmic! Dessert & VIP Viewing Experience
🅰 Echo Lake

⑤⑤⑤

← The Twilight Zone Tower of Terror on Sunset Boulevard (© Disney), and a Mickey Mouse topiary (inset)

↑ Visitors watching impressive stunts at the Indiana Jones™ Epic Stunt Spectacular!

③ ECHO LAKE

Set around a central lagoon modeled after Los Angeles' own Echo Park Lake, this one offers more charm by way of a soaring dinosaur and the nearby First Time in Forever: A Frozen Sing-Along Celebration. Indiana Jones™ Epic Stunt Spectacular! re-creates well-known film scenes to deliver daredevil feats that thrill the audience, some of whom are pulled from the crowd to participate.

Star Tours® – The Adventures Continue, a thrilling motion simulator mimicking galactic battles and locales often seen in the movies, is a sensational journey with encounters from familiar characters that can't be skipped. There are multiple scenarios to enjoy so you can visit the ride over and over again and have a different experience each time. When all that adventure works up an appetite, grab a

bite to eat at the charming 50's Prime Time Café *(p155)*, a delightfully retro homestyle eatery with comical waitstaff, or enjoy character dining at Hollywood & Vine.

> **Indiana Jones™ Epic Stunt Spectacular! re-creates well-known film scenes.**

④ COMMISSARY LANE

TOP 4 CHARACTER ENCOUNTERS

Incredibles
Join the family and Edna Mode at Pixar Place.

Chewbacca
Meet the warrior at the Star Wars Launch Bay in Animation Courtyard.

Mickey & Minnie
Seek out the iconic duo on Commissary Lane.

BB-8
Greet the sidekick at the Star Wars Launch Bay.

This small area is the perfect spot for relaxation and great food, especially at the famous Sci-Fi Dine-In Theater Restaurant *(p155)*, which seats patrons in makeshift cars looking out upon reels of old-timey science fiction films. Didn't make a reservation? Head to ABC Commissary restaurant, modeled after a film studio cafeteria, for quick-service eats.

For those simply strolling through the short pathway, be sure to pop into The Writer's Stop. This doubles up as a great spot to pick up a coffee or pastry, as well as some Disney souvenirs and stationery to take home. You

can even browse a fantastic selection of children's books, or pick up the latest thriller to enjoy during your stay.

The area is also home to Mickey and Minnie Starring in Red Carpet Dreams, a meet-and-greet that can be found at the end of the lane, near the Sci-Fi Dine-In. Witness Minnie on the set of her new film, *Hollywood Dreams*, wearing an elegant pink dress to dazzle on the red carpet. Meanwhile, Mickey reprises his role as the Sorcerer's Apprentice from *Fantasia*, with the costume to match. Have your camera at the ready and don't forget to ask for an autograph.

⑤ STAR WARS: GALAXY'S EDGE

Set within a trading outpost on the fictional planet of Batuu, the *Star Wars*-themed land is full of experiences that bring the epic film franchise to life. The attraction is occupied by a vast array of characters – both familiar and not so well-known – from aliens to humanoids, in order to create an experience as close to the legendary *Star Wars* films as possible. Look out for Rey and Chewbacca. Construction on Galaxy's Edge began in 2016, and the first phase was completed in 2019.

The setting of the planet Batuu will be familiar to fans of the 2018 *Star Wars: Thrawn: Alliances* novel, or the five-issue comic miniseries released ahead of the park's opening, which introduced the area of Batuu to the public. Visitors can expect a development that takes architectural and cultural inspiration from locations such as Morocco and Istanbul.

The land offers unique shopping experiences, souvenirs, and themed dining, as well as two hyper-realistic attractions. The first of these attractions, Millennium Falcon: Smugglers Run, lets passengers pilot Han Solo's famous ship as they embark on a secret mission. The second experience, an immersive 28-minute-long battle between the First Order and the Resistance on *Star Wars: Rise of the Resistance*, is housed in the biggest

INSIDER TIP
Disneybounding

While kids can dress up at Disney World, guests over 14 are not allowed to wear costumes. "Disneybounding" is a popular alternative, and involves dressing in regular attire inspired by the color schemes of characters – such as a yellow skirt and blue top for Snow White.

building that Disney has created for a dark ride.

Even when the rides are over, visitors can immerse themselves in the *Star Wars* experience by downloading the special Datapad app that lets you scan, translate, and hack your way around Batuu.

Naturally, Galaxy's Edge is also full of legendary characters to meet such as Chewbacca and BB-8 – and even the First Order storm-troopers don't mind posing for a photo or two.

← Stormtrooper in white battle armor on duty in the park

↑ Darth Vader approaching a towering, life-size Imperial AT-AT walker

⑥ GRAND AVENUE

Given that this downtown Los Angeles–inspired area formerly existed as Muppets Courtyard, it still retains its comical charm by way of a gift shop and PizzeRizzo restaurant, as well as the Muppet*Vision 3D theater attraction. In this highly enjoyable, slapstick 3D movie (starring the Muppets), trombones, cars, and rocks launch themselves out of the screen at spectators; they are so realistic that children grasp the air expecting to touch them. Mama Melrose's Ristorante Italiano offers fantastic Italian food in a "converted" backlot and BaseLine Tap House has over a dozen California beers on tap, wine, and worthy bites. Grand Avenue also serves as a main thoroughfare leading into Star Wars: Galaxy's Edge, so expect long lines at times.

> **BaseLine Tap House has over a dozen California beers on tap, wine, and worthy bites.**

⑦ ANIMATION COURTYARD

The original idea behind Animation Courtyard was not just to give visitors an inside look into the history and process of animation, but also a glimpse at all forthcoming Disney animated movies as they were being made.

Walt Disney Presents is home to a small-scale museum of Disney history and rotating character meet-and-greets; Mike Wazowski and Sulley from Monsters, Inc. are often featured. The Incredibles also meet with guests within the neighboring Pixar Place area, which formerly housed Toy Story attractions.

Animation Courtyard also hosts a Voyage of the Little Mermaid stage show, one of the most popular in the park, with puppetry and Audio-Animatronic® characters, while Disney Junior Dance Party!, aimed at youngsters, blends music and dancing with characters from shows like "Vampirina" and "The Lion Guard"; Doc McStuffins, Vampirina, and Sofia also offer one-on-one interactions and photo opportunities.

↑ The Magic of Disney Animation Sign at Animation Courtyard

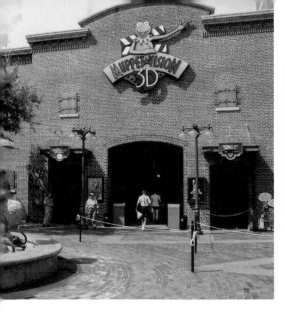

 INSIDER TIP
Play Disney Parks App

This digital app, which launched with the opening of Toy Story Land in 2018, provides interactive games within two of the three attraction lines, so that waiting in line can become playtime in itself.

← Fountain with statues of the Muppets at the Muppet*Vision 3D attraction

⑧ TOY STORY LAND

A large-scale backyard filled with oversized game pieces and everyday objects make visitors feel as though they're as small as a toy. A newish addition to Hollywood Studios, Toy Story Land has cemented itself as a family favorite as much for the fun, photogenic setting as for the great rides.

Board Slinky Dog Dash, an effortlessly fun family coaster with vehicles set within Andy's playthings, and climb into colorful carts that whip in circles on Alien Swirling Saucers. The Toy Story Mania! 4D interactive ride offers five unique midway shooting games

packed with cartoon whimsy, enabling visitors to knock down barnyard animal targets with eggs in Game 1: Hamm & Eggs, break plates with baseballs in Game 3: Green Army Men Shoot Camp, and throw rings at the Little Green Men in Game 4: Buzz Lightyear's Flying Tossers. Be sure to look out for the Green Army Drum Corps, a band of talented drummers who

lead a makeshift parade across the land, performing lively and catchy sequences. Meanwhile, Woody, Jessie, and Buzz Lightyear meet with guests throughout the day. Stop for a bite at Woody's Lunch Box – open for breakfast, lunch, and dinner – providing fun, child-friendly fare including tasty s'mores, perfect french toast, and tempting, melty grilled cheese sandwiches.

← Woody perched by the colorful entrance to Toy Story Land

Did You Know?

Effects that accompany the games at Toy Story Mania! 4D include water sprays and air blasts.

↑ Mickey and friends at the entrance to Epcot® during the annual garden festival

EPCOT®

🅰 A6 🏠 200 Epcot Center Dr. 🚌🚃 🕐 Times vary, check website
🌐 disneyworld.disney.go.com

Though imagined as a utopian Experimental Prototype Community of Tomorrow by Walt Disney himself, Epcot® opened in 1982 as a world's fair, intent on blending education with entertainment. From 2022, the 250-acre (101-ha) park will be divided into four sections: World Showcase, representing the culture and cuisine of countries around the globe, and World Discovery, World Celebration and World Nature, formerly all parts of Future World.

① WORLD DISCOVERY AND WORLD CELEBRATION

Here, Epcot®'s thrill rides abound and the park retains its science-and-technology edge. Build the concept car of tomorrow on Test Track®, and you'll put your prototype head-to-head with other passengers in a series of road tests. On Mission: SPACE®, take a journey beyond the horizon in a four-seat capsule that culminates with a landing on Mars. Select the Green experience for a tamer ride around Earth; opt for Orange and feel g-forces simulating an actual shuttle launch.

(It is the only attraction at Walt Disney World® offering motion sickness bags.)

The World Celebration area is anchored by the emblematic Spaceship Earth, which hosts a delightful journey through the history of communication, while World Discovery will soon be home to some of Disney World's biggest debuts. Space 220, a space station themed restaurant, is likely to be open in 2022, alongside Guardians of the Galaxy: Cosmic Rewind, a Marvel-themed roller coaster.

↑ The Test Track® ride at World Discovery and World Celebration (© Disney)

② WORLD NATURE

While at The Land pavilion, be sure to take a hang-gliding journey past sights like The Great Wall of China and the Eiffel Tower on Soarin' Around The World™, one of Walt Disney World®'s finest attractions. It's also home to Living with the Land, a greenhouse cruise providing lessons in sustainability and produce to select Disney restaurants, with character dining offered at Garden Grill Restaurant on the cruise.

The Seas with Nemo & Friends features a slow namesake attraction, where guests embark on a journey into the sea on "clamobiles" and meet characters from

Finding Nemo along the way, including favorites Marlin and Dory, on a quest to find Nemo. The adjacent Seas with Nemo & Friends Pavilion displays real clown fish, sharks and more in a massive 5.7-million-gallon saltwater aquarium. Observe them up close from here or the dining room of Coral Reef Restaurant, and interact with famed animated sea dwellers in Turtle Talk with Crush, where characters from Disney•Pixar Finding Nemo films converse with

↑ Views at the Soarin' Around The World™ attraction (© Disney)

children in a fantastical way. Also worthwhile for young children in this part of Epcot® is the slow-paced Journey Into Imagination With Figment. This colorful attraction takes visitors through a series of labs that call upon the imagination and all five senses. The interactive play area here is a particular highlight, as visitors are free to explore activities driven by the senses.

Character meets with Mickey and Minnie can also be experienced here at Epcot® Character Spot.

11,324

The number of aluminum and plastic-alloy triangles covering Spaceship Earth.

Map labels:
P, P, Main Entrance, The Seas with Nemo & Friends, Spaceship Earth®, Guardians of the Galaxy: Cosmic Rewind, World Discovery, The Land, ② World Nature, Mission: SPACE®, Imagination!, Test Track®, Canada, Showcase Plaza, Mexico, United Kingdom, Norway, World Showcase ③, China, France, Germany, Morocco, Italy, Japan, The American Adventure

HIDDEN MICKEYS

Mickey Mouse may not have a large presence within Epcot®, but the iconic character can be spotted everywhere throughout Walt Disney World® resort – if you look closely. Tile patterns, flooring, even hotel shower curtains host three semi-hidden intertwined circles, paying homage to the mouse who started it all.

③ WORLD SHOWCASE

The temples, town squares, and towering structures of the 11 pavilions each boast traditional decor with authentic details. At over a mile around, it's recommended to dedicate at least a half-day to explore this area.

However, food remains the highlight at World Showcase. Restaurants like Le Cellier Steakhouse in Canada and France's Monsieur Paul provide some of the best fine dining at Walt Disney World®, while bars aplenty have encouraged guests to sip avocado margaritas in Mexico or a Black & Tan in the United Kingdom as they "drink around the world." Choice snacks include caramel sweets inside Germany's Karamell-Küche, gelato in Italy, and Morocco for mint tea and hummus fries.

The shops also sell high-quality local products; visit Mitsukoshi for a taste of sake and silly toys – it's an offshoot from the popular Japanese department store – or Germany for beautiful and delicate Christmas ornaments sold year-round. The entertainment at all 11 pavilions is also superb. Acts from a Chinese acrobatic troupe, Mexican mariachi band, and humorous

> 💬 INSIDER TIP
> **Getting There**
>
> The best way to get to Epcot® is to take the monorail from Magic Kingdom®, with a quick transfer at the Transportation and Ticket Center. You can also take a ferry, a bus, or a Skyliner gondola.

Norway

▽ *Frozen* fans can rejoice at this charming, immersive pavilion. Restaurant Akershus is a highlight, with Disney Princesses circulating.

Germany

▽ This is the best spot for those on the hunt for a refreshing beer. Biergarten and Sommerfest have a wide range on offer.

Mexico

▲ This indoor pavilion – the only one at the World Showcase – is all about nightlife and set up like a Mexican marketplace.

China

▲ Along with live entertainment, visitors can expect exhilarating acrobatics and the 360-degree film "Wondrous China."

SHOP

The Fjording
Be sure to leave with authentic Norweigan toys, perfume, and Viking helmets.
🏰 Norway

Trading Post
Seek out authentic Canadian maple syrup, lumberjack clothing, and official NHL merchandise.
🏰 Canada

House of Good Fortune
A brilliant spot for unique items, including Chinese lanterns and Beijing teapots.
🏰 China

Norseman perform daily as Disney characters pose for photos around the waterfront loop. Following its *Frozen* reinvention, the Norway Pavilion now hosts a beautiful meet-and-greet with Anna and Elsa at their Royal Sommerhus. Visitors can also enjoy a Frozen Ever After boat ride. Mexico's Gran Fiesta Tour sees the Three Caballeros on tour, but one

↑ The Norway pavilion at Epcot®'s World Showcase (© Disney)

of the most fun attractions, Remy's Ratatouille Adventure – based on the namesake film – opened in 2021.

Annual seasonal festivals here are also a big draw. The Epcot International Flower & Garden Festival in spring and

Epcot® International Food & Wine Festival in fall are big hits with themed food and drink stalls, celebrity musicians, and pop-up experiences, while newer entries, including Epcot International Festival of the Arts, which celebrates visual and performing arts from around the globe, are gaining momentum.

> **The shops also sell high-quality local products; visit Mitsukoshi for a taste of sake and silly toys – it's an offshoot from the popular Japanese department store.**

Morocco
▽ Commissioned by Morocco's King Hassan II and built by Moroccan artisans, this pavilion allows for a truly cultural experience.

UK
▽ The vast range of buildings here, including castles, homes, and even the classic pub, showcase the best of Britain throughout time.

Japan
△ Matsuriza, a group of traditional Taiko drummers, provide ample entertainment daily here at the bottom of the pagoda.

France ⚐
△ With some of the best food on offer, visitors can enjoy snacks from *crepes* and ice cream to croissants and *macarons*.

④ 🎿 🍴 🖥 🛍

DISNEY'S ANIMAL KINGDOM®

A A7 **📍** 2901 Osceola Pkwy **🕐** Times vary, check website **W** disneyworld. disney.go.com

Part theme park, part animal sanctuary, this mystical expanse filled with geographical-themed lands is a unique home to hundreds of animal species.

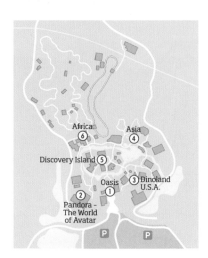

① OASIS

Elsewhere, an entrance is just an entrance, but here it's home to all-encompassing greenery where water-dwelling creatures and magnificent animals abound. Take either winding road – both lead toward the front of the park – and do your best to allow time to witness the various inhabitants and little surprises tucked within the foliage-festooned area.

As well as wallabies, giant anteaters, spoonbills, barking deer, and plenty of other animals, Oasis is also home to various wonderful birds, including storks and hummingbirds. With picturesque waterfalls, rope bridges, stunning flora, and gentle streams, this attraction is the perfect spot to relax quietly and lose oneself within nature.

> ### ANIMAL KINGDOM® AT NIGHTTIME
>
> Many experiences now stay open past sun-down, with Kilimanjaro Safaris® offering evening expeditions and nightfall making for haunting experiences on popular outdoor rides like Kali River Rapids®. Stumble upon entertainment, such as The Tree of Life, which comes alive with projections.

Embarking on Disney's Animal Kingdom® sanctuary

Unusual floating mountains in Pandora – The World of Avatar ↑

② PANDORA – THE WORLD OF AVATAR

Opened in 2017, the mythical land of Pandora (from James Cameron's movie *Avatar*) features floating mountains, fantastical alien flora growing among real tropical plants, and the sights and sounds of non-terrestrial wildlife. Beautiful by day and magical after dark, the Valley of Mo'ara is enticing, as is its Avatar Flight of Passage, a simulated ride designed to make visitors experience sea cliffs, astonishingly detailed caves, and charming forests from atop a winged banshee. The experience remains a phenomenon, clocking the longest wait in the park several years after its debut. An attached gift shop sells take-home banshee puppets, a best-seller.

Na'vi River Journey's lifelike Audio-Animatronic® and luminescent surroundings also impress, but don't quite pull at the heartstrings. Come mealtime, Satu'li Canteen offers customizable grain bowls with protein toppings.

Visit the attraction at nighttime and watch as the walkways glow a wonderful greenish-blue hue.

> **INSIDER TIP**
> **Avatar Flight of Passage**
>
> FastPass+ is difficult to obtain for this attraction, so arrive 90 minutes before the park opens (early access for Disney guests on certain days), or try before dinner.

③ DINOLAND U.S.A.

This quirky land lets visitors travel back in time to witness the dinosaurs, featuring a children's play area, one of Disney's Animal Kingdom®'s three rides, and even a nature trail. On the popular ride DINOSAUR, guests board a mobile motion simulator which bucks and weaves in an attempt to ensnare and avoid carnivorous dinosaurs before a meteor hits Earth. A wild ride that's mostly in darkness and features loud sounds that may startle young visitors, it's best enjoyed by older children; younger ones will enjoy digging for dino bones in The Boneyard® or carnival-style rides like TriceraTop Spin, which is within Chester & Hester's Dino-Rama, a colorful mini park area with plenty of games and rides to enjoy.

→ A green dinosaur greeting visitors at the entrance to Dinoland U.S.A.

④ ASIA

This highly evocative land features gibbons, exotic birds, and a Komodo dragon set in a mystical re-creation of post-Colonial Indian ruins, as magnificent Sumatran tigers roam palace remnants within the Maharajah Jungle Trek®. Look out for the brilliant murals along the walls of the paths during this trek.

Expedition Everest – Legend of the Forbidden Mountain™ takes passengers on a high-speed train adventure across the rugged terrain and icy slopes of the Himalayas, culminating in an unexpected encounter with a mythical beast. Its hyper-detailed theming and perfect execution make for what many consider the best attraction in all of Walt Disney World® Resort.

Kali River Rapids®, a raft ride with a vague anti-logging missive often leaves riders drenched – ideal on blistering hot days in Florida – while UP! A Great Bird Adventure Show combines the magic of Pixar films with the mystery of nature.

↑ Expedition Everest - Legend of the Forbidden Mountain™

EAT

Tiffins
Serious foodies only need apply at this tucked-away restaurant, one of Disney's best. If you can't indulge in the mouthwatering menu, which features a wide range of dishes from various cuisines, at least stop by its Nomad Lounge bar for lush greenery, small plates, and creative concoctions.

🔲 Discovery Island

⑤ DISCOVERY ISLAND

Looming tall in the center of Animal Kingdom® is the mesmerizing Tree of Life® – a massive, 14-story structure and signature landmark of the park that holds sway over a pageant of brightly colored shop fronts and a multitude of pools and gardens, each housing a naturistic escape. Below its delicately carved trunk is It's Tough to Be a Bug®, a 3D theater presentation with special effects inspired by the insects themselves. The Discovery Island Trails, including many tranquil paths and foot bridges, are a great way to see the Tree of Life® in great detail, as well as the stunning landscape and wildlife that surrounds it, from white storks and red kangaroos to macaws and lemurs.

← Admiring the imposing Tree of Life® and the serene surroundings

| TOP 3 | PHOTOGRAPH SPOTS |

Behind Tree of Life®
As the front is often overcrowded, head to the walkway between Africa and Asia for a more naturalistic view.

Walkway in Asia
This walkway toward Expedition Everest offers a mountainous display with Discovery River in the foreground.

Avatar Flight of Passage Line
Make the most of your time standing in line by taking perfect shots of the valley.

⑥ AFRICA

Enter through the village of Harambe to board a truck on Kilimanjaro Safaris® and prepare to be whisked away to an astonishing replica of an East African landscape. The 20-or-so minute drive over creaking bridges and dirt paths provides guests the opportunity to see many African animals including hippos, rhinos, giraffes, and elephants, all roaming free and undisturbed. It is not unusual for a white rhino to roam close enough to sniff the truck. Though this is the park's busiest attraction, it becomes much quieter in the afternoon.

Exit toward the Gorilla Falls Exploration Trail to experience up-close gorilla encounters amid a world of streams and waterfalls, or take in Harambe's street entertainment, set against surroundings modeled after

↑ One of the open-sided trucks on Kilimanjaro Safaris® venturing into a convincing replica of East Africa

regional architecture and structures. Festival of the Lion King, located nearby, is an exceptionally well choreographed and costumed production, featuring extravagant and colorful costumes and incredible acrobats, housed in an air-conditioned auditorium that proves extra popular in summer months.

167

EXPERIENCE MORE

Disney Springs®

AB6 **A**1486 Buena Vista Dr, Orlando **O**10am–midnight Sun–Thu (to 2am Fri & Sat) **W**disneysprings.com

This lovely outdoor waterfront mall underwent a massive reinvention from the former Downtown Disney® to now host a multitude of restaurants, nightlife, shopping, and entertainment across four well maintained "neighborhoods."

Visitors can enjoy free musical performances, a two-story bowling alley, VR experiences, a movie theater, and concerts at House of Blues® Orlando. Once the park closes, over-18s can spend a night out on the town; a portion of its thriving bars are open till 2am on weekends.

World of Disney, the largest merchandise store at Walt Disney World® Resort, is also located here – be sure to stop by for last-minute indulgences before traveling back home.

Disney's Blizzard Beach Water Park

AA7 **A**1534 Blizzard Beach Dr, Orlando **O**10am–5pm daily **W**disneyworld. disney.go.com

Disney legend has it that this was once a would-be ski resort. Now a fun-filled water park, Blizzard Beach's novelty winter theme is divinely quirky. The park's more significant rides, including the Teamboat Springs river raft and Summit Plummet – with its 12-story drop and speeds reaching up to 60 mph (97 km/ph) – make for fun excursions. Another favorite is the Downhill Double Dipper, two side-by-side chutes that allow you to race a friend to the bottom. Those in search of tamer experiences should explore the Cross Country Creek lazy river or Melt-Away Bay's large-scale waves, while children will enjoy Tike's Peak play zone.

↑ The sprawling World of Disney store in Disney Springs®, lit up at night

← Buildings towering above the horizon at Disney Springs® theme park

7

Disney's Typhoon Lagoon Water Park

🅰 B6 📍 1145 East Buena Vista Dr, Orlando ⏰ 10am–5pm daily 🌐 disneyworld.disney.go.com

According to another Disney legend, a typhoon swept through the area and left the "Miss Tilly" shipwreck atop Mount Mayday, an enormous geyser that erupts with water throughout the day.

The park has bolder rides than Blizzard Beach, and is home to an enormous wave pool at its center. Several tube slides offer fun for all thrill levels, but only daredevils should attempt the near-vertical five-story drop of Humunga Kowabunga. Gangplank Falls, Miss Adventure Falls raft ride, and the Crush 'n' Gusher water coaster will excite those averse to extreme drops, while the entire family will enjoy Typhoon Lagoon Surf Pool, with its gently shelving shallow end and wild six-foot waves.

Blizzard Beach closes for a few months for refurbishment each winter, at which time Typhoon Lagoon, its sister park, will remain open – and vice versa, so there's always a Disney World water park on offer.

> **The park has bolder rides than Blizzard Beach, and is home to an enormous wave pool in its center.**

EAT

Disney Springs® has become a popular outpost for world-class restaurants owned by celebrity chefs. Here are our top picks.

Wolfgang Puck Bar & Grill
🅰 Town Center
🌐 wolfgangpuck.com

$ $ $

Morimoto Asia
🅰 The Landing
🌐 patinagroup.com/morimoto-asia

$ $ $

Jaleo by José Andrés
🅰 West Side
🌐 jaleo.com

$ $ $

Erin McKenna's Bakery NYC
🅰 The Landing
🌐 erinmckennasbakery.com

$ $ $

Frontera Cocina
🅰 Town Center
🌐 fronteracocina.com

$ $ $

Typhoon Lagoon's lazy river, winding through a dense tropical forest ↑

ORLANDO AND THE SPACE COAST

Orlando started out as an army post, which was established during the Seminole Wars. A town later developed, but even through the first half of the 20th century Orlando and neighboring towns such as Kissimmee were only small, sleepy places dependent on cattle and the citrus crop. Everything changed in the 1960s. First came the job opportunities associated with the space program at Cape Canaveral. Then Walt Disney World® Resort started to take shape, with its first theme park opening here in 1971. Its success generated a booming entertainment industry in Greater Orlando as an increasing number of attractions appeared on the scene, all eager to cash in on the captive market.

With everything from roller coasters to rocket launches, the Orlando area is undeniably a family-oriented fantasyland and the undisputed theme park capital of the world. However, the region also has a subtle beauty, with hundreds of lakes bordered by moss-draped oaks or stands of cypress trees, spring-fed rivers, ancient forests, and verdant farmlands. The barrier islands across the broad Indian River boast 72 miles (116 km) of stunning sandy beaches, and there are two nature preserves rich in birdlife.

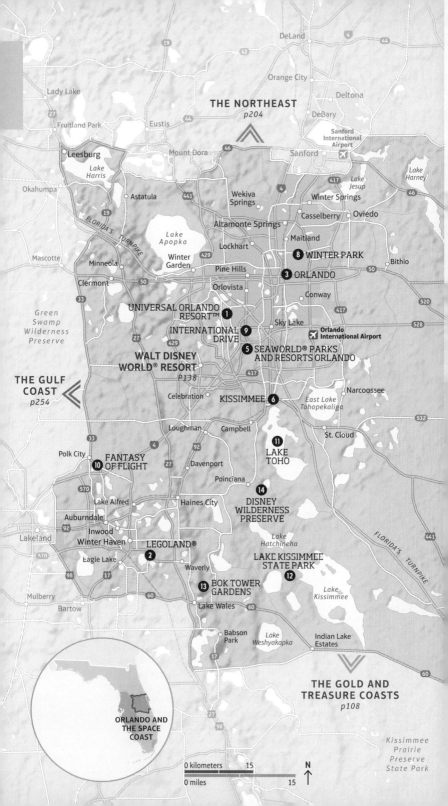

ORLANDO AND THE SPACE COAST

Must Sees

1. Universal Orlando Resort™
2. LEGOLAND®
3. Orlando
4. Kennedy Space Center

Experience More

5. SeaWorld® Parks and Resorts Orlando
6. Kissimmee
7. American Police Hall of Fame
8. Winter Park
9. International Drive
10. Fantasy of Flight
11. Lake Toho
12. Lake Kissimmee State Park
13. Bok Tower Gardens
14. Disney Wilderness Preserve
15. Valiant Air Command Warbird Air Museum
16. Canaveral National Seashore and Merritt Island
17. Cocoa Beach
18. Cocoa

New Smyrna Beach
Edgewater
95
1
Oak Hill
Apollo Beach
Mosquito Lagoon
16 CANAVERAL NATIONAL SEASHORE
Playalinda Beach
Mims
16 MERRITT ISLAND
402
Titusville
4 KENNEDY SPACE CENTER
AMERICAN POLICE HALL OF FAME
7
50
405
Merritt Island
15
VALIANT AIR COMMAND WARBIRD AIR MUSEUM
Banana River
Cape Canaveral
Sharpes
528
Cape Canaveral
COCOA 18
Lake Poinsett
532
Rockledge
Merritt Island
17 COCOA BEACH
A1A
419
Satellite Beach
Indian Harbour Beach
Eau Gallie
192
Melbourne International Airport
Melbourne
Deer Park
West Melbourne
Melbourne Beach
Palm Bay
Malabar
Atlantic Ocean
Bayside Lakes
Micco
Sebastian
Fellsmere
Blue Cypress Lake
Wabasso
Yeehaw Junction
Gifford
60
Vero Beach
441
FLORIDA'S TURNPIKE
Lakewood Park

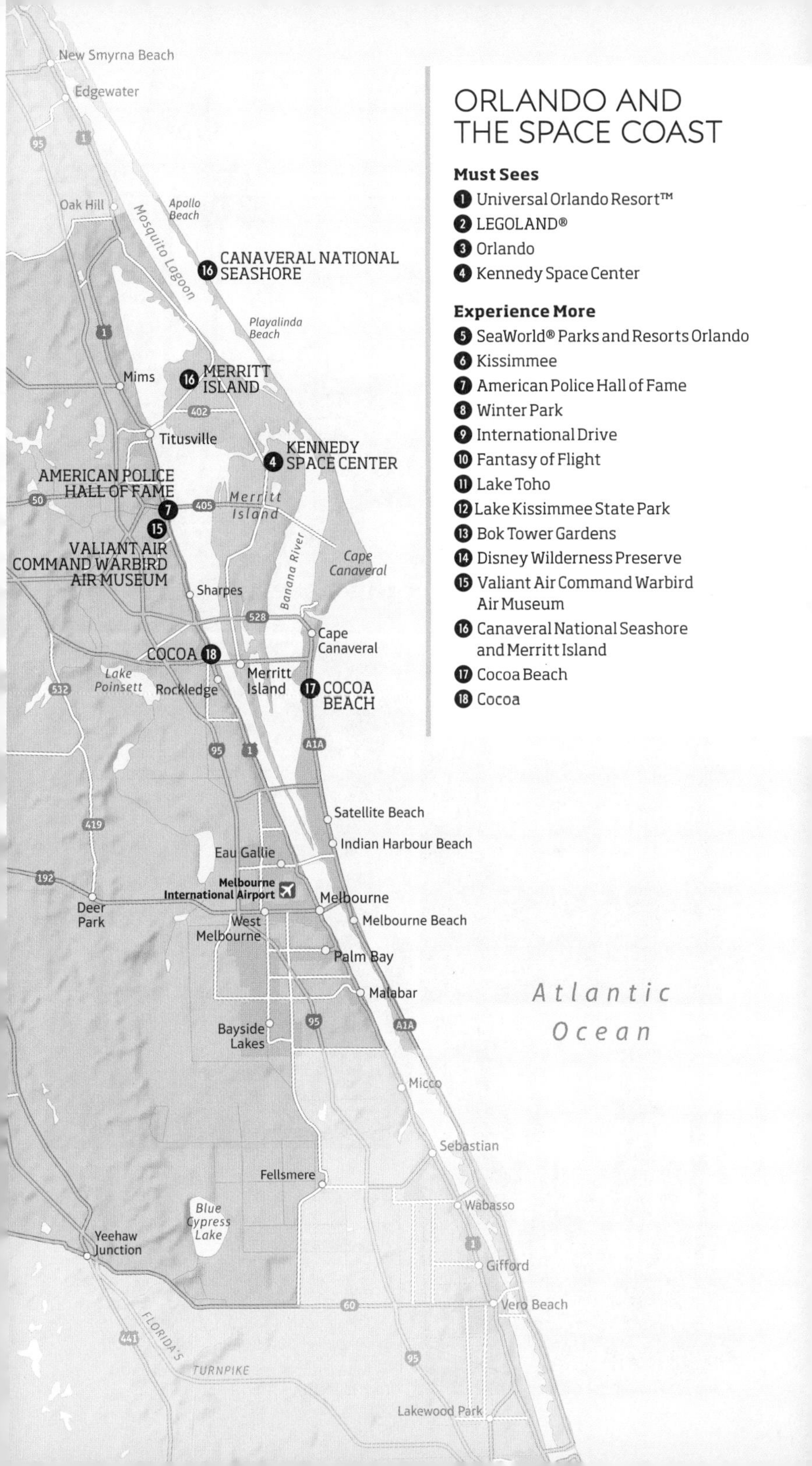

←

 A vibrant street in Universal Orlando Resort™.

② The Leaky Cauldron™ restaurant at Universal Studios Florida™.

③ The imposing *Saturn V* rocket at Kennedy Space Center.

④ A colorful art exhibit at Cornell Fine Arts Museum within Rollins College.

5 DAYS

in Orlando and the Space Coast

Day 1

Morning Breakfast early at your hotel in order to beat the crowds at family-favorite Universal Orlando Resort™ (p178).

Afternoon After a morning of movie-themed rides, grab some lunch then cool off with an afternoon of Hawaiian-themed aquatic fun in Volcano Bay™ (p184).

Evening CityWalk™ (p184) stays open late for dining, clubs, and shows. The world's largest Hard Rock Cafe is a good bet for those hoping to combine all three.

Day 2

Morning Another early start is essential to tackle the lines at the Wizarding World of Harry Potter™ (p180), which is spread across two of the parks at Universal Orlando Resort™.

Afternoon Stay in Potter mode for lunch at The Leaky Cauldron™ in Diagon Alley™, before filling the rest of the day with high tech fun at Marvel Super Hero Island® and Jurassic Park River Adventure™.

Evening Stick with your fantasy theme and opt for dinner in the cave-like world of Mythos Restaurant™ at Univesal Islands of Adventure.

Day 3

Morning Allow yourself a well-deserved lie-in and leisurely breakfast, before spending the morning exploring the state-of-the-art Orlando Science Center (p188).

Afternoon Follow lunch at White Wolf Cafe (1829 N Orange Ave), a pleasantly folksy option, with a stroll through the spectacular Harry P. Leu Gardens (p188).

Evening Outlet shoppers should make the most of late opening hours at Orlando's University Drive. Celebrate your bargains with an Italian feast at Vincenzo Cucina Italiana (www.vincenzos orlando.com).

Day 4

Morning Breakfast at Another Broken Egg (410 Orlando Avenue), then stroll through the art-oriented town of Winter Park (p197).

Afternoon Follow a lunch of crepes at the charming Café de France (www.lecafede france.com) with a stroll through the leafy campus of Rollins College and a visit to their Cornell Fine Arts Museum (p197).

Evening Splurge for dinner at the excellent BoVine Steakhouse (bovine steakhouse.com). To continue the luxury overnight, book into the Alford Inn at Rollins College (www.thealfordinn.com).

Day 5

Morning Just over an hour's drive leads to the thrilling Kennedy Space Center (p190). Tickets include a two-and-a-half hour bus tour, but you'll want to stay much longer to explore the extraordinary exhibits.

Afternoon Grab a quick lunch on-site and continue your tour of the displays. By mid-afternoon, it's time for a break; a short drive will take you to Cocoa Beach (p202) for a relaxing end to your trip.

Evening Dine on first-rate seafood at the Fat Snook (464 S Atlantic Ave) along the waterfront. Come sundown, the Inn at Cocoa Beach is a pleasant local motel choice (www.theinnatcocoabeach.com).

The colorful and brightly-lit skyline across Eola Lake

ORLANDO
BEYOND THE PARKS

Many visitors may only head to Orlando to spend time at its theme parks. But the city iself is another Florida highlight, with a thriving downtown area, that makes a relaxing and rewarding getaway when you're tired of the theme resorts.

Cultural Orlando

Culture in this part of the world extends far beyond the film characters and roller-coasters of the local theme parks. The city's Amway Center – home to the Orlando Magic basketball team – hosts many touring musical and theatrical events. The Orlando Museum of Art *(p189)* houses a world-class selection of art from the ancient cultures of the Americas. City Arts Factory *(39 S Magnolia Ave)* has more of a contemporary slant and is well worth a visit. Two large festivals bring in the culture crowd, too – the Orlando Jazz Festival in September, and the Mount Dora Arts Festival in February.

→

The Amway Center, a sports and culture center in downtown Orlando

The Real Deal

Downtown Orlando is a more authentic city center than you might imagine. All the tourist-centric attractions are found around the theme parks, so the heart of the city is a proper Floridian experience, offering lots of opportunities to explore, relax, and get to know the real Florida. One of its most attractive neighborhoods is Thornton Park, with its laid-back atmosphere, quirky boutiques and oak trees laden in Spanish Moss. Nearby is the tranquil greenery of Lake Eola Park, which boasts fountains and swan boats. The Orlando Farmer's Market also takes place here every Sunday, creating the perfect chance for a picnic lunch. A short drive north brings you to Wekiwa Springs State Park, which encompasses a huge expanse of green space, including some superb hiking trails.

A DAY FOR FOODIES IN ORLANDO

A food tour of the city is a great way to explore and treat your taste-buds. Have breakfast at Se7en Bites (*617 Primrose Dr*) for elevated Southern classics. Enjoy an eclectic American lunch menu at the Stubborn Mule (*www.thestubborn muleorlando.com*), followed by organic beers at Orlando Brewing (*1301 Atlanta Ave*). End with dinner at Artisan's Table (*55 W Church St Suite 128*) and a nightcap at The Hen House Bar (*11 Wall St*).

The elegant, elevated walkway of Church Street Station at sunset ↑

Al fresco dining at trendy and colorful restaurants ↑

Wining and Dining

If you visit Orlando's theme parks, you may end up eating a lot of fast food on the go – but head downtown and you'll find attractive neighborhoods providing alternatives to treat your culinary senses. The trendiest eateries are probably to be found around the city's Milk District, where artisanal cafes line up to serve thoughtfully prepared menus, from Southern comfort food to creative sandwich shops and vegan hotspots. Church Street is in the heart of Downtown Orlando, and has gastropubs and fine dining aplenty. Time your visit with one of the food festivals – Downtown Food and Wine Fest (February) and Central Florida Soul Fest (March) are the best.

① ⚡ 🍴 🖥 🛍

UNIVERSAL ORLANDO RESORT™

🅰 B5–B6 🏠 6000 Universal Blvd 🚌 21, 37, 40 from Orlando ⏰ Times vary, check website ⓦ universalorlando.com

Universal Orlando Resort™ is home to Universal's Islands of Adventure™ and Universal Studios Florida™, two theme parks where animated characters, and action films come to life by way of technologically advanced ride systems. Disney may think it has a stronghold on this town, but The Wizarding World of Harry Potter™ is an unmissable sight for any Orlando vacation.

Sip a Duff Beer in Moe's Tavern, meet SpongeBob SquarePants, and fight alongside Optimus Prime – here, experiences that are only available on screen become reality. The rides range from tame to towering roller coasters, so the parks offer attractions catering to thrill-seekers young and old.

If you're lucky, you may see live filming on the backlot within the park. From September to December you could even be in the audience for the taping of a TV show. Tickets for recordings are issued on the day at the Studio Audience Center located near Guest Services, on a first-come, first-served basis.

← Strolling along a picturesque palm-tree lined street in Universal Orland Resort™

TOP 4 THRILLS TO EXPERIENCE

Waterslide through Krakatau™ Volcano
Dive into a glistening waterfall on a four-person canoe.

Sit front row on The Incredible Hulk Coaster®
It's worth the wait to be the first one catapulted out at intense speeds.

Choose-Your-Own Music on Hollywood Rip Ride Rockit™
Control the soundtrack to your ride by selecting from a list of songs.

Survive the Jurassic Park River Adventure™ drop
Brace yourself for the 85-ft (26-m) plummet.

Seasonal Timeline

Summer

Fantastic entertainment abounds for Fourth of July celebrations – the busiest week of the summer here. Expect music from Orlando's most famous movies, great food, and a spectacular fireworks show, plus all the best attractions are open to enjoy till late.

Winter

▽ Christmastime in The Wizarding World of Harry Potter™ sees festive decor, themed entertainment, and piping hot Butterbeer™ abounding, while Universal's Holiday Parade featuring Macy's brings larger-than-life character balloons and seasonal fanfare to Universal Studios Florida™.

Spring

△ Mardi Gras, a park-wide party at Universal Studios Florida™, takes place from February through early April with street performers, New Orleans-style revelry, and live concerts from superstar artists, all included with admission.

Fall

The ticketed fright-filled festivity Halloween Horror Nights™ brings bone-chilling haunted houses themed to both cult classic slasher movies and twisted original ideas to Universal Studios Florida™ on select nights in September, October, and early November.

① WIZARDING WORLD OF HARRY POTTER™

TOP 4 WAYS TO ENJOY BUTTERBEER™

Soft Serve
A mix of Butterbeer™ and ice cream, it's served best at Florean Fortescue's at Diagon Alley™, as well as Three Broomsticks™ in Hogsmeade™.

Frozen
The standard drink may be served cold, but the frozen version is great for very hot days. Head to Hog's Head Pub™ in Hogsmeade or the Leaky Cauldron™ in Diagon Alley.

Potted Cream
An interesting choice, this adds a smooth texture to the drink. Three Broomsticks in Hogsmeade is the place to go.

Hot
Only available in the winter, you can find it at the Leaky Cauldron in Diagon Alley.

Spanning across both parks, The Wizarding World of Harry Potter™ operates the famed Hogwarts™ Express – complete with Platform 9¾™ and a wonderful in-cabin experience unique to each direction of travel – for a seamless visit to both ends of the themed expanse.

Pass through the somewhat hidden entrance for The Wizarding World of Harry Potter™ – Diagon Alley™ and you'll find yourself in a setting seemingly extracted from the film series, packed with familiar shops and eateries including Leaky Cauldron™ and Weasleys' Wizard Wheezes novelties for tricksters. The Harry Potter and the Escape from Gringotts™ attraction here packs coaster-style thrills, mythical troll bankers, and an encounter with Lord Voldemort into an extraordinarily well executed experience. While the fire-breathing dragon atop Gringotts™ draws plenty of attention, don't let it distract from a visit to the darkened Knockturn Alley and scoops from Florean Fortescue's Ice-Cream Parlour, which are only sold here.

Board at King's Cross Station to reach The Wizarding World of Harry Potter™ – Hogsmeade™ at Universal's Islands of Adventure®, home to Three Broomsticks™ restaurant, Hog's Head™ pub, Honey-dukes™ candy shop and other haunts straight from the book, along with a nightly light show and an array of

> **The Wizarding World of Harry Potter™ operates the famed Hogwarts™ Express - complete with Platform 9¾™ and a wonderful in-cabin experience.**

↑ Quaint and picturesque streets at The Wizarding World of Harry Potter™

Did You Know?

To board at King's Cross or Hogsmeade™ station, a 2-Park admission is required.

bewitched attractions. Take a winding path through Hogwarts™ castle to face Dementors and other familiar frights on broomstick aboard Harry Potter and the Forbidden Journey™, or ride the family-friendly Flight of the Hippogriff™ coaster past Hagrid's hut. The Care of Magical Creatures teacher is also the star of Hagrid's

Magical Creatures Motorbike Adventure™, a roller-coaster that opened in 2019.

Magic abounds in The Wizarding World of Harry Potter™ right down to the interactive wand souvenirs, which trigger water effects, levitations, object animations, and other experiences throughout Hogsmeade™ Village and Diagon Alley™. An interactive show at Ollivanders™ wand shop, located in both parks, will see one lucky wizard paired with their intended wand. A visit to the shop itself allows guests to customize interactive wands to their liking. The creamy butterscoth non-alcoholic Butterbeer™ beverage, a long-time favorite of Hogwarts™ students, can also be indulged around the park.

↑ The iconic and imposing Hogwarts™ castle on a sunny day

→ Statue outside Gringotts™ Bank in Diagon Alley™

> 💬 **INSIDER TIP**
> **Wizards Only**
>
> To keep The Wizarding World of Harry Potter™ completely immersive, no modern branded products – including soda and water – are sold inside. Ice cream flavors, candies, beverages, and even exclusive beers were created for the theme park; the only exceptions are British snacks sold inside London's would-be King's Cross station and select draft beers.

② ISLANDS OF ADVENTURE™

Set in eight themed lands surrounding a central lagoon, most experiences here center around franchises of comics, books, and big-budget films like *Jurassic Park* and *King Kong*. There is no transportation system within the park other than small boats which crisscross the lake. A day will suffice to experience all the attractions.

The first island you encounter moving clockwise is the Marvel Super Hero Island®, which represents the original comic book characters through inventive rides like The Amazing Adventures of Spider-Man®'s vivid 3D battle and The Incredible Hulk Coaster®, which launches passengers 150 ft (45 m) toward an over-water track with seven inversions topping out at nearly 70 mph (112 km/h) – often regarded as the best coaster in Florida.

Skull Island: Reign of Kong and Jurassic Park® tackle more down-to-earth menaces. Jurassic Park River Adventure® provides a 85-ft (26-m) plummet into water, while Skull Island signals the return of the legendary ape to the park as visitors board jungle vehicles for a thrill-ride through an ancient temple and a series of caves before confronting the colossal Kong

↑ Colorful Seuss Landing™, and The Incredible Hulk Coaster® *(inset)*

himself. A new rollercoaster with four inversions, the Jurassic World VelociCoaster, opened in 2021.

On hotter days, seek out Toon Lagoon's two water rides, which will leave you soaked but nonetheless refreshed. Camp Jurassic®'s Pteranodon Flyers, Raptor Encounter, and the entirety of Seuss Landing™ are also brilliant colorful rides, with character experiences and ornate, playful architecture that make for a visual treat.

> **Skull Island signals the return of the legendary ape to the park as visitors board jungle vehicles for a thrill-ride.**

RIDES AT THE RESORT

Revenge of The Mummy™
Expect total darkness and warrior mummies.

The Amazing Adventures of Spider-Man®
A 3D adventure experienced alongside Marvel characters.

TRANSFORMERS: The Ride-3D
An immersive journey that places you directly into a war zone.

Harry Potter and the Forbidden Journey™
This highly popular ride uses incredible technology to fly you above Hogwarts™.

③ UNIVERSAL STUDIOS FLORIDA™

With lands loosely grouped into geographical locations, this cinematic park packs the most punch in terms of familiarity; here, you can meet Hello Kitty, watch *The Secret Life of Pets'* Duke and Gidget pass by on parade floats, and experience attractions themed to *Despicable Me*, *Shrek*, *Fast & The Furious*, *Transformers* and *The Tonight Show Starring Jimmy Fallon*, or take in an homage to film at the nightly Cinematic Celebration™.

Some rides based on less recent franchises, like Men in Black™ – Alien Attack™, don't hold up as well as others, but Revenge of the Mummy™, an indoor coaster plunging riders into darkness as they attempt to escape the wrath of Imhotep from the *Mummy* film franchise, is one of the best. ET Adventure®, based on the 1982 classic film, is also not to be missed, as visitors board the famous flying bike with ET and soar into the sky.

With colorful details culled from the cult cartoon, Springfield, also known as Simpsons Land, is a veritable highlight. Guests can explore the Kwik-E-Mart, visit Duff Brewery, and even meet Krusty The Clown or the entire Simpsons clan before embarking on the screen-simulated The Simpsons Ride™ that takes you directly into cartoon Springfield.

An expansive play area tucked within Woody Woodpecker's Kid Zone hosts a playplace comprised of oversized objects at Fievel's Playland and a fantastical multi-story Curious George water splash zone. Universal's Superstar Parade™ is another excellent attraction, which dead-ends near Mel's Drive-In for a Character Party Zone featuring fantastic floats and music; use this ideal opportunity to snap photos with Gru and Agnes from *Despicable Me*, *SpongeBob SquarePants'* Patrick and Squidward, and the cast of *Dora The Explorer*.

Lisa, Bart, Marge, and Homer welcoming visitors to The Simpsons Ride™ ↑

④ VOLCANO BAY™

With lush foliage, over a dozen waterslides, and its towering 200-ft-tall (60-m) centerpiece, Universal's Volcano Bay™ is easily the most beautiful water park in Orlando, themed to an impressive mythical paradise combining a variety of Polynesian cultures into a tiki-lined tropical escape. This is by far the most relaxing park within the resort, but nonetheless offers some impressive thrill rides to enjoy. Do note that ticketing here is separate from Universal's other two parks.

Volcano Bay™ is tech-nologically advanced in both its rides and procedures – here, you'll never carry a tube or raft up stairs – so you can enjoy state-of-the-art slides without waiting in hours-long lines, thanks to a virtual queue system and complimentary TapuTapu™ wristbands. (Be sure to bring a towel, though, as they charge for rentals.)

Attractions range from multi-person raft rides like Honu ika Moana™ to the 70-degree drop on Ko'okiri Body Plunge™, but its best is Krakatau™ Aqua Coaster, a gravity-defying adrenaline rush up and down a series of hills through the park's emblematic mountain. Kids can splash around in three themed lagoons, while thrill-averse adults should head for the slow and relaxing Kopiko Wai Winding River™, wade through The Reef, or walk through the volcano's center for a picturesque view and interactive encounter with Vol, its charming spirit.

Waturi Beach, a beautiful lagoon by Krakatau™, is the perfect spot to swim in the warm waves or admire the stunning, glistening waters here.

> 💬 INSIDER TIP
> **TapuTapu™**
>
> This wristband allows guests to "check in" at rides and hold their place in a virtual line. Simply hold the wristband to a ride totem and it will signal when to return.

↑ The tempting Toothsome Chocolate Emporium and Savory Feast Kitchen™

⑤ CITYWALK™

The stretch between Universal Orlando Resort's parking garage and the entryway to both Universal's Islands of Adventure™ and Universal Studios Florida™ is filled with shopping, dining, and nightlife. It offers visitors the opportunity to continue their Universal experience long after the parks have closed.

Popular chain restaurants including Bubba Gump Shrimp Co.™ and Jimmy Buffet's Margaritaville® operate locations here, but families love the inventive sushi-and-burgers menu at The Cowfish™, and Jamaican food at Bob Marley – A Tribute to Freedom, which is based on the Jamaican singer's house. Toothsome Chocolate Emporium & Savory Feast Kitchen® is a highlight that can't be missed. However, reservations are not taken at this steampunk-inspired haven for chocolate lovers, so wait for a table or grab a towering milkshake to go.

The best bet for couples remains VIVO Italian Kitchen™ or Antojitos Authentic Mexican Food™, which offer exciting food and extensive drink menus. For after-hours entertainment, the complex also hosts a large Universal™ Cinemark movie theater, and a music venue at Hard Rock Live® Orlando. Traveling without kids? Enjoy dueling pianos at Pat O' Brien's® or club vibes at the groove™ and Red Coconut Club™, and Voodoo Doughnut's sugary delights for a delicious nighttime treat after a ong day.

Did You Know?

You can find every kind of regional hot dog at the Hot Dog Hall of Fame® stand.

←

Relaxing by Krakatau™ mountain, and having fun at Volcano Bay™ *(inset)*

Must See

EAT

Most of the best restaurants in Universal Orlando Resort™ are located in the CityWalk™ complex. Ranging from Mediterranean and sushi to Italian and grilled meats, the following places offer something for each taste bud, with ample entertainment to enjoy alongside your meals.

Fusion Bistro Sushi & Sake Bar™
🅰 CityWalk™

⑤⑤⑤

NBC Sports Grill & Brew ™
🅰 CityWalk™

⑤⑤⑤

Red Oven Pizza Bakery™
🅰 CityWalk™

⑤⑤⑤

Bigfire
🅰 CityWalk™

⑤⑤⑤

The Cowfish® Sushi Burger Bar
🅰 CityWalk™

⑤⑤⑤

Bob Marley-A Tribute to FreedomSM
🅰 CityWalk™

⑤⑤⑤

VIVO Italian Kitchen™
🅰 CityWalk™

⑤⑤⑤

LEGOLAND®

F4 **1 Legoland Way, Winter Haven** **Times vary, check website**
legoland.com/florida

This family-friendly, cheerful theme and water park highlights
characters and experiences from within the LEGO® universe
and hosts a handful of brilliant attractions.

Thrills here come by way of LEGO® NINJAGO® The Ride, an
interactive multiplayer competition, and many roller coasters –
Flying School suspended coaster, The Dragon steel coaster, and
The Great LEGO® Race, which offers virtual reality integration.

The LEGO® Movie™ World land brings shops, restaurants,
and three new rides themed to the blockbuster movie. Board a
"Triple Decker Flying Couch" for a flying attraction set opposite
a full dome screen on *The LEGO® Movie*™ Masters of Flight, ride
Unikitty's Disco Drop, and experience Downtown Bricksburg's
Taco Everyday eatery.

On weekends, PirateFest sees the whole park taken over by
Brickbeard's pirates, with Junior Pirates recruited for fun and
games. Past the amusements is the LEGOLAND® Water
Park, which requires an added fee. Here, a wave pool, water
slides, and a Build-a-Raft River allows guests to attach large-
scale LEGO® pieces onto specially designed inflatable tubes.
LEGOLAND® also retains the botanical gardens portion of the
former Cypress Gardens theme park for a natural counterpart
to the creations from its famed creativity-enhancing bricks.

> **PICTURE PERFECT**
> **Unique Photo**
> **Opportunities**
>
> The large red dinosaur
> just past LEGOLAND®'s
> entrance is a visitor
> favorite, but silly LEGO®
> structures, like those
> outside Pepper & Roni's
> Pizza Stop, are fantastic
> as well. Look out for
> characters referencing
> pop culture icons, and
> a LEGO® plumber
> hilariously carrying
> an all-lego toilet outside
> the restrooms.

↑ Fantastic LEGO® model of New York, populated with figures

STAY

LEGOLAND® Hotel
A LEGO® castle, elevator disco dance parties, and a brick pit give this kid-friendly hotel an edge over standard lodging.

⑤⑤⑤

Pirate Island Hotel
A kid-friendly option with nightly pirate-themed entertainment, in-room treasure hunts, and bunk beds in family rooms.

⑤⑤⑤

Beach Retreat
LEGO® bungalows, a resort-style pool, and beach vibes set this motel-like option apart. Trundle bunk beds for three are available and there are plenty of outdoor play areas.

⑤⑤⑤

1 The park offers meet-and-greets with characters, such as Wyldstyle, President Business, and fan favorite, Emmet, from *The LEGO® Movie™*.

2 With its playful exterior, staying at the LEGO® hotel is an unmissable experience.

3 Build-a-Raft River is best enjoyed on a hot Florida day.

The bright lights of downtown Orlando, set around Lake Eola ↑

3

ORLANDO

⌂F3 ✈🚌 **ℹ8723 International Drive; www.visit orlando.com**

Until the 1950s, Orlando was not much more than a sleepy provincial town. Its proximity to Cape Canaveral and the theme parks, however, helped to change all that. Downtown Orlando beckons mostly at night, when tourists and locals flock to the bars and restaurants around Orange Avenue. During the daytime, take a stroll in the park around Lake Eola, to get a taste of Orlando's (comparatively) early history.

①

Harry P. Leu Gardens

⌂1920 N Forest Ave
🕙9am–5pm daily
🌐leugardens.org

The Harry P. Leu Gardens, which were donated by Leu and his wife to the City of Orlando in 1961, offer 50 acres (20 ha) of serenely beautiful gardens. Features such as Florida's largest rose garden are formal and pristine, while elsewhere nature has been allowed a freer rein, and you can find mature woods of spectacular live oaks and cypresses, festooned with Spanish moss. In winter, seek out the stunning camellias.

②

Maitland Art Center

⌂231 W Packwood Ave
🕙Art Center: 11am–4pm Thu–Sun; Grounds: daily
🌐artandhistory.org

This art center located in the leafy suburb of Maitland, north of downtown Orlando, occupies studios and living quarters that were designed in the 1930s by artist André Smith as a winter retreat for fellow creatives. Set around gardens and court-yards, the buildings are lovely, with abundant use made of Mayan and Aztec motifs. The studios are still used, and there are exhibitions of contempo-rary American arts and crafts.

③

Orlando Science Center

⌂777 East Princeton St
🕙10am–5pm daily
🌐osc.org

This center aims to provide a stimulating environment for experiential science learning through its huge range of state-of-the-art, interactive exhibits. Covering 207,000 sq ft (19,200 sq m) of floor space, these include the Dr. Phillips CineDome, a movie theater

> Loch Haven Park is also home to the Orlando Shakespeare Theater, which hosts the city's Fringe Festival in spring.

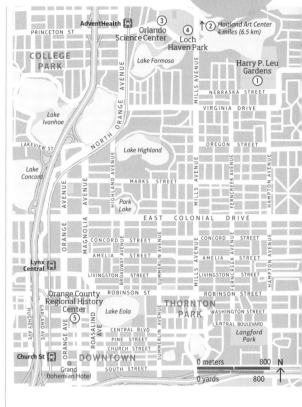

that doubles as a planetarium. Exhibits change frequently, but the DinoDigs area, with its collection of dinosaur fossils, is perennially popular with kids, as is the orange packing plant, where youngsters eagerly pick and pack plastic oranges.

The original museum was opened in 1960 at Loch Haven Park and was called the Central Florida Museum, before being renamed in 1984. The present building, six times larger than its previous home, opened in February 1997.

---

④
Loch Haven Park

📍 N Mills Ave at Rollins St

Loch Haven Park, 2 miles (3 km) north of downtown, is home to a trio of small museums. The most highly regarded is the **Orlando Museum of Art**, which has four permanent collections: pre-Columbian artifacts, with figurines from Nazca in Peru; African art; Contemporary art and graphics; and American paintings of the 19th and 20th centuries. Loch Haven Park is also home to the Orlando Shakes Theater, which hosts the city's Fringe Festival in spring.

Orlando Museum of Art
🕙 10am–4pm Tue–Fri, noon–4pm Sat & Sun
🌐 omart.org

---

⑤
Orange County Regional History Center

📍 65 E Central Blvd 🕙 10am–5pm Mon–Sat, noon–5pm Sun 🌐 thehistorycenter.org

Housed in the 1927 courthouse downtown, the Center crams 12,000 years of Central Florida's past into three floors. Don't miss the diorama of the sink-hole that swallowed buildings and cars in Winter Park in the 1980s.

↑ The curved, sand-colored exterior of the Orlando Science Center

④ 🛝 🎿 🍴 🛍️

KENNEDY SPACE CENTER

🅐F3 🅐Brevard County 🚌 🕐From 9am daily (closing time varies by season, check website) 🆆kennedyspacecenter.com

NASA has been an exciting presence in Florida since the late 1960s, and this impressive visitor's center gives everyone a chance to experience their own space adventure.

Less than an hour's drive east of Orlando, the Kennedy Space Center captured the world's attention when the launch of *Apollo 11* in July 1969 realized President Kennedy's dream of landing a man on the moon. The center is one of the homes of NASA (National Aeronautics and Space Administration), and was the preparation and launch facility for the crewed Space Shuttle (*p194*). The Visitor Complex offers events, attractions, and interactive programs throughout the year.

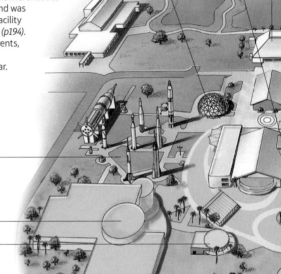

Apollo/Saturn V Center is dominated by a Saturn V rocket and a reconstructed control room.

Astronaut Encounter

Children's Play Dome

Rocket Garden is filled with a group of towering rockets that each represent a different period of space flight's history.

The Heroes & Legends exhibit includes the US Astronauts Hall of Fame.

Information

Entrance

Timeline

1958
First American satellite, the *Explorer 1*, is launched (Jan 31).

1969
◀ Neil Armstrong and Buzz Aldrin (*Apollo 11*) walk on the moon (Jul 24)

1961
◀ Alan Shephard is the first American in space; Kennedy commits nation to moon landing.

1965
Edward White is the first American to walk in space (Jun 3).

1981
Columbia is the first shuttle in space (Apr 12).

1986
▲ The *Challenger* explodes, killing all its crew (Jan 28).

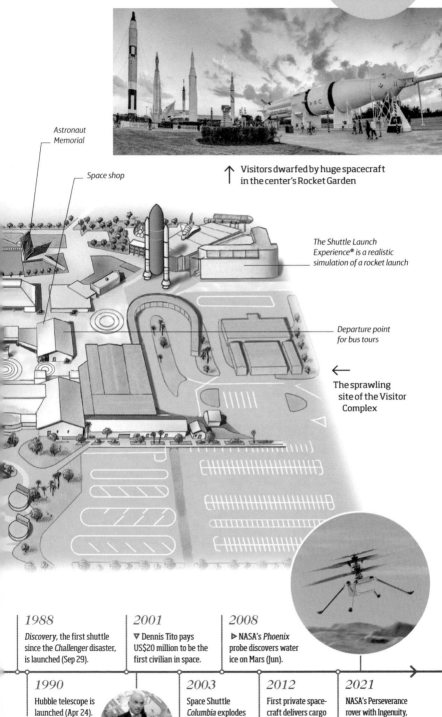

↑ Visitors dwarfed by huge spacecraft in the center's Rocket Garden

Astronaut Memorial

Space shop

The Shuttle Launch Experience® is a realistic simulation of a rocket launch

Departure point for bus tours

← The sprawling site of the Visitor Complex

1988

Discovery, the first shuttle since the *Challenger* disaster, is launched (Sep 29).

1990

Hubble telescope is launched (Apr 24).

2001

▽ Dennis Tito pays US$20 million to be the first civilian in space.

2003

Space Shuttle *Columbia* explodes on re-entry, killing all its crew (Feb 1).

2008

▷ NASA's *Phoenix* probe discovers water ice on Mars (Jun).

2012

First private spacecraft delivers cargo to the International Space Station.

2021

NASA's Perseverance rover with Ingenuity, a helicopter, touches down on Mars.

VISITOR COMPLEX

Built in 1967 for astronauts and their families to view space center operations, today the Visitor Complex is host to more than 1.5 million tourists each year. The 131 sq mile (340 sq km) facility offers guests a comprehensive space experience to be explored at their own pace, including the Space Shuttle Atlantis, excellent IMAX® films, astronaut encounters, and the Apollo/Saturn V Center – the climax of the video-enhanced bus tour. One all-inclusive ticket admits visitors on the KSC Tour, both IMAX® films, the US Astronaut Hall of Fame at Heroes & Legends, and all exhibits.

The place everyone heads first is the Shuttle: A Ship Like No Other exhibit, where you can see the dramatic placement of the actual Atlantis orbiter, viewed as it would have been by space-walking astronauts. You can then head to the thrilling Shuttle Launch Experience, where you feel the G-forces as the simulation hurtles you toward space, then for an instant you hang weightless. Next on the list, or whenever you feel a need to escape the Florida heat, is the IMAX® Theater at Nasa Now and Next.

Top of the bill is *Hubble 3D*, an IMAX film narrated by Leonardo DiCaprio, which offers an inspiring look into the legacy of the Hubble Space Telescope. The film illustrates the impact the telescope has had on the way we view the universe, and features footage from the final Hubble repair

> ### GREAT VIEW
> ### Rocket Launch
>
> The Kennedy Space Center Visitor Complex, just a few miles away from the launch pads, is by far the best place to view spacecrafts liftoff and leave Earth. Tickets to see the rocket launch can be purchased online.

mission. Another film on offer is *Journey to Space*, narrated by Sir Patrick Stewart. The film uses actual space footage to explore NASA's plans to reach out into deep space. The Astronaut Encounter at the Universe Theater offers visitors an opportunity to meet someone who has flown in space.

The US Astronaut Hall of Fame® commemorates the astronauts of Mercury, Gemini, Apollo, and the Space Shuttle Program, and has many of their personal items on display. Nearby a "Space Mirror" tracks the movement of the sun, reflecting its light onto the names inscribed on the Astronaut Memorial. This honors the 16 astronauts who have given their lives in service of space exploration.

> **Head to the thrilling Shuttle Launch Experience, where you can feel the G-forces as the simulation hurtles you toward space, then for an instant you hang weightless.**

A gleaming rocket, ↑ dominating an exhibit in the Visitor Complex

KSC BUS TOUR

↑ Young visitors transfixed by an exhibit in the Apollo/Saturn V Center

KSC Tour buses leave every few minutes from the Visitor Complex and offer an exceptional tour of the space center's major facilities. The tour includes the Apollo/Saturn V Center and takes guests into secured areas, where guides explain the inner workings of each of the facilities. Visitors can take as long as they wish to explore the Apollo/Saturn V Center.

The bus tour begins with a 40-minute drive through NASA's property at Cape Canaveral, narrated by space guide (and TV scientist) Emily Calandrelli. It usually includes the monumental Vehicle Assembly Building, Launch Complex 39, and all of the facilities in between (though tour routes may be altered at any time because of ongoing operations).

The tour ends at the Apollo/Saturn V Center, which features an actual 363 ft (110 m) Saturn V moon rocket. Visitors will see the historic launch of Apollo 8, the first manned mission to the moon in the Firing Room Theater, followed by a film at the Lunar Theater, which shows footage of the moon landing.

The Treasures Gallery contains everything from Alan Shepard's moon-dust covered spacesuit to the Apollo 14 Command Module, as well as various pieces of rare equipment and other spacesuits from the original moon missions.

SPECIAL INTEREST TOURS AND ADD-ONS

There are additional special-interest tours, for an extra charge, throughout the center, including: Cape Canaveral: Then & Now Tour, which is an historic tour of the Mercury, Gemini, and Apollo launch pads, as well as the Air Force Space and Missile Museum; and the KSC Up-Close Tours, which provide an insider's view of the entire space program.

There is also the Astronaut Training Experience®, along with sister program Mars Base 1. The 4–5 hour astronaut training program (for those aged 10 and older) involves practicing spaceship docking, navigating Mars terrain, and experiencing the sensation of spacewalking in microgravity, all using immersive technology.

The 5–7 hour Mars Base 1 program takes guests virtually to Mars to live and work for the day; tasks include working at the Mars Base Operations Center, tending vegetables in the Botany Lab, and programming robots.

A shorter add-on (30 min) is the Cosmic Quest, a live action gaming experience which allows players to construct a Martian habitat, conduct experiments on the International Space Station, and launch a NASA Mars probe. Finally, "Dine With An Astronaut" offers a buffet lunch with a real astronaut (the general Astronaut Encounter presentations are included with entry).

Tours sell out daily, so should be reserved in advance. Those keen to experience all of the tours – which is well worth doing – should aim to do so on separate days, as they cover vast areas in great detail.

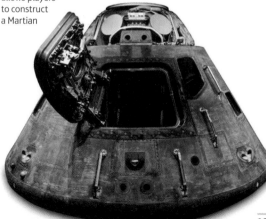

→ The *Apollo 14* capsule, housed within the Apollo Treasures Gallery

THE SPACE COAST

By the late 1970s, the cost of sending astronauts into space had become too much. Hundreds of millions of dollars were spent with little reward. The time had come to develop reusable spacecraft. The answer was the Space Shuttle *Columbia*, which was launched into space on April 12, 1981. The shuttle's large cargo capacity enabled it to take satellites and probes into space, and it was used to lift materials for the construction of the International Space Station.

BEYOND THE SHUTTLE PROGRAM

The future of space seems to lie in the hands of private entrepreneurs. Their companies, which include SpaceX, Virgin Galactic, and Blue Origin, have begun to take over the work traditionally undertaken by NASA, which shares its Kennedy Space Center launch pads and resources with them. Rockets designed by these companies launch from the Space Center regularly (launch schedules are available online), and visitors can see them during tours of the space center, or from across the lagoon.

Amazon owner Jeff Bezos founded Blue Origin in 2000, to develop safe, reliable, cost-effective human access to space. Working in partnership with NASA, the company has successfully tested an innovative launch-pad escape system, and launched sub-orbital rockets. In the future, Blue Origin plans to take tourists into space, and deliver astronauts into orbit.

However, not all space exploration has moved to the private sector. Current NASA missions include three Artemis missions, scheduled between 2021 and 2024, which will use its Orion crew module systems for the beginning of human journeys toward the Moon, asteroids, and Mars. Visitors to Kennedy Space Center can find out more about these missions, as well as six future Artemis launches and the Lunar Gateway – a planned space station for lunar orbit.

↑ *Delta II* launching from Cape Canaveral Air Force Station

SPOTS TO WATCH THE LAUNCHES

Titusville
🅰 Across the lagoon from KSC

Marina Park
🅰 501 Marina Rd

Sand Point Park
🅰 101 N Washington Ave (US 1)

Space View Park
🅰 8 Broad St

Manzo Park
🅰 3335 S Washington Ave (US 1)

The Crawler backed away once the shuttle was in place.

The crawlerway, 180 ft (55 m) wide, was designed to withstand the weight of the shuttle as it was taken to the launch pad by gigantic crawlers. The rock surface overlies a layer of asphalt and a bed of stone.

Tracks enabled the tower to be moved away before liftoff.

→ A launch pad at Kennedy Space Center

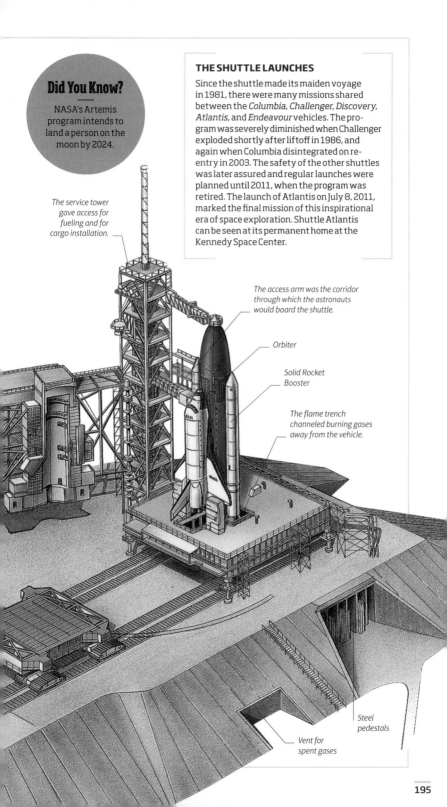

THE SHUTTLE LAUNCHES

Since the shuttle made its maiden voyage in 1981, there were many missions shared between the *Columbia*, *Challenger*, *Discovery*, *Atlantis*, and *Endeavour* vehicles. The program was severely diminished when Challenger exploded shortly after liftoff in 1986, and again when Columbia disintegrated on re-entry in 2003. The safety of the other shuttles was later assured and regular launches were planned until 2011, when the program was retired. The launch of Atlantis on July 8, 2011, marked the final mission of this inspirational era of space exploration. Shuttle Atlantis can be seen at its permanent home at the Kennedy Space Center.

The service tower gave access for fueling and for cargo installation.

The access arm was the corridor through which the astronauts would board the shuttle.

Orbiter

Solid Rocket Booster

The flame trench channeled burning gases away from the vehicle.

Steel pedestals

Vent for spent gases

↑ Visitors enjoying a thrilling, watery ride at SeaWorld® Parks and Resorts Orlando

EXPERIENCE MORE

5

SeaWorld® Parks and Resorts Orlando

🅰E3 🏠7007 SeaWorld Dr 🕒Times vary, check website 🆆seaworld.com

This entertainment complex comprises three parks, each providing distinct aquatic entertainment.

The most famous park in the complex is SeaWorld® Orlando. Among the main attractions are the Kraken® and Mako rollercoasters, and the Antarctica: Empire of the Penguin ride, where the audience can follow the fictional adventures of Puck the Penguin before exploring the icy world of a penguin colony. Turtle Trek is home to rescued turtles, which are too injured to survive on their own in the wild, and other animals can be seen in walk-through exhibits or sit-down stadium shows. For an overview of the park, take the six-minute ride up the 400-ft (122-m) Sky Tower.

SeaWorld® Orlando has a rehabilitation program of rescuing stranded marine animals and, whenever possible, releasing them back into the wild. However, less positive aspects of SeaWorld® Orlando have come to light since the release of the documentary film Blackfish.

Across the street, the Discovery Cove park offers some unforgettable experiences, such as an opportunity to spot beautiful marmosets, or take an underwater walking tour around the Grand Reef.

The third park in the complex is Aquatica, SeaWorld's Waterpark®, which captures the essence of an aquatic paradise. Lagoons, wave pools, relaxing rivers, racing rides, and water slides are all set amidst shady cabanas and vibrant flora.

6

Kissimmee

🅰E3 🏠Osceola County 🚗🚌 🛈1925 E Irlo Bronson Memorial Hwy and 5770 W Irlo Bronson Mem Hwy, Old Town; www.experience kissimmee.com

In the early 20th century, cows freely roamed the streets of this cattle boom town. Now, the only livestock you are likely to see are those that appear in the twice-yearly rodeo at Kissimmee's **Silver Spurs Arena**.

Kissimmee means "Heaven's Place" in the language of the

> **BLACKFISH DOCUMENTARY**
>
> The 2013 documentary film Blackfish questioned the ethics and highlighted the dangers of keeping killer whales in captivity. After the film's release, SeaWorld® Orlando received strong criticism for its treatment of its killer whales and saw a downturn in public opinion, as well as a drop in the number of visitors to its theme parks. SeaWorld has since ceased its orca breeding program and refocused all performances with orcas to be more educational.

Calusa, but despite the romantic name, many people only stop here to make use of the glut of cheap motels close to Walt Disney World® Resort, along the US 192. After a day in a theme park, however, you may prefer to visit Kissimmee's Old Town. This re-created pedestrian street of early 20th-century buildings has eccentric shops offering psychic readings, tattoos, Irish linen, candles, and so forth. There is also an entertaining haunted house and a small fairground with antique equipment.

Warbird Adventures, by the Kissimmee municipal airport, offers visitors the opportunity to learn to fly in an original World War II Advanced T-6 Navy Trainer or a classic MASH helicopter.

Silver Spurs Arena

⊛ 🄰 Osceola Heritage Park 🄲 For shows 🅦 silverspurs rodeo.com

Warbird Adventures

⊛ 🄰 N Hoagland Blvd
🄲 9am–5pm Mon–Sat
🅦 warbirdadventures.com

American Police Hall of Fame

🄰 F3 🄰 6350 Horizon Dr 🄱 Titusville 🄲 10am–4pm Tue–Sat 🅦 aphf.org

Few visitors are unmoved by the Hall of Fame's vast marble memorial, engraved with the names of more than 5,000 American police officers who have died in the line of duty. Yet some of the exhibits, while fascinating, are gory and sensationalist. The *RoboCop* mannequin and weapons disguised as lipstick and an umbrella are innocuous enough. Some visitors, however, may find inspecting the gas chamber harder to stomach.

Winter Park

🄰 E2 🄱🄳 🄸 150 N New York Ave; www.winterpark.org

This town took off in the 1880s when wealthy northerners started to build winter retreats here. The aroma of expensive perfume and coffee radiates along its main street, Park

Avenue. The **Charles Hosmer Morse Museum of American Art** holds probably the world's finest collection of works by Louis Comfort Tiffany. Nearby Rollins College is home to **Cornell Fine Arts Museum** and a collection of fine Italian Renaissance paintings.

Charles Hosmer Morse Museum of American Art

⊛ 🄰 445 Park Ave N 🄲 9:30am–4pm Tue–Sat, 1–4pm Sun 🅦 morse museum.org

Cornell Fine Arts Museum

🄰 1000 Holt Ave 🄲 10am–4pm Tue–Fri, noon–5pm Sat & Sun 🅦 rollins.edu/cornell-fine-arts-museum

↑ People enjoying the buzzing nightlife along Kissimmee's pedestrianized Old Town

The upside-down building housing WonderWorks, and a visitor looking at the exhibits (inset) ↑

9 🍴 🛍️

International Drive

E2 Orange County Orlando i 8723 International Drive; www.international driveorlando.com

Anchored by Universal Studios Florida™ and SeaWorld® at either end, International Drive, or "I-Drive," is a tawdry 3-mile (5-km) ribbon of restaurants, hotels, shops, and theaters.

I-Drive's biggest draw is the ICON Park complex, which offers excellent, family-oriented entertainment through several popular attractions. Tickets for the various sites can be bought individually, though packages often offer multiple entries and discounts.

ICON Park's most popular attraction is the **The Wheel at ICON Park™**, a huge ferris wheel that offers a view of Central Florida in one of 30

air-conditioned, transparent capsules. Compass marks on the ceiling give directions, while a recorded commentary points out the landmarks.

Waxworks of celebrities from the worlds of music, movies, television, art, science, history, and sports line the halls of **Madame Tussauds Orlando**. Snap a selfie with Taylor Swift or Aquaman, share the table with Audrey Hepburn in her *Breakfast at Tiffany's* attire, or see Neil Armstrong wearing his moon-walk suit.

In the same building as Madame Tussauds Orlando, **SEA LIFE Aquarium Orlando** offers a glimpse into the lives of more than 5,000 sea animals in 32 displays reflecting the different oceans of the world. In one room, sardines swim in a silvery vortex above visitors'

heads, and sharks and rays swim above and below visitors walking through a 360-degree ocean tunnel.

The **7D Motion Theater** offers thrilling shows with seven dimensions, including wind, sound, and movement.

Filled with fantastic objects, illusions, and movie footage of strange feats, **Ripley's Believe It or Not!** is a fun attraction at I-Drive. It is one of a worldwide chain of museums that was born out of the 1933 Chicago World Fair's so-called Odditorium – the creation of an American broadcaster, cartoonist and anthropologist, Robert Ripley, who traveled the globe in search of the weird and wonderful.

WonderWorks, an upside-down structure, offers interactive family fun with a simulated earthquake and laser tag games. **Titanic – The Experience**, dedicated to commemorating the ship that sank in 1912, is also worth a visit, with movie memorabilia, and re-creations of the ship's

> I-Drive's biggest draw is the ICON Park complex, which offers excellent, family-oriented entertainment through several popular attractions.

rooms and grand staircase. Back on I-Drive is **Pointe Orlando**, an outdoor shopping mall with upscale eateries, nightclubs, and shops, along with other attractions such as an IMAX® movie theater, B.B. King's Blues Club, and an Improv Comedy Club.

Anyone with a sweet tooth will love **Chocolate Kingdom – Factory Adventure Tour**, which offers an introduction to chocolate making. Kids will also enjoy the wooden elevated go-kart tracks, bumper cars and boats, carousel, and massive arcade at **Magical Midway Thrill Park**, while teens and elders enjoy **Escape Game Orlando**, an "escape room" attraction where the challenges include finding a work of art or breaking out of jail.

The Wheel at ICON Park™
🎫 🏠8401 I-Drive
🕙 Times vary, check website
🌐 iconparkorlando.com

Madame Tussauds Orlando
🎫😊 🏠8387 I-Drive
🕙 10am-10pm daily (to 11pm Fri & Sat) 🌐 madame tussauds.com/orlando

SEA LIFE Aquarium Orlando
🎫😊👶 🏠849 I-Drive
🕙 Times vary, check website
🌐 visitsealife.com/orlando

💬 INSIDER TIP
I-Ride Trolley System

The most convenient and affordable way to get around the I-Drive area, this transportation costs $2 per ride for adults, and $1 for children aged 3-9. Trolleys operate from 8am-10:30pm Thu-Sun.

7D Motion Theater
🎫 🏠8401 I-Drive 🕙10am-10pm daily (to midnight Fri & Sat) 🌐 inthegame. net/iconpark

Ripley's Believe It or Not!
🎫 🏠8201 I-Drive 🕙9am-midnight daily 🌐 ripleys. com/orlando

WonderWorks
🎫 🏠9067 I-Drive
🕙 10am-11pm Sat, 10am-10pm Sun-Fri 🌐 wonder worksonline.com

Titanic - The Experience
🎫 🏠7324 I-Drive 🕙10am-10pm Sun-Fri, 10am-11pm Sat 🌐 premierexhibitions. com/exhibitions

Pointe Orlando
🎫😊👶 🏠9101 I-Drive
🕙 11am-10pm daily (to 8pm Sun) 🌐 pointe orlando.com

400 ft
The height of the Wheel at ICON Park™ (122 m).

Chocolate Kingdom - Factory Adventure Tour
🎫😊👶 🏠9901 Hawaiian Ct (off I-Drive) 🕙11am-5pm Tue-Sun 🌐 chocolateking dom.com

Magical Midway Thrill Park
🎫😊👶 🏠7001 I-Drive
🕙 Noon-midnight daily
🌐 magicalmidway.com

Escape Game Orlando
🎫 🏠8145 I-Drive 🕙8am-1am daily 🌐 theescape game.com/orlando

→
The Wheel at ICON Park™, offering superb views of Central Florida

Fantasy of Flight

E3 **Polk County**
1400 Broadway Blvd SE,
Polk City **Winter
Haven** **Times vary,
check website** **fantasy
offlight.com**

Fantasy of Flight may have
the edge over Florida's many
other aviation attractions
because it provides the
very sensations of flying.
A series of vivid walk-through
exhibits takes visitors into
a World War II B-17 Flying
Fortress during a bombing
mission, and into World
War I trenches in the
middle of an air raid.

For an extra fee visitors
can ride a World War II fighter
aircraft simulator in a dog-
fight over the Pacific. In the
cockpit, there will be a pre-
flight briefing and advice
from the control tower about
takeoff, landing, as well as the
presence of enemy aircraft.

A hangar full of the world's
greatest collection of mint
antique airplanes contains the
first widely used airliner in the
US, the 1929 Ford Tri-Motor,
which appeared in the film
*Indiana Jones and the Temple
of Doom*, and the Roadair 1,
a combined plane and car
that flew just once, in 1959.

Several tours are available,
including a look behind the
scenes at the huge storage
bays, or a visit to the
Restoration Shop where
visitors will meet expert
craftsmen who rebuild
the engines. There is
also the opportunity
to watch a pilot fly
one of the aircraft
in a private air
show – or take
to the skies.

↑ A visitor climbing into the 1944 Short
Sunderland flying boat at Fantasy of Flight

Lake Toho

F3 **Osceola County 3
miles (5 km) S of Kissimmee**
Kissimmee **From Big
Toho Marina on Lakeshore
Blvd, Kissimmee**

At the headwaters of the
Florida Everglades, and
approximately 20 miles
(32 km) from downtown
Orlando, Lake Tohopekaliga
(or Toho, as the locals call it)
is famous for its wide variety
of exotic wildlife. Makinson
Island, in the middle of the
lake, is a 135-acre (55-ha)
nature preserve and county
park, where visitors can
observe a range of flora
and fauna in their natural
surroundings. Alligators, bald
eagles, ospreys,
herons, and
egrets
can all be
observed on a
2 mile (3 km)
hiking trail
around the pre-
serve. Visitors must
arrange their own trans-
portation to reach the
island. Approximately one
third of the 30 sq-mile
(77 sq-km) lake is made
up of maidencane grass
and bullrush reeds.

→ A great blue heron,
one of Lake Toho's
winged residents

Anglers come from all over
the world to compete in
events at Lake Toho, which
is one of the best places
in Florida for catching
trophy bass.

Lake Kissimmee
State Park

F4 **14248 Camp Mack
Rd, Lake Wales** **florida
stateparks.org**

This wonderful park of
live oak forest, prairie, and
floodplains is one of the
best places in central Florida
to witness native wildlife:
wild turkeys, white-tailed
deer, gopher tortoises,
owls, alligators, hawks and
bald eagles, as well as loads
of armadillos are often
seen on the 20 miles
(32 km) of hiking trails,
and around the well-
maintained campground.
The Cracker Shack shop
sells basic camping supplies
and snacks, while Cow
Camp is an 1876-era cattle
camp that hosts demon-
strations on the lives of
19th-century Florida cow
hunters. Other activities in
the park include canoeing,
kayaking, fishing, biking
and horseback riding.

13

Bok Tower Gardens

F4 **Polk County, 1151 Tower Blvd, Lake Wales** **Winter Haven** **Lake Wales** **8am–6pm daily** **boktowergardens.org**

Edward W. Bok arrived in the US from Holland in 1870 at the age of six, and subsequently became an influential publisher. Shortly before his death in 1930, he presented 128 acres (52 ha) of beautiful woodland gardens to the American public "for the success they had given him."

The sanctuary now encompasses 250 acres (100 ha) at the highest spot in peninsular Florida – a dizzying 298 ft (91 m) above sea level – in the center is the Singing Tower, which shelters Bok's grave at

Did You Know?

The endangered Florida panther has been spotted in Disney Wilderness Preserve.

its base. The tower cannot be climbed, but try to attend its 45-minute live carillon concert, played daily at 3pm.

14

Disney Wilderness Preserve

F4 **2700 Scrub Jay Trail, 12 miles (18 km) SW of Kissimmee** **Kissimmee** **Apr–Oct: 9am–4:30pm Wed–Fri, 8:30am–4:30pm Sat; Nov–Mar: 9am–4:30pm daily** **nature.org**

This wilderness preserve is a peaceful place. A partnership between Disney and the Nature Conservancy, the 20 sq-mile (50 sq-km) preserve consists of tranquil lakes and swamps that are a haven for native plants and animals. The preserve is bordered by one of the last remaining undeveloped lakes in Florida.

More than 160 different species of wildlife live here, including Florida scrub-jays, Florida sandhill cranes, and Sherman's fox squirrels.

Unlike the other Disney attractions, there are no thrills or rides here. Visitors can follow one of the three hiking

FLORIDA'S GATORS

Around one million alligators live in Florida's fresh and brackish water areas, including lakes, rivers, and even golf-course ponds. Despite such large numbers, alligators remain on the endangered list. Fatal attacks on humans are rare but do occasionally occur (the latest was in 2018).

trails that lead to the shores of Lake Russell. The shortest walk is the interpretive trail, a pleasant 0.8 miles (1.2 km), where there is the chance to learn first-hand about nature along the way. The longer trails are partially unshaded, so water and sunscreen should be brought along during the hotter months.

Visitors can also take an off-road buggy tour, which starts with a 20-minute introductory video about the preserve, before a embarking upon a trip through the swampland with a guide. Do bear in mind that, despite its name, this is not a theme park. The alligators and snakes are very real. Visitors should always remain alert and exercise caution when they explore these regions.

→ The imposing Singing Tower at the center of Bok Tower Gardens

A wood stork, one of the many birds inhabiting the marshes of Merritt Island

16

Canaveral National Seashore and Merritt Island

🅰F3 🏠Brevard County 🚌Titusville 🌐nps.gov

These adjacent preserves share a wide range of habitats including saltwater estuaries, marshes, pine flatwoods, and hardwood hammocks. The variety is due to the meeting of temperate and subtropical climates here. You can often see alligators, as well as endangered species such as manatees, but it is the birdlife that makes the greatest visual impact.

The **Canaveral National Seashore** incorporates Florida's largest undeveloped barrier island beach – a magnificent 24-mile (39-km) strip of sand backed by dunes strewn with sea oats and sea grapes. Apollo Beach, at the northern end, is accessible along Route A1A, while Playalinda Beach is reached from the south, along Route 402; no road connects the two. Be aware that swimming conditions can be hazardous,

Valiant Air Command Warbird Air Museum

🅰F3 🏠6600 Tico Rd, Titusville, Brevard County 🚌Titusville 🕙10am–6pm daily 🌐vacwarbirds.org

At this museum an enormous hangar houses military planes from World War II and later – all lovingly restored to flying condition. The pride of the collection is a working Douglas C-47 called Tico Belle: the aircraft saw service during World War II before becoming the official carrier for the Danish royal family.

Every March there is an air show, with mock dogfights. Several of the restored planes fly regularly, including a US Navy TBM Avenger, which underwent a 15-year rehabilitation. This plane honors the five bombers of the infamous Flight 19, which disappeared over the Bermuda Triangle in 1945. Visitors interested in aircraft restoration may explore the Larkin/Lindsay Restoration Hangar (accompanied by a staff member) and observe the detailed work on various ongoing warbird projects, carried out by its dedicated volunteers. Another section of the museum displays a large collection of military aviation memorabilia, including uniforms, insignia, equipment, weapons, models, and artifacts.

and there are no lifeguards. Behind Apollo Beach, Turtle Mound is a 40-ft-(12-m-) high rubbish dump of oyster shells created by the Timucua between AD 800 and 1400. Climb the boardwalk to the top for a view over Mosquito Lagoon, flecked with myriad mangrove islets.

Route 402 to Playalinda Beach offers great views of the Kennedy Space Center's shuttle launch pads rising out of the watery vastness. This route also crosses **Merritt Island National Wildlife Refuge**, most of which lies within the Kennedy Space

↑ Admiring an aircraft at the Valiant Air Command Warbird Air Museum

← Surfers and swimmers enjoying the waves at Cocoa Beach

Center and is out of bounds. To experience the local wildlife first hand, follow the 6-mile (10-km) Black Point Wildlife Drive. East along Route 402 toward Playalinda, the Merritt Island Visitor Information Center has excellent displays on the habitats within the refuge. A mile (1.5 km) farther east, the Oak Hammock and Palm Hammock trails have boardwalks for birdwatching.

Canaveral National Seashore

⊛ ⌂ Route A1A, 20 miles (32 km) N of Titusville ◷ Summer: 6am–8pm daily; winter: 6am–6pm daily ⓦ nps.gov

Merritt Island National Wildlife Refuge

⌂ Route 406, 4 miles (7 km) E of Titusville ◷ Sunrise-sunset daily ⓦ merritt island.fws.gov

> Cocoa's historic district, near where Route 520 crosses the Indian River to Cocoa Beach, is an attractive enclave known as Cocoa Village.

Cocoa Beach

🄰 G3 🚋 Merritt Island 🄷 400 Fortenberry Rd; www.visitcocoabeach.com

This no-frills resort calls itself the surfing capital of the east coast. With the pier hosting "win your weight in beer" competitions, the area is better suited to laid-back college kids than it is to families. Motels and chain restaurants characterize the main thoroughfare, but are all eclipsed by the **Ron Jon Surf Shop**, a neon palace selling surfboards galore. In front of its flashing towers, beach bum sports figures are frozen in modern sculpture.

Ron Jon Surf Shop

⌂ 4151 N Atlantic Ave ◷ 9am–11pm daily ⓦ ronjonsurfshop.com

Cocoa

🄰 F3 🚋 🄷 400 Fortenberry Rd, Merritt Island; www. cityofcocoabeach.com

Cocoa is the most appealing community among the sprawl of conurbations along the

💬 INSIDER TIP
Space Coast Birdlife

The magnificent and abundant birdlife of the Space Coast is best viewed early in the morning or shortly before dusk. Between November and March, in particular, the marshes and lagoons teem with migratory ducks and waders, as up to 100,000 arrive from colder northern climes.

Space Coast mainland. Its historic district, near where Route 520 crosses the Indian River to Cocoa Beach, is an attractive enclave known as Cocoa Village – with buildings dating from the 1880s and replica gas street lamps.

On the eastern edge of the village is the Classical Revival **Porcher House**, built of coquina stone in 1916. Note the heart, diamond, and club carvings on its portico wall: Mrs. Porcher was an extremely avid bridge player.

Porcher House

⊛ ⌂ 434 Delannoy Ave ☎ (321) 633-0806 ◷ 8am–5pm Mon–Fri

COLON[I]

St.

GIFT SHO[P]

THE NORTHEAST

Florida's post-Colonial history begins here on the aptly named First Coast. Juan Ponce de León first stepped ashore here in 1513, and Spanish colonists established St. Augustine, now a well-preserved town guarded by the mighty San Marcos fortress, in 1565. The Northeast also saw the first influx of pioneers and tourists during the 19th-century steamboat era, and in the 1880s Henry Flagler's railroad opened up the east coast to wealthy visitors who flocked to his grand hotels in St. Augustine and Ormond Beach. Broad, sandy beaches flank the popular resort of Daytona, which has been synonymous with car racing ever since the likes of Henry Ford and Louis Chevrolet raced automobiles on the beach during their winter vacations.

Venturing inland, west of the St. Johns River, is the wooded expanse of the Ocala National Forest; the woods then thin out to reveal the rolling pastures of Marion County's billion-dollar thoroughbred horse industry. Nearby, charming country towns and villages such as Micanopy have been virtually untouched by the 20th century.

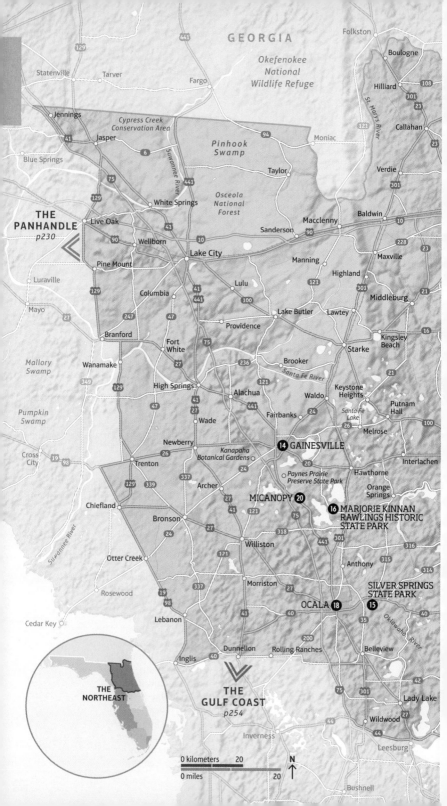

THE NORTHEAST

Must Sees

Must Sees

1 Jacksonville
2 St. Augustine

Experience More

3 Fernandina Beach
4 Fort Caroline National Memorial
5 Kingsley Plantation
6 Talbot Island State Parks
7 Daytona Beach
8 World Golf Hall of Fame
9 Washington Oaks Gardens State Park
10 Bulow Plantation Ruins Historic State Park
11 Daytona International Speedway
12 Ponce de León Inlet Lighthouse
13 Sanford
14 Gainesville
15 Silver Springs State Park
16 Marjorie Kinnan Rawlings Historic State Park
17 Ocala National Forest
18 Ocala
19 Mount Dora
20 Micanopy
21 Ormond Beach
22 Blue Spring State Park

Skyscrapers of downtown Jacksonville, reflected in St. Johns River ↑

JACKSONVILLE

🅐F1 🏠Duval County 🚗🚌🚆 ℹ️550 Water St; www.
visitjacksonville.com

Jacksonville, the capital of the First Coast of Florida, was founded in 1822. Named after General Andrew Jackson, the town boomed as a port and rail hub in the 1800s. Today the sprawling city spans the St. Johns River, and features an impressive commercial district.

① Jacksonville Beaches

🏠Duval County, St. Johns County 🚌🚆Jacksonville 🚌BH1, BH2, BH3 🌐jacksonvillebeach.org

East of downtown Jacksonville, half a dozen beaches stretch along the Atlantic shore. In the south, Ponte Vedra Beach is known for its sports facilities, particularly golf. Jacksonville Beach is the busiest spot, and is home to Adventure Landing, a year-round entertainment complex and summer season water park. Heading north, Neptune Beach and Atlantic Beach are both quieter and are popular with families. By far the nicest spot in the region is the **Kathryn Abbey Hanna Park**, with its fine white sand beach, woodland trails, and camping areas. The park lies just south of the fishing village of Mayport, which still boasts its own shrimping fleet and is home to a US Navy base.

Kathryn Abbey Hanna Park

 🏠500 Wonderwood Dr
📞(904) 249-4700 🕐8am–8pm daily (Nov–Mar: to 6pm)

② Cummer Museum of Art and Gardens

🏠829 Riverside Ave
🕐Times vary, check website
🌐cummermuseum.org

This excellent museum stands in exquisite formal gardens that lead down to the St. Johns River. With a permanent collection of 4,000 objects, the 12 galleries exhibit a small but satisfying selection of both decorative and fine arts. These range from Classical and pre-Columbian sculpture and ceramics through Renaissance paintings to the jewel-like Wark Collection of early Meissen porcelain.

Other notable pieces include Rubens' tiny *Entombment of Christ* (c 1605), and a striking collection of Japanese netsuke. Also on show is work by American Impressionists and such 19th-and-20th-century artists as John James Audubon and Philip Evergood.

↑ A 6th-century Greek vase, on display in the Cummer Museum of Art

③

Museum of Contemporary Art Jacksonville

🏠 333 North Laura St
🕐 Times vary, check website 🌐 moca jacksonville.unf.edu

Located in the heart of the city, this five-gallery museum is home to the largest collection of modern and contemporary art in Southeast USA.

④

Museum of Science and History

🏠 1025 Museum Circle
🕐 Times vary, check website 🌐 themosh.org

This ever-expanding museum houses an eclectic collection of exhibits, and provides a user-friendly guide to local history. The 12,000-year-old culture of the Timucua and their predecessors is illustrated with tools and other archaeological finds. Sections deal with the ecology and history of the St. Johns River

↑ The unassuming facade of the Museum of Science and History

and the *Maple Leaf*, a Civil War steamship that sank in 1864. The Bryan Gooding Planetarium runs laser shows on Fridays and Saturdays.

⑤

Jacksonville Zoo and Gardens

🏠 870 Zoo Parkway 🕐 9am-5pm daily 🌐 jacksonville zoo.org

Opened in 1914, this zoo features about 1,800 animals, from anteaters to zebras, in re-creations of their natural habitats. Lions, elephants, and kudu roam the African veldt, while dik-dik deer, African crocodiles, and porcupines can be found along the zoo's Okavango Trail. Other attractions include the largest collection of jaguars in the US, an aviary, and a Magellanic penguin area. For a broader picture, take the 15-minute miniature rail journey that loops around half of the site.

SHOP

Sweet Pete's Candy Factory

Located in a former political club dating back to 1903, Sweet Pete's is one of the biggest independent candy makers in the country. Head here to stock up on handcrafted candies in a fun environment – there's a rooftop patio on site, as well as a tempting dessert bar.

🏠 400 N Hogan St
🕐 Times vary, check website 🌐 sweet petescandy.com

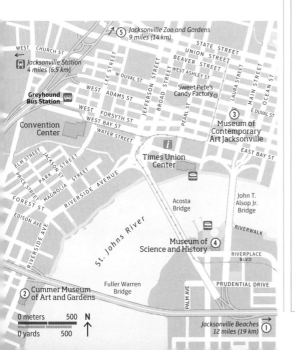

2

ST. AUGUSTINE

 F2 ☐ 🛈 10 Castillo Drive; www.visitstaugustine.com

America's oldest continuously occupied European settlement was founded by Pedro Menéndez de Avilés on the feast day of St. Augustine in 1565. The town was burned down by British troops in 1702 but was soon rebuilt; much of the old town dates to this early period. Today, visitors flock to its lovely beaches and marinas.

1

Colonial Quarter

🏠 33 St. George St
🕙 10am–5pm daily
🔒 During special events
Ⓦ colonialquarter.com

Experience life in 16th–18th-century St. Augustine, and learn about the cultures that left their mark on it – from Minorcans and American Indians to the Spanish, British, and African Americans – on this large plot in the downtown historic district. Guided tours operate several times a day, and interactive events, such as musket drills

in the 17th-century fortified town, are fun for all ages.

The Colonial Quarter also showcases archaeological evidence of one of the town's first wooden forts, as well as 16th-century boat-building and blacksmith skills. Climb the watchtower for views of the Castillo de San Marcos and the bay.

2

The Oldest Wooden Schoolhouse

🏠 14 St. George St 🕙 10am–7pm Fri & Sat, 10am–5pm Sun–Thu Ⓦ oldestwooden schoolhouse.com

Built some time before 1788 and tucked beside the City Gate, this is purportedly the oldest wooden schoolhouse in

The imposing city hall of St. Augustine, before a palm-dotted plaza

America. Walls of cypress and red cedar are held together by wooden pins and cast-iron spikes, and a massive chain anchors it in high winds. The well-preserved interiors and gardens are open to the public.

③

Peña-Peck House

🏠 143 St. George St
🕐 10:30am–5pm Mon-Sat, 12:30–5pm Sun 🌐 pena peckhouse.com

This restored house was built in the 1740s for the Spanish Royal Treasurer, Juan de Peña. In 1837 it became the home and office of Dr. Seth Peck, whose family lived here for almost 100 years. The estate was donated to the city of St. Augustine in 1931. Inside, the house is furnished in mid-19th century style, and is home to the Woman's Exchange of St. Augustine.

← The exterior of the Oldest Wooden Schoolhouse in St. Augustine

④

Governor's House Cultural Center and Museum

🏠 48 King St 🕐 10am–5pm daily 🌐 staugustine.ufl.edu

Government House, adorned with Spanish-style loggias, overlooks the Plaza de la Constitucion and houses a museum, managed by the University of Florida. The museum's exhibitions focus on St. Augustine and North Florida history.

⑤

Spanish Military Hospital Museum

🏠 3 Aviles St 🕐 9am–5pm daily 🌐 smhmuseum.com

Offering a rare glimpse into the kind of care that was given to soldiers in the late 1700s, this military hospital doubles as a museum. Rooms here include an apothecary and cot-lined ward. A short presentation can be attended, and on display is a list of hospital rules and gory medical practices.

DRINK

A1A Ale Works Restaurant & Taproom
The seasonal beers from the onsite brewery keep people returning to this pub. There's also live music on the weekend.

🏠 1 King St
🌐 a1aaleworks.com

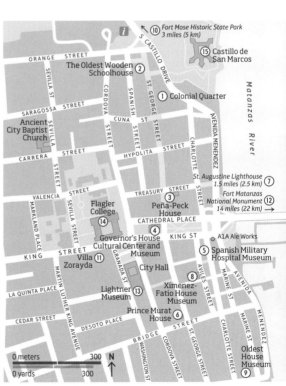

⑥ Prince Murat House

🏠 246 St. George St
🌐 thecollectorinn.com

Once part of the Dow Museum of Historic Homes, this house was rented by Prince Murat, nephew of Napoleon Bonaparte. The atmospheric home has been renovated and turned into a boutique hotel that offers the unbeatable experience of staying in one of the oldest buildings in the entire country.

⑦ St. Augustine Lighthouse

🏠 81 Lighthouse Ave
🕐 9am-6pm daily 🌐 st augustinelighthouse.com

This working historical lighthouse offers lofty views of St. Augustine. Various workshops are offered on site, and visitors can learn about

→

The jaunty black-and-white tower of St. Augustine Lighthouse

the changing coastline, the origins of the shrimping industry, and traditional wooden boat-building (for the latter, call ahead for times). There are also activities aplenty for children, from the walk-in kaleidoscope to knot-tying lessons and a play shipyard.

⑧ Ximenez-Fatio House Museum

🏠 20 Aviles St 🕐 10am-5pm Mon-Sat 🌐 ximenez fatiohouse.org

This lovely house was built in 1797 as the home and store of a Spanish merchant. Today, run by the National Society of Colonial Dames, it is a lifestyle museum that re-creates the genteel boarding house it became in the 1830s, when invalids, developers, and adventurers escaped to Florida from the harsh northern winters during the region's first tourism boom. The interiors are decorated with period artworks and furnishings.

⑨ Oldest House Museum

🏠 14 St. Francis St
📞 (904) 824-2872 🕐 10am-5pm daily

Also known as the González-Alvarez house, this building can trace its history through almost 300 years. There is even evidence that the site was first occupied in the early 1600s, though the existing structure postdates the English raid of 1702.

The coquina walls were part of the original one-story home of a Spanish artilleryman, Tomas González. A second story was added during the English occupation of 1763–83. The building is now a museum, which is owned and operated by the St. Augustine Historical Society. Tours run every half hour, and each room is furnished in a style relevant to the different periods of the house's history.

⑩ Fort Mose Historic State Park

🏠 15 Fort Mose Trail
📞 (904) 823-2232
🕐 9am-5pm Thu-Mon

In 1738, this 40-acre (16-ha) site became America's first legal free African settlement, for those fleeing slavery from the colonies in the Carolinas. In 1994 the site became a National Historic Landmark, and in 2009, a precursor site on the National Underground Railroad Network to Freedom. Guests can explore the land – which includes a winding observation and birding boardwalk – visitor center, and museum. On the first Saturday of every month, the Fort Mose Militia practice firing drills with antique weapons such as muskets. With members dressed in 18th-century costumes, it makes for an excellent photo opportunity.

Villa Zorayda

📍 83 King St 🕐 10am-5pm
Mon-Sat, 11am-4pm Sun
🌐 villazorayda.com

Included on the US National Register of Historic Places, this is a one-tenth scale replica of part of the Alhambra Palace in Granada, Spain. Built in 1883 with 40 windows differing in size, shape, and color, it contains valuable art and artifacts from the Middle East. The most bizarre item on display here is the "Sacred Cat Rug," a 2,400-year-old carpet fashioned from the hair of ancient Egyptian cats. Visitors can take self-guided audio tours in both English and Spanish.

---

⑫
Fort Matanzas National Monument

📍 8635 A1A South
🕐 9am-5:30pm daily
🌐 nps.gov/foma

This Spanish outpost fort was built between 1740–1742 to guard the Matanzas Inlet, and to warn St. Augustine of enemies advancing from the south. The fort has a long and bloody history; "matanza" translates as "slaughter" in English. Today, Fort Matanzas is a reminder of Spain's early empire in the Americas. The site hosts regular reenactments and history demonstrations, particularly during summer.

The park is situated on barrier islands along the Atlantic shores and Matanzas estuary, providing salt marshes, scrub, and maritime hammock to attract and to protect endangered species. Visitors must take a short, free ferry that runs hourly.

> **The fort has a long and bloody history; "matanza" translates as "slaughter" in English. Today, Fort Matanzas is a reminder of Spain's early empire in the Americas.**

Ponce de León Hotel and its ornate rotunda *(inset)* at Flagler College

⑬
Lightner Museum

📍 75 King St
🕐 9am-5pm daily
🌐 lightnermuseum.org

Formerly the Alcazar Hotel, set up by Henry Flagler in 1889, this Hispano-Moorish building is now shared between City Hall and a museum devoted to the Gilded Age. It was selected by Chicago publisher Otto C. Lightner, who transferred his collections of Victorian arts here in 1948. There's a glittering display of superb glass and artworks, plus mechanical musical instruments and toys. The Grand Ballroom houses an exhibit of "American Castle" furniture.

⑭
Flagler College

📍 King St at Cordova St
🕐 Daily 🌐 legacy.flagler.edu

Originally the Ponce de León Hotel, another of Flagler's splendid endeavors, this building opened in 1888, and was heralded as "the world's finest hotel." It became part of the newly established Flagler College in 1968. Guided tours take in the stunning Rotunda, with its Tiffany glass sunroof, oak carvings, gold gilding, and murals by artist George Maynard; the ornate dining room complete with Tiffany stained-glass windows and more murals by Maynard; and the stately Grand Parlor (aka the Flagler Room).

CASTILLO DE SAN MARCOS

📍 1 South Castillo Dr ⏰ 9am–5pm daily 🌐 nps.gov/casa

This impressive historical structure dates back to the late 17th century. Explore the old military fort and see weapons demonstrations for a glimpse into Florida's dramatic past.

Despite its role as protector of the Spanish fleets en route back to Europe, St. Augustine was guarded for over 100 years only by a succession of wooden forts. After suffering a century of attacks, including one by Sir Frances Drake and many more by pirates, the Spanish colonizers began to build a stone fortification in 1672. The resulting Castillo de San Marcos is the largest and most complete Spanish fort in the US. After the US gained Florida in 1821, the castillo was renamed Fort Marion. It was used chiefly as a military prison and storage depot for the rest of the 19th century.

The fort is now a fascinating historical attraction where you can easily spend an afternoon exploring the old barracks or just enjoying the river views.

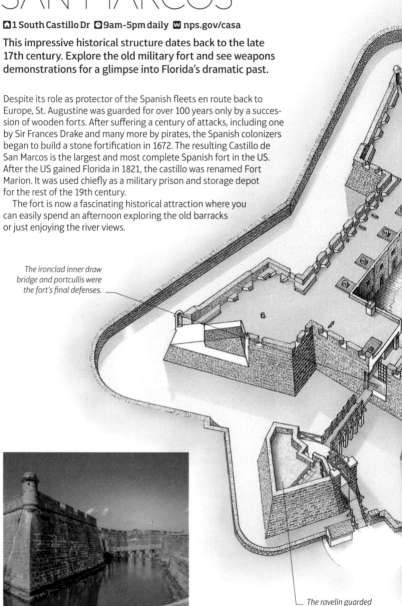

The ironclad inner draw bridge and portcullis were the fort's final defenses.

The ravelin guarded the entrance from enemy attack.

↑ The moat around the fort, which was originally kept dry

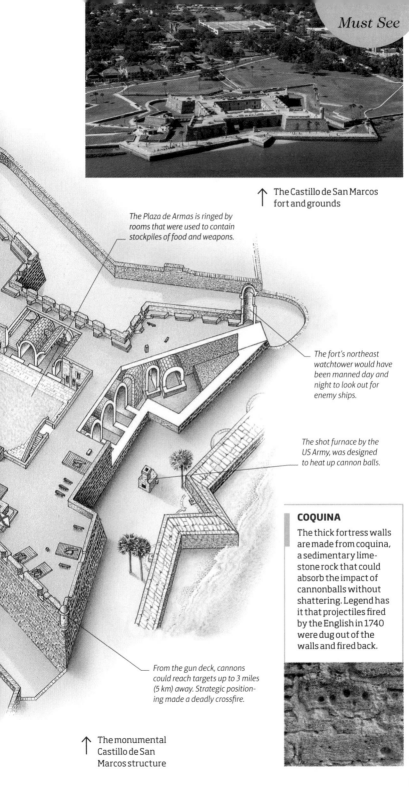

↑ The Castillo de San Marcos fort and grounds

The Plaza de Armas is ringed by rooms that were used to contain stockpiles of food and weapons.

The fort's northeast watchtower would have been manned day and night to look out for enemy ships.

The shot furnace by the US Army, was designed to heat up cannon balls.

COQUINA

The thick fortress walls are made from coquina, a sedimentary limestone rock that could absorb the impact of cannonballs without shattering. Legend has it that projectiles fired by the English in 1740 were dug out of the walls and fired back.

From the gun deck, cannons could reach targets up to 3 miles (5 km) away. Strategic positioning made a deadly crossfire.

↑ The monumental Castillo de San Marcos structure

A SHORT WALK
ST. AUGUSTINE

Distance 1.5 miles (2 km) **Time** 25 minutes

The historic heart of St. Augustine, with its picturesque, narrow streets, is a pleasant area to walk around. The streets are lined by attractive buildings made of Indigenous coquina rock, which date from the 18th century. Part of the fun is escaping off the busy main streets and wandering down shady side turnings, peering into courtyards, and discovering quiet corners where cats bask in the sunshine and ancient live oaks trail curtains of gray-green Spanish moss.

When Henry Flagler honeymooned in St. Augustine in 1883, he was so taken by the place that he later returned to found the Ponce de León Hotel, now Flagler College, and soon the gentle trickle of visitors became a flood. St. Augustine has been a major stop on the tourist trail ever since.

Tiles and other Spanish touches were used in the architecture of **Flagler College**, a former Flagler hotel.

START

GRANADA STREET

KING STREET

Cleopatra (c 1890) by Romanelli is one of the exhibits from Florida's Gilded Age on display at the **Lightner Museum**.

Casa Monica became Flagler's third hotel in town in 1888.

Governor's House Museum is home to the University of Florida's exhibit "First Colony: Our Spanish Origins," which tells the story of the founding of St. Augustine.

FINISH

ARTILLERY LANE

AVILES STREET

Ximenez-Fatio House was built as a private house in 1797. In the mid-19th century it became a boarding house.

← Imposing marble lions at the Bridge of Lions

↑ St. Augustine's stunning town square, illuminated at night

7 ft

The width of Treasury Street, the narrowest street in the US (2 m).

The **Peña-Peck House**, dating from the 1740s, is the finest First Spanish Period home in the city.

The heart of the Spanish settlement is the **Plaza de la Constitucion**. This leafy square is host to a program of concerts, and is flanked by the Governor's House Museum and the Cathedral Basilica.

Marble lions guard the **Bridge of Lions**, which opened across Matanzas Bay in 1927.

| 0 meters | | 75 |
| 0 yards | | 75 |

N ↗

The **Spanish Military Hospital** (p210), a reconstruction of a ward, re-creates the spartan hospital conditions available to Spanish settlers in the late 18th century.

EXPERIENCE MORE

Fernandina Beach

F1 961687 Gateway Blvd, Nassau County; www. ameliaisland.com

The town of Fernandina Beach on Amelia Island, just across the St. Marys River from Georgia, was renowned as a pirates' den until the early 1800s, its deep-water harbor drawing a motley crew of foreign armies and adventurers. Nicknamed the Isle of Eight Flags, today Fernandina is a charming Victorian resort and Florida's primary source of sweet Atlantic white shrimp – more than two million pounds (900,000 kg) are caught by the shrimping fleet each year.

Did You Know?

The Isle of Eight Flags Shrimp Festival is held in Fernandina Beach on the first weekend of May.

The original Spanish settlement was established at Old Fernandina, a sleepy backwater just north of the present town. In the 1850s, the whole town moved south to the eastern terminus of Senator David Yulee's cross-Florida railroad. The move, coupled with the dawn of Florida tourism in the 1870s *(p45)*, prompted the building boom that created the much-admired heart of today's Fernandina – the 50-block Historic District.

The legacy of Fernandina's golden age is best seen in the Silk Stocking District, which occupies more than half of the Historic District, and is so-named for the affluence of its original residents. Sea captains and timber barons built homes here in a variety of styles: Queen Anne houses decorated with fancy gingerbread detailing and turrets jostle graceful Italianate residences and fine examples of Chinese Chippendale furniture.

Watching the shrimp boats put into harbor at sunset is a local ritual. The fleet is commemorated by a monument at the foot of downtown Center Street, where chandleries and naval stores once held sway. These weathered brick buildings now house antique shops and upscale gift shops. The 1878 Palace Saloon still serves a wicked Pirate's Punch at the long mahogany bar adorned with hand-carved caryatids.

Down on 3rd Street, the 1857 Florida House Inn is the state's oldest tourist hotel, and a couple of blocks farther south, the **Amelia Island Museum of History** occupies the former jail. Guided, 90-minute tours cover the island's turbulent past – from the time of the first Native American inhabitants to the early 1900s. Guided tours of the town are also offered, but be sure to reserve ahead.

Amelia Island Museum of History

233 S 3rd St For construction; will reopen in 2022 ameliamuseum.org

→

Sunset over the sea at a remote beach in Talbot Island State Parks

Charming store-lined street in Fernandina Beach, known as the Isle of Eight Flags

4

Fort Caroline National Memorial

 F1 🏠 12713 Fort Caroline Rd, Jacksonville, Duval County ⏱ Times vary, check website 🌐 nps.gov/timu

The actual site of Fort Caroline was washed away when the St. Johns River was dredged in the 1880s. At Fort Caroline National Memorial, a reconstruction of the original 16th-century defenses illustrates the style of the first European forts in the Americas.

In the attempt to stake a claim to North America, three small French vessels carrying 200 men, led by explorer René de Goulaine de Laudonnière, sailed up the St. Johns River in June 1564 and made camp 5 miles (8 km) inland. Local Timucua people helped them to build a triangular wooden fort, named La Caroline in honor of Charles IX of France. A year later, with the settlers close to starvation, a large

fleet of reinforcements under Jean Ribault arrived. The Spanish, however, took the fort in September 1565.

Fort Caroline also hosts the Timucuan Preserve Visitor Center, the hub of the Timucuan Ecological and Historic Preserve which encompasses much of the area, including Fort George Island.

5

Kingsley Plantation

F1 🏠 11676 Palmetto Ave, Fort George, Duval County ⏱ 9am–5pm daily 🌐 nps.gov/timu

One of the oldest plantation houses in Florida, the Kingsley Plantation sits at the northern end of Fort George Island. It is thought that the house was originally built by John McQueen in 1798, but it is now named for Zephaniah Kingsley, who moved here in 1814. Kingsley owned 32,000 acres (12,950 ha) of land stretching from Lake George near the Ocala National Forest north to the St. Marys River. This area used to encompass four major plantations; the Kingsley plantation itself had as many as 100 enslaved

people working in its fields of cotton, sugarcane, and corn.

Confronting the realities of slavery and the role that the plantation played is a major focus of the site. Free tours take in the grounds and the plantation house, which is topped by a small rooftop parapet called a "widow's walk," once used to survey the surrounding fields. The plantation is known for the 25 cabins in the woods that once housed enslaved people. Constructed of durable tabby, these basic dwellings have survived the years, and one is now restored.

6

Talbot Island State Parks

F1 🏠 12157 Heckscher Dr, Jacksonville, Duval County ⏱ 8am–sunset daily 🌐 floridastateparks.org

Much of Amelia Island and the neighboring islands of Big Talbot, Little Talbot, and Fort George remain undeveloped and a natural haven for wildlife such as otters, marsh rabbits, fiddler crabs, and herons. Bobcats hide out in the woods, manatees bob about in the Intracoastal waters, and in summer turtles lay their eggs on the beach (p130). In fall, whales travel here to calve offshore.

Daytona Beach

F3 🚗 🚌 ℹ️ **126 E Orange Ave, Volusia County; www.daytonabeach.com**

Extending south from Ormond Beach is brash and boisterous Daytona Beach. As many as 200,000 students descend on the resort every Spring Break, even though Daytona has tried to discourage them. Its famous 23-mile (37-km) beach is one of the few in Florida where cars are allowed on the sands – a hangover from the days when motor enthusiasts raced on the beaches (p223).

Daytona is still a mecca for motorsports fans. The nearby speedway (p222) attracts huge crowds, especially during the Speedweek in February and the Motorcycle Weeks in March and October. Downtown Daytona, known simply as "Mainland," lies across the Halifax River from the beach. Most of the action, though, takes place on the beach, which is lined with hotels. The Boardwalk still retains some of its arcades and carnival-style atmosphere, but the area has been regenerated and offers updated rides, including a roller coaster. The Daytona Lagoon water park and the bandstand still draw crowds. Down on the beach, jet skis, windsurf boards, buggies, and bicycles can be rented. Across the Halifax River, in the restored downtown area, the **Halifax Historical Museum** occupies a 1910 bank building. Local history displays include a model of the Boardwalk in about 1938, with chicken-feather palm trees and a Ferris wheel.

West of downtown is the excellent **Museum of Arts and Sciences**. The Florida prehistory exhibit is dominated by the 13-ft (4-m) skeleton of a giant sloth, while Arts in America features arts from 1640 to 1920. There are also notable Cuban and African collections, and a planetarium.

Gamble Place is run by the same museum. Built in 1907 for James Gamble, of Procter & Gamble, this hunting lodge, surrounded by open porches, sits on a bluff above Spruce Creek. The furnishings are all period pieces. Tours are available by reservation through the museum, and take in the Snow White House – an exact copy of the one in Disney's 1937 classic – built in 1938 for Gamble's great-grandchildren.

Halifax Historical Museum

 📍 **252 S Beach St** 🕐 **10:30am–4:30pm Tue–Fri, 10am–4pm Sat** 🌐 **halifaxhistorical.org**

Museum of Arts and Sciences

 📍 **1040 Museum Blvd** 🕐 **10am–5pm Mon–Sat (from 11am Sun)** 🌐 **moas.org**

Gamble Place

 📍 **1795 Taylor Road, Port Orange** 🕐 **8am–5pm Wed–Sun** 🌐 **crackercreek.com**

---

❽ World Golf Hall of Fame

F2 📍 **1 World Golf Place** 🕐 **10am–6pm Mon–Sat, noon–6pm Sun** 🌐 **worldgolf halloffame.org**

Set within the vast World Golf Village complex of condos and golf courses is this museum,

Did You Know?

Alexander Winton set the land speed racing record of 68 mph (109 km/h) at Daytona Beach in 1903.

A gazebo in a luxuriant corner of Washington Oaks Gardens State Park

takes you to the ruins of the old sugar mill, which resemble the remains of some ancient South American temples.

About 10 miles (16 km) north of Bulow Plantation is historic **Flagler Beach**, a charming old-world town with a fishing pier, quaint museum, and ocean-front eateries serving fantastic food with splendid views.

Flagler Beach
🏠 20 Airport Rd, Suite C, Palm Coast 🌐 cityofflagler beach.com

STAY

The Shores Resort & Spa

The bright and breezy rooms at this resort deliver a seaside chic that's enhanced by four-poster beds and splendid ocean views. There's also a full-service spa and a brilliant tiki bar to retire to in the evening.

🅰 F3 🏠 2637 S Atlantic Ave, Daytona Beach 🌐 shoresresort.com

$$$

Streamline Hotel

For fans of the retro look, this three-story, mint-green Art Deco building (dating back to the 1940s) will be just the ticket. One of the oldest hotels on Daytona Beach, it underwent a major renovation in 2017. Worth it for the views from the rooftop cocktail bar alone.

🅰 F3 🏠 140 S Atlantic Ave, Daytona Beach 🌐 streamlinehotel.com

$$$

an extensive tribute to all things golf. It charts the history of the sport, beginning in Scotland, and covers early golf stars, such as Tom Morris and Bob Hope. There's also a drive simulator, a substantial collection of golf memorabilia, and an 88-ft- (27-m-) Wall of Fame. The on-site restaurant, Bill Murray's Caddy Shack, is recommended for a bite to eat.

9

Washington Oaks Gardens State Park

🅰 F2 🏠 6400 N Ocean Shore Blvd, Flagler County 🚌 St Augustine 🕐 8am–sunset daily 🌐 floridastate parks.org

Beneath a canopy of oaks and palms, a huge area of former plantation land has been transformed into beautiful gardens of hydrangeas, azaleas, and ferns, plus a rose garden and trails through a coastal hammock to the Matanzas River. Across the A1A, a boardwalk leads down to the lovely beach, strewn with coquina boulders and tidal pools

The Boardwalk at Daytona Beach, with its roller coaster and neon-lit Ferris wheel

eroded from the soft stone. This state park is perfect for a relaxing stroll, an afternoon picnic, or even simply spending a day at the beach. There are also plenty of picturesque photo opportunities.

10

Bulow Plantation Ruins Historic State Park

🅰 F2 🏠 3501 Old Kings Rd S, Flagler Beach, 3 miles (5 km) S of SR 100 🚌 Daytona Beach 🕐 9am–5pm Thu–Mon 🌐 floridastateparks.org

Somewhat off the beaten path, the ruins of this 19th-century plantation stand in a dense hammock where sugarcane once grew. The site is part of the 4,675 acres (1,890 ha) of land adjacent to a creek that Major Charles Bulow bought in 1821. Enslaved people cleared half this area, planting rice, cotton, and sugarcane. The plantation, known as Bulowville, was abandoned after Native American attacks during the Seminole Wars (p45). Today, Bulow Creek is a state canoe trail, and you can rent canoes to explore this backwater. On its banks are the foundations of the plantation house; a ten-minute stroll

Daytona International Speedway

🅰F3 🅰1801 W International Speedway Blvd, Volusia County 🚌9 ⏰9am–5pm daily 🌐daytonainternational speedway.com

Daytona's very own "World Center of Racing," the Daytona International Speedway, which opened in 1959, attracts thousands of race fans and visitors every year. People travel from all around the world to attend the eight major racing weekends held annually at the track – which can hold about 160,000 spectators. The Speedway plays host to NASCAR (National Association for Stock Car Auto Racing) meets in addition to sports car, motorcycle, and even karting races.

The most famous and prestigious of the NASCAR meets held here is the Daytona 500. Also known as "The Great American Race," this important 500-mile-long (800-km) race, which takes place annually in mid- to late February, is a must-see event for all racing fans and attracts the most visitors to the speedway.

The Motorsports Hall of Fame of America is also based here, with displays honoring stock cars, motorcycles, drag racing, land speed records, power-boating, and aviation. It is also home to Sir Malcolm Campbell's Bluebird V, the car that set a land speed record on nearby Ormond Beach in 1935.

A half-hour trolley tour around the track at Daytona International Speedway is available on days when no races are due to take place. Other worthwhile tours last between 30 minutes and three hours. A trip around the track, along the infield and down the pit road, gives visitors an idea of what the drivers go through during a race. Speed fanatics can choose from one of the many driving experiences on offer, or even opt to be the passenger as a professional instructor reaches exhilarating speeds of up to 165 mph (266 km/h).

> **A half-hour trolley tour around the track at Daytona International Speedway is available on days when no races are due to take place.**

Ponce de León Inlet Lighthouse

🅰F3 🅰4931 S Peninsula Dr, Volusia County ⏰10am–6pm daily (to 9pm Jun–Sep) 🌐ponceinlet.org

This lighthouse dates from 1887 and guards the entrance to a hazardous inlet at the tip of the Daytona peninsula. The lighthouse tapers sky-ward for 175 ft (53 m), its beacon is visible 19 miles (30 km) out to sea, and there are far-reaching views from the windswept observation deck. One of the former keepers' cottages at its base has been restored to its 1890s appearance, another houses the Cuban Rafts Exhibit, and a third contains a magnificent 17-ft-(5-m-) high Fresnel lens.

→ The Ponce de León Inlet Lighthouse, and the stairs to its observation deck *(inset)*

THE BIRTHPLACE OF SPEED

Daytona's love affair with the car started in 1903, when the first timed automobile runs took place on the sands at Ormond Beach, the official "Birthplace of Speed." The speed trials were enormously popular and attracted large crowds. Speed trials continued until 1935, when Malcolm Campbell set the last world record on the beach. Stock cars began racing at Ormond Beach in 1936, and the first Daytona 200 motorcycle race took place there the following year. Development forced the racetrack to be moved in 1948, and in 1959 Daytona International Speedway opened and racing on the beach was abandoned.

RACING ON THE BEACH

In 1902, a guest at the Ormond Hotel noticed just how easy it was to drive his car on the hard sandy beach. He organized the first speed trials, which continued for the next 32 years at Ormond Beach.

Olds' Pirate was the first car to race on the beach that year. The first official race was held in the next year, when Olds challenged Alexander Winton and Oscar Hedstrom on a motorcycle. Winton won in his car, Bullet No 1.

Years later, the Bluebird was driven to a new world record for the measured mile by Malcolm Campbell at Ormond in 1935. Powered by a Rolls-Royce engine, the car reached speeds greater than 276 mph (444 km/h).

THE "WORLD CENTER OF RACING"

In 1953, Bill France, who had entered the inaugural stock car race, realized that the growth of Daytona Beach would soon put an end to the beach races. He proposed the construction of Daytona International Speedway, today one of the world's leading racetracks. The speedway hosts the 500-mile- (805-km-) long Daytona 500 motor race every February. The event is the most prestigious in the National Association for Stock Car Auto Racing (NASCAR).

LEE PETTY

In 1959, Petty won the first Daytona 500 at Daytona International Speedway, controversially beating Johnny Beauchamp by a mere 2 ft (50 cm). The 500-mile (800-km) competition was watched by a crowd of 41,000 and involved 59 cars.

↑ Vehicles line up at the start line at Daytona International Speedway

⓭ Sanford

▲F3 🚆🚌 ℹ️ 400 E 1st St, Seminole County; www. sanfordfl.gov

Built during the Seminole Wars (p45), Fort Mellon was the first permanent settlement on Lake Monroe. Sanford was founded nearby in the 1870s. It became a major inland port thanks to the commercial steamboat from Jacksonville on the St. Johns River, which eventually brought Florida's early tourists.

Restored downtown Sanford dates from the 1880s, the height of this steamboat era. Several of the old red-brick buildings (a rarity in Florida) house antique shops, and the area can easily be explored on foot in a couple of hours. Today's visitors are more likely to arrive on the Auto Train or by SunRail than by river, but short pleasure cruises are still available.

EAT

Bolay
Popular health-forward spot that offers protein and veggie bowls.

▲E2 🏠2905 SW 42nd St #80, Gainesville 🌐bolay.com

💲💲💲

La Cocina de Abuela
Homey decor and Colombian-style dishes such as oxtail soup.

▲E2 🏠125 NW 23rd Ave, Gainesville 📞(352) 204-5561 🚫Sun & Mon

💲💲💲

Beque Holic
This Korean barbecue restaurant allows you to grill your own meats.

▲E2 🏠3812 W Newberry Rd, Gaines-ville 🌐bequeholic.com

💲💲💲

The Top
A typically American burger joint with vegetarian options.

▲E2 🏠30 N Main St, Gainesville 🌐thetop gainesville.com

💲💲💲

⓮ Gainesville

▲E2 ✈️🚌 ℹ️ 300 E University Ave, Alachua County; www.visit gainesville.com

A lively university town, the cultural capital of north central Florida, and home of the Gators football team, Gainesville is a comfortable blend of town and gown.

In the restored downtown historic district are brick buildings that date from the 1880s to the 1920s, several of which house cafes and restaurants. The university campus is dotted with fraternity houses and two important museums.

Leave plenty of time for the first of these, the excellent **Florida Museum of Natural History**. The natural science collections contain more than 10 million fossil specimens, plus superb butterfly and shell collections. There are displays dedicated to the various natural environments of Florida and an anthropo-logical journey through the state's history up to the 19th century. The **Harn Museum of Art** is one of the largest and best-equipped university

↑ Red-brick buildings along 1st Street, in Sanford's historic downtown

↑ Kayakers and glass-bottom tour boats on the placid Silver River at Silver Springs

art museums in the country. Its excellent permanent collection of fine art and crafts includes a broad range of east Asian ceramics, African ceremonial objects, Japanese woodcuts, and European and American paintings.

Just southwest of town, the lovely **Kanapaha Botanical Gardens** are at the height of their beauty from June to September, although visitors in springtime are rewarded by masses of azaleas in bloom. A trail circles the large sloping site, whose beauty was first noted by the American naturalist William Bartram in the late 1800s. The paths meander beneath vine-covered arches and through bamboo groves. Other distinct areas that are worth visiting include a desert garden, a lakeside bog garden, and a colorful hummingbird garden.

Florida Museum of Natural History

⊚ ⌂ Hull Rd at SW 34th St 🕙 10am–5pm Mon–Sat; 1–5pm Sun 🔲 florida museum.ufl.edu

Harn Museum of Art

⊚⊚⊚ ⌂ Hull Rd (off SW 34th St) 🕙 11am–5pm Tue–Fri, 10am–5pm Sat, 1–5pm Sun 🔲 harn.ufl.edu

Kanapaha Botanical Gardens

⊚⊚ ⌂ 4700 SW 58th Dr (off Route 24) 🕙 9am–5pm Fri–Wed, 9am–7pm Sat & Sun 🔲 kanapaha.org

Silver Springs State Park

🅰 E3 ⌂ 5656 E Silver Springs Blvd 🕙 8am–sunset daily 🔲 silversprings.com

Glass-bottom boat trips at Silver Springs have been revealing the natural wonders of the world's largest artesian spring since 1878. Florida's oldest commercial tourist attraction, Silver Springs became a state park in 2013 after undergoing a $4-million makeover, which included removing exotic animals and amusement rides. The boat trips offer the opportunity to catch a glimpse of the Florida outback, where the early Tarzan movies starring Johnny Weismuller were filmed.

On a quieter note, at the camping entrance to the park – 2 miles (3 km) southeast of Silver Springs – visitors can take a 15-minute walk along a trail through a hardwood hammock and a cypress swamp area, leading to a swimming hole in a bend of the river.

Also to be found here are a replica of a 19th-century pioneer cracker village and the Silver River Museum and Environment Center, which has exhibits on the history of Marion County and the natural history of Florida.

> **FLORIDA'S BUBBLING SPRINGS**
>
> Most of Florida's 320 known springs are located in the northern half of the state. The majority are artesian springs, formed by waters forced up deep fissures from underground aquifers (rock deposits containing water). Those that gush more than 100 cu ft (3 cu m) per second are known as first-magnitude springs. Filtered through the rock, the water is extremely pure and sometimes high in salts and minerals. These properties, plus the sheer beauty of the springs, have long attracted visitors for both recreational and health purposes.

↑ The aqua waters of Silver Glen Springs in Ocala National Forest

16

Marjorie Kinnan Rawlings Historic State Park

🅰 E2 🏠 S CR 325, Cross Creek, Alachua County 🚌 Ocala ⏰ Grounds: 9am–5pm daily; house (by guided tour only): Oct–Jul: 11am–3pm Thu–Sun 🌐 floridastateparks.org

The author Marjorie Kinnan Rawlings arrived in the tiny settlement of Cross Creek in 1928. Her rambling farmhouse remains largely unchanged, nestling in a well-tended citrus grove where ducks waddle up from the banks of Orange Lake.

The writer remained here during the 1930s and then visited on and off until her death in 1953. The local scenery and characters fill her autobiographical novel, *Cross Creek* (1942), while the big scrub country

to the south inspired her famous novel *The Yearling* (1938), a coming-of-age story about a boy and his fawn.

Guided tours explore the Cracker-style homestead, built in the 1880s, which has been imaginatively preserved and contains Rawlings' original furnishings: bookcases full of contemporary writings by authors such as John Steinbeck and Ernest Hemingway, a secret liquor cabinet, a typewriter, and a sunhat on the veranda. Lived-in touches like fresh flowers make it look as though the owner has just gone out for a stroll around the garden.

→ The typewriter used by the author Marjorie Kinnan Rawlings

17

Ocala National Forest

🅰 E3 ⏰ 24 hours daily ℹ 45621 State Rd 19 Altoona 🌐 fs.usda.gov

Between Ocala and the St. Johns River, the world's largest sand pine forest covers 366,000 acres (148,000 ha), crisscrossed by spring-fed rivers and numerous hiking trails. It is one of the last refuges of the endangered Florida black bear and also home to deer and otters. Birds, including bald eagles, ospreys, barred owls, the non native wild turkey, and many species of wader (which frequent the river swamp areas), can all be spotted here.

Dozens of hiking trails vary in length from boardwalks and short loop trails of just under a mile (1.4 km), to a 66-mile (106-km) stretch of the cross-state National Scenic Trail. Bass fishing is popular on the many lakes scattered through the forest, and recreation areas such as Salt Springs, Alexander Springs, and Fore Lake offer swimming holes, picnic areas, and campgrounds. The 7-mile (11-km) canoe run down

Juniper Creek from the **Juniper Springs Recreation Area** is one of the finest in the state; reserve in advance via the Juniper Springs Recreation Area.

Birdwatching is particularly good along the Salt Springs Trail, and wood ducks congregate on Lake Dorr. Information and guides can be picked up at the main visitor center on the western edge of the forest, or at the smaller centers at Salt Springs and Lake Dorr, both on Route 19.

Juniper Springs Recreation Area

🏠 26701 State Rd 40, Astor ⏰ 8am–8pm daily 🌐 recreation.gov

Ocala

🅰 E3 🚗🚌 ℹ Chamber of Commerce, 110 E Silver Springs Blvd, Marion County; www.ocalamarion.com

Surrounded by undulating pastures, Ocala is the seat of Marion County and the center of Florida's thoroughbred horse industry. The grass in this region is enriched by a subterranean limestone aquifer, and the resulting calcium-rich grazing helps to contribute to the light, strong bones of championship horses. Florida's equine industry has produced many champions, including five Kentucky Derby winners.

There are hundreds of thoroughbred farms and breeding centers around Ocala, many of which can be visited. Expect to see Arabians, Paso Finos, and miniature horses on the farms; contact the Ocala Chamber of Commerce for up-to-date information regarding visits. East of

→ Charming Steamboat Gothic Donnelly House, in downtown Mount Dora

1,200

The number of horse farms in Ocala, the "Horse Capital of Florida."

Ocala, the **Appleton Museum of Art** was built in 1984 by the industrialist and horsebreeder Arthur I. Appleton. His collection includes pre-Columbian and European antiquities and Meissen porcelain, and is known for its strong core of 19th-century European art.

Appleton Museum of Art

♿ 🏠 4333 NE Silver Springs Blvd ⏰ 10am–5pm Tue–Sat, noon–5pm Sun 🌐 appleton museum.org

---

Mount Dora

🅰 F3 ℹ 341 N Alexander St, Lake County; www.mountdora.com

Set among the former citrus groves of Lake County, this town is one of the prettiest Victorian settlements left in the state. Its name comes from both the relatively high local elevation of 184 ft (56 m), and the small lake on which it sits. The town was originally known as Royellou, after Roy, Ella, and Louis, the children of the first postmaster.

Mount Dora's attractive tree-lined streets are laid out on a bluff above the lakeshore. The historic tour takes in quiet neighborhoods of late 19th-century clapboard homes and the restored downtown district, with its many antique shops.

On Donnelly Street, the splendid Donnelly House, now a Masonic Hall, is a notable example of ornate Steamboat architecture. The Modernism Museum on 4th Avenue houses a collection which perfectly showcases the movement. Nearby, the small **Mount Dora History Museum** depicts local history in the old fire station, which later became the jail. Down on Lake Dora, fishing and watersports are available.

Mount Dora History Museum

♿ 🏠 450 Royellou Lane ⏰ 1–4pm Sat 🌐 mountdorahistory museum.com

Herlong Mansion, an elegant example of Greek Revival architecture in Micanopy

⑳ Micanopy

🅰E2 🎫30 E University Ave, Gainesville, Alachua County; www.micanopy town.com

Established in 1821, Florida's second oldest permanent white settlement was a trading post on Native American lands, originally known as Wanton. Renamed Micanopy in 1826, after a Seminole chief, this time-warp village is now as decorous as they come, and a haven for filmmakers and antique lovers. Planted with live oaks trailing Spanish moss, the main street, Cholokka Boulevard, is lined with Victorian homes and a strip of craft galleries and brick-fronted shops stuffed with bric-a-brac. Here, too, is the grandest building in Micanopy, the imposing red-brick antebellum Herlong Mansion, supported by four massive Corinthian columns. Built by a 19th-century lumber baron, today it serves as a bed and breakfast.

Micanopy's picturesque cemetery, established in 1825, is located on a canopied street off Seminary Road, en route to I-75. Shaded by spreading live oaks and majestic cedars, and covered with velvety moss, it exudes a suitably mournful vibe.

During the 17th century one of the largest and most successful Spanish cattle ranches in Florida was located to the north of present-day Micanopy. Cattle, horses, and hogs once grazed on the lush grass of **Paynes Prairie Preserve State Park**, where a small herd of wild American bison can some-times be seen, as well as more than 200 species of local and migratory bird.

Passing through the preserve is the pleasant 17-mile (27-km) Gainesville-Hawthorne State Trail, a rail trail used by hikers, riders, and cyclists.

> 💬 INSIDER TIP
> ## Antique Treasures
>
> Micanopy is one of Florida's best cities for antiques shopping. Cholokka Boulevard and Antique City Mall *(17020 Southeast, Co. Rd 234)* have the best finds.

Paynes Prairie Preserve State Park

⊗ 🅰100 Savannah Blvd, US 441, 1 mile (1.5 km) N of Micanopy ⊙8am-sunset daily floridastateparks.org

㉑ Ormond Beach

🅰F2 🚌 🎫110 E Granada Blvd, Ormond Beach, Volusia County; www. ormondbeach.org

Ormond Beach was one of the earliest winter resorts on Henry Flagler's railroad. No longer standing, his fashionable Ormond Hotel boasted a star-studded guest list including Henry Ford and John D. Rockefeller.

Rockefeller bought a house just across the street in 1918 after overhearing that another guest was paying less; despite his immense wealth, the millionaire chief of Standard Oil guarded his nickels and dimes closely. His winter home, **The Casements**, has been restored and is today a museum and cultural center, housing Rockefeller-era

memorabilia, such as the great man's high-sided wicker beach chair. There's also a period-style room and a rather incongruous Hungarian arts and crafts display.

A short walk from The Casements, the **Ormond Memorial Art Museum** is set in a small but charming tropical garden. Shady paths wind around lily ponds inhabited by basking turtles. The museum hosts changing exhibitions of works by contemporary Florida artists as well as student shows.

The Casements

🅰 ⓐ 25 Riverside Dr
🕒 8am–5pm Mon–Sat
ⓦ thecasements.net

Ormond Memorial Art Museum

🅰 ⓐ 78 E Granada Blvd
🕒 10am–4pm Mon–Fri; noon–4pm Sat & Sun
ⓦ ormondartmuseum.org

㉒

Blue Spring State Park

🅰 F3 ⓐ 2100 W French Ave, Orange City 🕒 8am–sunset daily ⓦ florida stateparks.org

One of the country's largest first-magnitude artesian springs, Blue Spring pours out around 100 million gallons (450 million liters) of water a day. The temperature of the water is at a constant 68° F (20° C), and consequently the park is a favorite winter refuge for manatees (*p279*). Between the months of November and March, when the manatees escape the cooler waters of the St. Johns River, you can

→ A boardwalk in Blue Spring State Park, and a West Indian manatee (*inset*)

see hundreds of them from the park's elevated boardwalks. Snorkeling or scuba diving are available in the turquoise waters of the spring head, as is canoeing on the St. Johns. Thursby House, atop one of the park's ancient shell mounds, was built in the late 19th century.

About 2 miles (3 km) north as the crow flies is wooded **Hontoon Island State Park**. Reached by a free ferry from Hontoon Landing, the island has an observation tower, camping and picnic areas, and a nature trail. Canoes can also be rented. In 1955, a wooden owl totem made by the local Timucua people was found here.

Hontoon Island State Park

🅰 ⓐ 2309 River Ridge Rd, De Land 🕒 8am–sunset daily ⓦ floridastateparks.org

THE PANHANDLE

There is a saying in Florida that "the farther north you go, the farther south you get." Certainly, the Panhandle has a history and sensibility closer to its Deep South neighbors of Georgia and Alabama than to the rest of the Florida peninsula. Climate, history, geography, and even time (the western Panhandle is one hour behind the rest of the state), distinguish this intriguing region from other parts of Florida.

The Panhandle was the site of the first attempt by the Spanish at colonizing Florida. A community was set up near present-day Pensacola in 1559, but was abandoned after a hurricane. It later reemerged and was the main settlement in the region until the 1820s, when Tallahassee was chosen as the capital of the new Territory of Florida. The Panhandle's lumber and cotton trade were big industries in the 1800s, but the region was bypassed by the influx of wealth that came to other parts of Florida with the laying of the railroads. Tourism in the Panhandle is a more modern development, even though its fine white-sand beaches are unparalleled in the state.

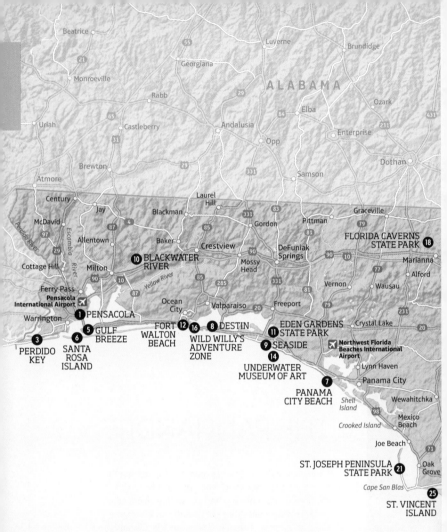

THE PANHANDLE

Must Sees
1. Pensacola
2. Tallahassee

Experience More
3. Perdido Key
4. Steinhatchee
5. Gulf Breeze
6. Santa Rosa Island
7. Panama City Beach
8. Destin
9. Seaside
10. Blackwater River
11. Eden Gardens State Park
12. Fort Walton Beach
13. Alfred B. Maclay Gardens State Park
14. Underwater Museum of Art
15. Monticello
16. Wild Willy's Adventure Zone
17. Torreya State Park
18. Florida Caverns State Park
19. Cedar Key
20. Wakulla Springs State Park
21. St. Joseph Peninsula State Park
22. Manatee Springs State Park
23. Apalachicola
24. Suwannee River State Park
25. St. Vincent, St. George, and Dog Islands

↑ Colorful buildings in the Seville Quarter, a complex of bars and restaurants

1

PENSACOLA

 A1 🚗🚊🚌 ℹ️ **1401 E Gregory St; www.visit pensacola.com**

This waterfront city was first settled by Spanish colonists in 1559. Much of the current city dates from a boom in the 1800s; several historic districts provide the most interesting areas to explore in Pensacola. While downtown is the main focus for sightseeing, the barrier island of Pensacola Beach, linked to the mainland by two bridges, is a pleasant place to stay.

T.T. Wentworth, Jr. Florida State Museum

📍 **330 S Jefferson St**
🕐 **Times vary, check website** Ⓦ **historic pensacola.org**

This museum is laid out in the former City Hall, an imposing Spanish Renaissance Revival building. The founder's eclectic collections include West Florida memorabilia, artifacts from Spanish shipwrecks, and weird and wonderful oddities from all over the world. These range from arrowheads and a "shrunken head" from pre-Columbian Central America, to a 1930s telephone exchange and old Coca-Cola bottles. The museum hosts well-thought-

out historical displays and dioramas illustrating points along Pensacola's Colonial Archaeological Trail, which links remains of fortifications dating from 1752–1821. One of the exhibits chronicles over 450 years of Pensacola history.

2

Pensacola Museum of Art

📍 **407 S Jefferson St**
🕐 **10am–5pm Tue–Thu, 10am–7pm Fri & Sat, noon–4pm Sun** Ⓦ **pensacola museum.org**

The cells of the old city jail, complete with steel-barred doors, have taken on a new life as whitewashed galleries

for this museum. Frequently changing exhibitions draw on the museum's broad-based collections, which include pre-Columbian pottery, 19th-century satinware glass, and Roy Lichtenstein's Pop Art.

3

Pensacola Children's Museum

📍 **115 E Zarragossa St**
🕐 **10am–4pm Tue–Sat**
Ⓦ **historicpensacola.org**

Housed in an 1885 building first known as the Gulf Saloon, this museum, run by the University of West Florida Historic Trust, offers an interactive learning experience of Pensacola history, showcasing military and multicultural histories plus those of the maritime and lumber industries. Child-friendly exhibits include the

Did You Know?

The average commute time in Pensacola is 19 minutes.

Panton Trading Post, Lavalle Cottage, the Fort, Native American Village, and Kiddie Corral. The second floor houses artifacts geared toward adults, but also offers a rail set, building blocks, and dress-up clothes that kids will enjoy.

④

Pensacola Lighthouse & Museum

🏠 2081 Radford Blvd
🕐 10am-4pm Tue-Thu, 10am-5pm Fri-Sun
🌐 pensacolalighthouse.org

Opposite the aviation museum inside Naval Air Station Pensacola (NAS), (bring ID), the Pensacola Lighthouse & Museum features a 159-ft- (48-m-) lighthouse built in 1859 – from the top you can see all the way to Perdido Key. The museum is housed inside the 1869 keeper's quarters, with exhibits on the Native American Weedon Island culture, the 17th-century Spanish colony of Santa

↑ The pristine exterior of Old Christ Church, which is now home to a museum

María de Galve, and the first Pensacola Lighthouse, built in 1824.

⑤

Historic Pensacola Village

🏠 205 E Zarragossa St
🕐 10am-4pm Tue-Sat
🌐 historicpensacola.org

This collection of museums and historic houses is located in Pensacola's oldest quarter, called the Historic Pensacola Village. You can enjoy strolling through the village's streets, which offer a taste of the city as it was in the 19th century.

For a more in-depth look, take one of the guided tours that depart twice daily from Tivoli House on Zarragossa Street. In tourist season, tour guides liven up proceedings by dressing in period costume. The tours visit the French Creole Lavalle House (1805) and the gracious Dorr House (1871), the Old Christ Church (1832), and the Lear-Rocheblave House (1890), among others.

A single ticket, available from Tivoli House, covers the tour and entrance to all village properties for one week. This ticket will be required to visit the Museum of Commerce and Museum of Industry. Housed in a late 19th-century warehouse, the former museum provides an informative introduction to Pensacola's early development. Exhibits cover brick-making, fishing, and the lumber trade.

Forming a backdrop to Zarragossa Street's Museum of Commerce is a Victorian street scene complete with reconstructed stores including a printer's shop with a working press and a music store.

Overlooking leafy Seville Square is Old Christ Church, built in 1832, and one of the oldest churches in Florida still standing on its original site.

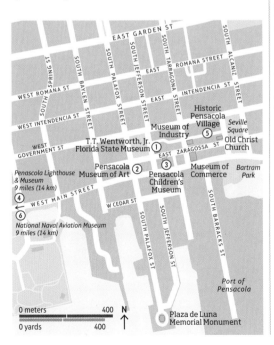

NATIONAL NAVAL AVIATION MUSEUM

🅰A1 🏠1750 Radford Blvd, NAS Pensacola 🕙10am-4pm Tue-Sun; ID required
Ⓦnavalaviationmuseum.org

Fans of aircraft and military history shouldn't miss the chance to visit this incredible free museum. See everything from the earliest military planes used in World War I to the latest technology and exciting simulators.

Opened in 1963, this museum has grown over the years to over 350,000 sq ft (32,500 sq m) of exhibit space, making it the world's largest Naval Aviation museum. More than 150 aircraft and spacecraft, as well as models, artifacts, and technological displays, cover the decks aboard Naval Air Station Pensacola, attracting nearly a million visitors annually. Representing Navy, Marine Corps, and Coast Guard aviation, the museum offers tours by volunteers, many of whom are military veterans.

The museum occupies two floors, or "decks," which are divided into two wings joined by an atrium. The west wing is devoted almost entirely to World War II carrier aircraft, while the south wing is more broadly historical. More aircraft can be found in Hangar Bay One, to the rear of the museum.

HIDDEN GEM
Fort Barrancas

A few minutes' walk from the museum is Fort Barrancas, part of the fortifications built by the Spanish in the 17th and 18th centuries. Fort Barrancas Visitor Center is open 9am-4:15pm Thu-Mon.

A Tomcat fighter jet on display in front of the National Naval Aviation Museum ↑

↑ Impressive and wide variety of aircrafts found inside the museum

Flying Boats

▽ During World War I the US navy developed a series of "flying boats" - or seaplanes - though the war ended before they could be deployed. In 1919 one of these aircraft, the NC-4, set off from Long Island across the Atlantic and became the first aeroplane to make a successful transatlantic flight, albeit with a number of stops en route.

Flying Tigers

▷ The painted jaws of these World War II fighters (the P-40B Tomahawk) were the trademark of Colonel Claire Chennault's American Volunteer Group (AVG), better known as the Volunteer Flying Tiger pilots, who fought in the skies over China and Burma. These plucky pilots quickly gained fame flying against overwhelming odds.

The Blue Angels

▽ The Blue Angels Atrium is the stunning centerpiece of the museum. Suspended in flight here are aircraft from the world-famous Blue Angels, the U.S. Navy's aerobatic display team. The Blue Angels are based at NAS Pensacola and regularly fly over the museum. Practice times vary throughout the year; check the schedule online.

A SHORT WALK
PENSACOLA

Distance 0.5 miles (1 km) **Time** 15 minutes

The city's first settlers were a party of Spanish colonists, led by Don Tristan de Luna, who sailed into Pensacola Bay in 1559. Their settlement survived for only two years before being wiped out by a hurricane. The Spanish returned, but Pensacola changed hands frequently: in the space of just over 400 years the Spanish, French, English, Confederate, and US flags all flew over the city. Pensacola took off in the 1880s, when much of the present downtown district was built. This area features a variety of architectural styles, ranging from quaint Colonial cottages to elegant Classical-Revival homes built during the late 19th-century timber boom. The route shown here focuses on the area known as Historic Pensacola Village (p235).

Did You Know?

Pensacola suffered $7.3 billion worth of damage during Hurricane Sally in 2020.

*The simple plan and bright color scheme of **Lavalle House**, an early 19th-century cottage, was designed to appeal to its French Creole immigrant tenants.*

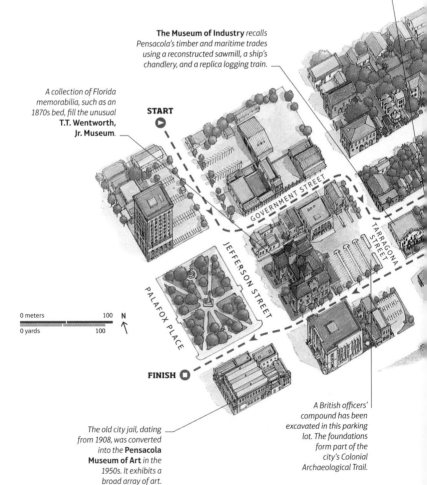

*The **Museum of Industry** recalls Pensacola's timber and maritime trades using a reconstructed sawmill, a ship's chandlery, and a replica logging train.*

*A collection of Florida memorabilia, such as an 1870s bed, fill the unusual **T.T. Wentworth, Jr. Museum.***

START

GOVERNMENT STREET

TARRAGONA STREET

JEFFERSON STREET

PALAFOX PLACE

0 meters 100
0 yards 100
N

FINISH

*The old city jail, dating from 1908, was converted into the **Pensacola Museum of Art** in the 1950s. It exhibits a broad array of art.*

A British officers' compound has been excavated in this parking lot. The foundations form part of the city's Colonial Archaeological Trail.

INSIDER TIP
JazzFest

Seville Square hosts many great festivals, including JazzFest in May, which has been going for over 30 years. Visit www.jazzpensacola.com for more details.

*Dating from the mid-19th-century steamboat era, the delightful **Steamboat House** echoes the shape of a riverboat. It comes complete with veranda "decks."*

Dorr House, *a fine Greek Revival mansion, is the last of its kind in western Florida.*

*Shaded by live oaks and magnolia trees, **Seville Square** lies at the heart of the Seville District, which was laid out by the British in the 1770s.*

GOVERNMENT STREET

ALCANIZ STREET

ADAMS STREET

CHURCH ST

ZARRAGOSSA STREET

Fountain Square *centers around a fountain decorated with plaques.*

BAYFRONT PARKWAY

*The **Museum of Commerce** holds many interesting exhibits in a cleverly constructed late-Victorian streetscape.*

→
The stunning façade of the T.T. Wentworth, Jr. Museum

↑ The Old Capitol building, with the New Capitol rising behind it

 ②

TALLAHASSEE

 C1 106 E Jefferson St; www.visittalla hassee.com

Just 14 miles (23 km) from the Georgia border, Tallahassee is gracious, hospitable, and uncompromisingly Southern. The former site of an Apalachee settlement, this remote spot was an unlikely place to found the capital of Territorial Florida in 1824. Tallahassee boomed during the plantation era, however, and elegant town houses sprung up that can still be enjoyed today.

 ①

Historic District

This area, which contains the city's fine 19th-century homes, is focused around Park Avenue and Calhoun Street, both quiet, shady streets planted with century-old live oak trees and southern magnolias. The Brokaw McDougall House on Meridian Street is a splendid Classical Revival building. Similar influences are evident in The Columns, an 1830 mansion on Duval Street. The Capitol Complex is at the very heart of downtown Tallahassee. Here, the venerable Old Capitol building has been beautifully restored to its 1902 state, with a pristine white

dome and striped awnings. Inside, visitors can see the Supreme Court chamber, the old cabinet meeting room, and also the Senate. The 22-floor New Capitol building behind, where the March–May legislative sessions take place, casts a shadow over its predecessor. But although it is a grim 1970s structure, it does at least offer a lovely view of Tallahassee from its top floor. The Visitor Center on Jefferson Street has walking-tour maps.

→

Bradley Cooley's *Indian Heritage Tableau,* outside the Museum of Florida History

②

Museum of Florida History

📍 500 S Bronough St
🕐 9am–4:30pm Mon–Fri, 10am–4:30pm Sat, noon–4:30pm Sun 🔗 museumof floridahistory.com

The museum tackles over 500 years of the region's history in entertaining style. Varied dioramas feature elements of Timucua, Apalachee, and Calusa culture, massive armadillos, and a mastodon skeleton made of bones found in

Did You Know?

Tallahassee is home to the largest magnet laboratory in the world.

Wakulla Springs (p251). Many artifacts and storyboards provide an excellent history from the Colonial era to the "tin can" tourists of the 1920s.

Tallahassee Museum

📍 3945 Museum Dr 🕑 9am-5pm Mon-Sat (from 11am Sun) 🌐 tallahassee museum.org

Located 3 miles (5 km) south-west of the city, the Tallahassee Museum is very popular with children. Its centerpiece is Big Bend Farm, a superb re-creation of late 19th-century rural life; employees dressed as farmhands tend goats and geese among authentic 1880s farm buildings. Bellevue, a small plantation home built in the 1830s, is among the other attractions. There is also an interactive discovery center and a zoo.

Knott House Museum

📍 301 East Park Ave 🕑 1-3pm Wed-Fri, 10am-3pm Sat 🌐 Aug 🌐 museumof floridahistory.com

This house is unusual in that it was built by a free Black builder in 1843 – 20 years prior to the liberation of Florida's enslaved people. It is now one of Tallahassee's most beautifully restored Victorian homes, and is named after the Knott family, who moved here in 1928 and completely refurbished the house. The attractive interior is evocative of the former owners. Poems that Luella Knott composed and tied to her antique furnishings are still in place today, earning the site the nickname of "The House That Rhymes." It opened to the public as a museum in 1992.

STAY

Hotel Duval

This boutique hotel features an attractive rooftop bar.

📍 415 N Monroe St 🌐 hotelduval.com

💲💲💲

Governor's Inn

Housed in a converted stable with charmingly rustic interiors.

📍 209 S Adams St 🌐 govinn tallahassee.com

💲💲💲

Aloft Tallahassee Downtown

A good-value hotel with quirky design touches and an outdoor pool.

📍 200 N Monroe St 🌐 marriott.com

💲💲💲

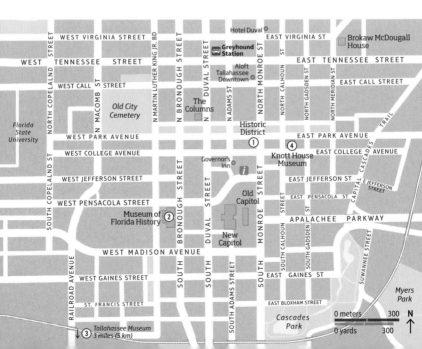

EXPERIENCE MORE

③
Perdido Key

🏠 A1 ℹ️ 15500 Perdido Key Dr, Pensacola; www.visit perdido.com

A 30-minute drive southwest from Pensacola are the pristine shores of Perdido Key, which regularly features in the list of the top 20 US beaches. There are bars and restaurants and facilities for water sports, fishing, and diving.

The eastern end of the island is accessible only by foot. The road runs as far as the **Johnson Beach** day use area section of the Gulf Islands National Seashore, just east of the bridge from the mainland. The sands extend for 6 miles (10 km) on both gulf and bay sides, and there are facilities for visitors, and a ranger station.

On the mainland opposite Perdido Key, **Big Lagoon State Park** combines sandy beach with salt-marsh areas offering excellent bird-watching and hiking. Enjoy sweeping views from the observation tower.

> **A 30-minute drive southwest from Pensacola are the pristine shores of Perdido Key, which regularly features in the list of the top 20 US beaches.**

Johnson Beach

 🏠 13300 Johnson Beach Rd 🕐 Mar–Oct: 5am–9pm daily; Nov–Feb: 5am–6pm daily 🌐 nps.gov/guis/

Big Lagoon State Park

 🏠 12301 Gulf Beach Hwy 🕐 8am–sunset daily 🌐 floridastateparks.org

---

④
Steinhatchee

🏠 D2 ℹ️ 428 N Jefferson, Perry; www.stein hatchee.com

Set back from the mouth of the Steinhatchee River, this is a sleepy old fishing town along the riverbank. To get a flavor of the place, stroll among the fish camps, bait shops, and boats tied up to the cypress wood docks. Trout fishing is big here, and people go crabbing along the coast.

About 26 miles (42 km) northwest is Keaton Beach, a tiny but popular coastal resort with good year-round fishing.

---

⑤
Gulf Breeze

🏠 A1 ℹ️ 409 Gulf Breeze Parkway, Santa Rosa County; www.gulfbreeze chamber.com

The affluent community of Gulf Breeze lies at the western end of a promontory reaching out into Pensacola Bay. The area east of the town is heavily wooded and once formed part of the huge swathes of southern woodlands that were set aside in the 1820s to provide lumber for shipbuilding.

The **Naval Live Oaks Area of the Gulf Islands National Seashore**, off US 98, was originally a government-owned tree farm and now it protects some of the remaining woodland. Visitors can follow trails through 1,300 acres (500 ha) of oak hammock woodlands, sand-hill areas, and wetlands, where wading birds feast off an abundance of marine life. A visitor center dispenses maps and information about local

A boardwalk through the marshes at Big Lagoon State Park, near Perdido Key

White-sand beach at Santa Rosa, a barrier island on the Gulf of Mexico

flora and fauna. It also has exhibits on the Native American settlements found here from as far back as 1000 BC. This visitor center acts as the main headquarters for the Gulf Islands National Seashore, a collective name for several national parks, each with a specific focus of natural or historic interest, lining 160 miles (257 km) of coastline between here and Mississippi.

Naval Live Oaks Area of the Gulf Islands National Seashore

📍 1801 Gulf Breeze Parkway
🕐 8am–sunset daily
🌐 nps.gov/guis

 6

Santa Rosa Island

🅰A1 ℹ️8543 Navarre Parkway, Navarre; www. visitpensacolabeach.com

A long, thin streak of sand, Santa Rosa stretches all the way from Pensacola Bay to Fort Walton Beach, a distance

of 45 miles (70 km). At its western tip **Fort Pickens**, completed in 1834, is the largest of four US forts constructed in the early 19th century to defend Pensacola Bay.

The famous Apache chieftain Geronimo was imprisoned in Fort Pickens from 1886–8, during which time people came from far and wide to see him. The authorities supposedly encouraged his transformation into a tourist attraction. The fort remained in use by the US Army until 1947. Now, visitors are free to explore the brick fort's dark passageways and small museum.

Santa Rosa Island boasts several fine white beaches. Pensacola Beach and Navarre Beach are both popular, each with a fishing pier and plenty of water sports activities. Between them is a beautiful, undeveloped stretch of sand where visitors can relax away from the crowds. There is also a camp ground, situated at the western end of the island, near Fort Pickens.

Fort Pickens

♿ 📍1400 Fort Pickens Rd (Route 399) 🕐5am–6pm daily (Mar–Oct: to 9pm)
🌐 nps.gov/guis

Panama City Beach

 B1 🚗🚌 ℹ️ 17001 Panama City Beach Parkway; www.visitpanama citybeach.com

The Panhandle's biggest resort, Panama City Beach is a 27 mile (43 km) "Miracle Strip" of hotels, amusement parks, and arcades, bordered by a gleaming quartz sand beach. Nicknamed the "wreck capital of the south," it caters both to the young crowds at Spring Break, and to families, who dominate in summer. The sports facilities are excellent.

Panama City Beach is also a famous diving destination. Besides a few natural reefs formed from limestone ridges in the sea bottom and the presence of older shipwrecks, it has more than 50 artificial diving sites created by wrecked boats. For the less energetic, **Capt. Anderson's Marina** and **Treasure Island Marina** offer glass-bottomed boat tours and trips to see wild dolphins. **St. Andrews State Park**, at the far eastern end of Panama City Beach, features pristine beaches free of development. Ferries run from here to similarly untouched Shell Island, across the inlet.

The **Museum of Man in the Sea** provides a homespun but educational look at the history of diving and marine salvage. Exhibits range from ancient diving helmets to salvaged treasures from the 17th-century Spanish galleon

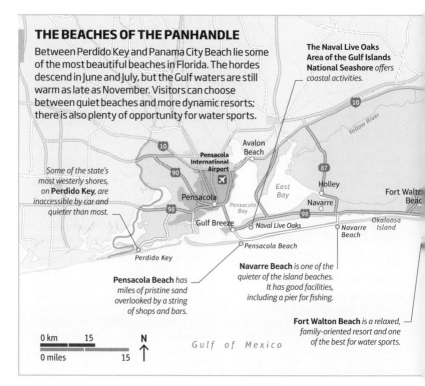

THE BEACHES OF THE PANHANDLE

Between Perdido Key and Panama City Beach lie some of the most beautiful beaches in Florida. The hordes descend in June and July, but the Gulf waters are still warm as late as November. Visitors can choose between quiet beaches and more dynamic resorts; there is also plenty of opportunity for water sports.

The Naval Live Oaks Area of the Gulf Islands National Seashore *offers coastal activities.*

Some of the state's most westerly shores, on **Perdido Key**, *are inaccessible by car and quieter than most.*

Pensacola Beach *has miles of pristine sand overlooked by a string of shops and bars.*

Navarre Beach *is one of the quieter of the island beaches. It has good facilities, including a pier for fishing.*

Fort Walton Beach *is a relaxed, family-oriented resort and one of the best for water sports.*

Yellow River

Avalon Beach

Pensacola International Airport

East Bay

Holley

Fort Walton Beach

Pensacola

Pensacola Bay

Navarre

Okaloosa Island

Gulf Breeze

Naval Live Oaks

Navarre Beach

Pensacola Beach

Perdido Key

0 km   15
0 miles   15

N ↑

Gulf of Mexico

← A roller coaster in Panama City Beach, the biggest resort in the Panhandle

Atocha (p300), plus a parking lot full of submarines. Moby Dick is a whale rescue vessel resembling a killer whale.

The 1,600 ft (490 m) Lazy River tube ride at **Shipwreck Island Water Park** is great, but there are also higher-energy options, such as the Zoom Flume, the Raging Rapids, or the 660 ft (201 m) White Knuckle River inner tube ride. There are gentler rides for youngsters, as well as a children's pool.

Coconut Creek Family Fun Park has two 18-hole mini-golf courses. There is also a giant maze the size of a football field, which has as its theme voyaging from one South Pacific island to another, and is the largest of its kind in the country.

Capt. Anderson's Marina
🏠 5550 N Lagoon Dr
🕐 9am-5pm Mon-Fri
🌐 captandersons
marina.com

Treasure Island Marina
🏠 3605 Thomas Dr
🕐 7:30am-4pm daily
🌐 treasureisland
marina.net

St. Andrews State Park
♿🅿 🏠 4607 State Park Lane 🕐 8am-sunset daily
🌐 floridastateparks.org/
standrews

Museum of Man in the Sea
♿ 🏠 17314 Panama City Beach Parkway 🕐 For tours only; 10am-4pm Thu-Sun
🌐 maninthesea.org

Shipwreck Island Water Park
♿🅿🚻 🏠 12201 Hutchison Blvd 🕐 Times vary, check website
🌐 shipwreckisland.com

Coconut Creek Family Fun Park
♿ 🏠 9807 Front Beach Rd
🕐 9am-11:30pm daily
🌐 coconutcreekfun.com

DRINK

No Name Lounge
The views of The Gulf from the terrace seats are worth the visit alone. Add cheap drinks and free table snacks and you've got a place loved by locals and visitors alike.

🅰 B1 🏠 5555 W Hwy 98, Panama City 🌐 facebook.com/
nonameloungepc

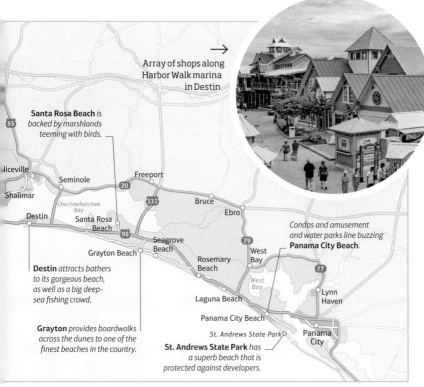

→ Array of shops along Harbor Walk marina in Destin

Santa Rosa Beach *is backed by marshlands teeming with birds.*

85

Niceville

Seminole

Freeport

Shalimar

Choctawhatchee Bay

20

331

Bruce

Ebro

Destin

Santa Rosa Beach

98

Seagrove Beach

Grayton Beach

Rosemary Beach

West Bay

79

West Bay

Laguna Beach

Panama City Beach

St. Andrews State Park

Panama City

Lynn Haven

77

Destin *attracts bathers to its gorgeous beach, as well as a big deep-sea fishing crowd.*

Condos and amusement and water parks line buzzing **Panama City Beach**.

Grayton *provides boardwalks across the dunes to one of the finest beaches in the country.*

St. Andrews State Park *has a superb beach that is protected against developers.*

 8

Destin

A1 🚗 ✈ **i** **4484 Legendary Dr, Suite A, Okaloosa County; www. destinfwb.com**

Situated between the Gulf of Mexico and Choctawhatchee Bay, Destin is a narrow strip of a town that runs parallel to the coastal highway, US 98. It started out in 1845 as a fishing camp but the town has since grown into what is claimed to be the "most prolific fishing village" in the United States. Deep-sea fishing is the big attraction, and charter boats come and go full of hopeful fishermen. The waters near Destin are particularly rich in fish because of a 100-ft (30-m) drop in the continental shelf only 10 miles (16 km) from the shore. The prime catches include amberjack, tarpon, and blue marlin. There is a busy calendar of fishing tournaments in Destin, the most notable being October's month-long Fishing Rodeo. Another important date is early October, when people flock here for the Destin Seafood Festival. Cockles, mussels, shrimp, and crab tempt the crowds.

With its stunning beaches and the clear waters so typical of the Emerald Coast, Destin

has also become a very popular seaside resort, offering opportunities for diving and snorkeling.

 9

Seaside

B1 **i** **25777 US Hwy 331 South, Walton County; www.seasidefl.com**

When Robert Davis decided to develop Seaside in the mid-1980s, the vanished resorts of his childhood provided his inspiration. Davis's vision was of a nostalgic vacation town of traditional wooden cottages, with wraparound verandas, steeply pitched roofs, and white picket fences. The original style was rapidly hijacked, however, by quaint gingerbread detailing, turrets, and towers.

The town's pastel-painted, Neo-Victorian charms have an unreal, Disneyesque quality, and when driving along US 98 it is hard to resist stopping for a quick peek. And then, of course, there is the additional appeal of the beach.

About 1 mile (1.5 km) west of Seaside, the **Grayton**

Beach State Park boasts another fine stretch of Panhandle shoreline, and one that regularly features high in the rankings of the nation's top beaches. In addition to its

Did You Know?

Seaside was the set location for *The Truman Show*, the 1998 movie starring Jim Carrey.

→

The southern-style mansion anchoring Eden Gardens State Park

A boat preparing to dock at Destin, a town renowned for its fishing opportunities

broad strand of pristine quartz-white sand, the park offers good surf, fishing, and boating facilities, a nature trail, and a campground. During the summer, families can take part in programs led by park rangers.

Grayton Beach State Park

 County Rd 30A, off US 98, 1 mile (1.5 km) W of Seaside ☉8am-sunset daily ✍floridastateparks.org

---

10

Blackwater River

🄰A1 🄰Santa Rosa County 🄰✉Pensacola 🄸5247 Stewart St, Milton; www.srcchamber.com

The Blackwater River starts in Alabama and flows for 60 miles (97 km) south to the Gulf of Mexico. One of the purest sand-bottom rivers in the world, its dark waters meander prettily through the forest, creating oxbow lakes and sand beaches.

The river's big attraction is its canoeing: one of the state's finest canoe trails runs for 31 miles (50 km) along its course. Canoe and kayak trips can be arranged through several operators in Milton, the self-styled "Canoeing Capital of Florida." These trips range from half-day paddles to three-day marathons.

The small **Blackwater River State Park**, located at the end of the canoe trail, offers swimming, picnicking areas, and the Chain of Lakes Trail. This 1-mile (1.5-km) nature trail runs through woodlands thick with oak, southern magnolia, and red maple trees.

Blackwater River State Park

 🄰7720 Deaton Bridge Rd, Milton ☉8am-sunset daily ✍floridastateparks.org

11

Eden Gardens State Park

🄰B1 🄰181 Eden Gardens Rd, Santa Rosa Beach ☉8am-sunset daily ✍floridastateparks.org

Along with the usual state park favorites like kayaking and hiking, Eden Gardens State Park also offers some fun for history and culture lovers at the **Wesley House**. Lumber baron William H. Wesley built this fine Greek Revival mansion overlooking the Choctawhatchee River in 1897. The two-story building, styled after an antebellum mansion, is furnished with antiques, and the estate's gardens are shaded by magnolia trees and live oaks. These lead to the river, near where the old lumber mill once stood. Whole trees were once floated from inland forests downriver to the mill, where they were sawed into logs, then sent along the Intracoastal Waterway to Pensacola.

Wesley House

 🄰181 Eden Gardens Rd ☉10am-3pm Thu-Mon ✍floridastateparks.org

12

Fort Walton Beach

Ⓐ A1 🚗🛥️🚌 **ℹ 34 Miracle Strip Parkway SE, Okaloosa County; www.fwb.org**

The city of Fort Walton Beach lies at the western tip of the Emerald Coast, a 24-mile (40-km) strip of dazzling beach stretching east to Destin and beyond. Diving shops and marinas line US 98, which skirts the coast and links Fort Walton to Santa Rosa Island. There is superb swimming as well as pier and deep-sea fishing, and this is a prime location for watersports, too. Also available is sailing, or windsurfing off the island's north shore, on sheltered Choctawhatchee Bay. For those who prefer dry land, the Emerald Coast boasts a dozen golf courses.

Downtown, the Indian Temple Mound Museum stands in the shadow of an ancient earthwork, a ceremonial and burial site of the Apalachee tribe. Built between 800 and 1400 AD, the earthen Fort Walton Temple Mound is thought to have been a religious center – what remains

is 12 ft (4 m) tall and 223 ft (68 m) across. The museum exhibits artifacts recovered from the mound and other historic sites nearby, and houses one of the finest collections of pre-contact ceramics in the southeast, while well-illustrated displays trace more than 10,000 years of human habitation in the Choctawhatchee Bay area. The museum is part of the **Heritage Park and Cultural Center** complex, which also includes the Camp Walton Schoolhouse Museum, the Garnier Post Office Museum, and the Civil War Exhibit Building, chronicling Florida's experience in the US Civil War.

Three miles (5 km) north of town at Shalimar, at the Eglin Air Force Base, the **US Air Force Armament Museum** displays aircraft, missiles, and bombs dating from World War II to the present day. There is an SR-71 "Blackbird" spy plane as well as high-tech laser equipment.

Heritage Park and Cultural Center

♿🅿️ **Ⓐ 139 SE Miracle Strip Parkway** ⏰ **10am-3pm Tue-Sat; mound: 8am-5pm daily** **fwb.org**

US Air Force Armament Museum

🅿️ **Ⓐ 100 Museum Dr (Route 85)** ⏰ **9:30am-5pm daily** 🌐**afarmamentmuseum.com**

---

13 🎨

Alfred B. Maclay Gardens State Park

Ⓐ C1 **Ⓐ 3540 Thomasville Rd, Leon County** ⏰ **8am-sunset daily** **florida stateparks.org**

These gorgeous gardens, north of Tallahassee, were laid out around Killearn, the 1930s winter home of New York financier Alfred B. Maclay. More than 200 varieties of plant are featured in the landscaped gardens, which surround the shores of Lake Hall. They remain eye-catching even in winter, when the camellias and azaleas are in full bloom (from January to April). Visitors can also swim, fish, go boating, or stroll along the Big Pine Nature Trail.

14

Underwater Museum of Art

Ⓐ B2 **Ⓐ 357 Main Park Rd, Grayton Beach** ⏰ **Noon-9pm Mon-Fri, 10am-10pm Sat, 10am-9pm Sun** 🌐**umafl.org**

It seems a logical progression that a region with world-class art and scuba diving would eventually combine the two. The Underwater Museum of Art is located just under a mile (1.5 km) off the coast

←

Sunset over the pier at Fort Walton Beach, on the Florida Panhandle

↑ A pond bordered by ferns and blooming iris at Alfred B. Maclay Gardens State Park

The museum is very much an eco-tourism venture, with environmentally friendly materials being used for the sculptures.

of Grayton Beach State Park (p246). In 2018, seven large sculptures, including a giant skull and an octopus, were submerged in and around the designated areas at a depth of around 60 ft (18 m). Every year, a new selection of sculptural works is installed.

The museum is very much an ecotourism venture, with environmentally friendly materials being used for the sculptures. This not only drives home a message of conservation, but also helps local marine life by providing new habitats, meaning that the artworks themselves transform over time as marine creatures and plants live among them.

Entry to the museum is free; however, visitors do need to ensure that they are certified divers who are comfortable in open water. Dive 30 (www. dive30a.com) and Emerald Coasts Scuba (www.divedestin. net) offer trips to the dive site.

15

Monticello

🅰 D1 ℹ️ 420 W Washington St, Jefferson County; www. cityofmonticello.us

Founded in 1827, Monticello (pronounced "Montisello") was named after the Virginia home of former President Thomas Jefferson. Lying at the heart of northern Florida's cotton-growing country, the town prospered at the expense of enslaved people and elegant homes were built here. Some of these are now guest houses, making the town an ideal base from which to explore the Tallahassee area.

Monticello radiates from the imposing courthouse on US 90. The historic district lies to the north, where there are tree-canopied streets and a wealth of lovely old buildings, ranging from 1850s antebellum mansions to Queen Anne homes with decorative wood-work and Gothic features.

Every year at the end of June, Monticello hosts its Watermelon Festival to celebrate a mainstay of the local agricultural economy. Pageants, dancing, rodeos, and the traditional watermelon seed spitting contest are among the festival's many attractions.

16

Wild Willy's Adventure Zone

🅰 A1 🏠 1306 Miracle Strip Parkway SE, Fort Walton Beach 🕙 10am–10pm daily 🌐 wwazone.com

This modern-looking theme park on Okaloosa Island can be reached by car over the Midbay Bridge from Destin. It offers a good mix of outdoor and indoor activities. The most intricate attraction is the Tree Top Challenge, which encompasses five increasingly challenging levels of ropes and obstacles, reaching heights up to 60 ft (18 m). There are also two miniature adventure golf courses with a dinosaur theme, each aimed at a different age group. The Redemption Arcade is a state-of-the-art collection of video games that also includes a few old favorites where tickets and prizes are available, such as Skee-Ball and Grab and Win. In the 4-D Movie Experience, 3-D movies combine with articulated seats and other special effects for a thrilling experience of dinosaurs and the Wild West. There are also bungee-tied trampolines for adrenaline fans.

Admiring the rock formations at Florida Caverns State Park

17

Torreya State Park

🅰C1 🚗Route CR 1641, 13 miles (21 km) N of Bristol 🚌Blountstown 🕐8am–sunset daily 🌐floridastateparks.org

More off the beaten path than most other parks in Florida, Torreya State Park is nevertheless well worth seeking out. Named after the Florida torreya, a rare and now endangered type of yew tree that once grew here in abundance, the park abuts a beautiful forested bend in the Apalachicola River. High limestone bluffs, into which Confederate soldiers would dig gun pits to repel Union gunboats during the Civil War, flank the river, offering one of the few high natural vantage points in Florida.

Gregory House, a fine 19th-century Classical Revival mansion, stands on top of the 150 ft (45 m) bluff. In 1935 it was moved here by conservationists from its first site downriver and has since been restored.

It is a 25-minute walk from Gregory House down to the river and back, or you can take the 7-mile (11-km) Weeping Ridge Trail. Both paths run through woodland and offer a chance to spot all types of birds, deer, beaver, and the unusual Barbours map turtle (so-called for the maplike lines etched on its shell).

18

Florida Caverns State Park

🅰B1 🚗3345 Caverns Rd, off Route 166, 3 miles (5 km) N of Marianna 🕐8am–sunset daily 🌐floridastateparks.org

The limestone that underpins Florida is laid bare in this series of underground caves hollowed out of the soft rock and drained by the Chipola River. The filtering of rainwater through the limestone rock over thousands of years has created a breathtaking subterranean cavescape of stalactites, stalagmites, columns, and glittering rivulets of crystals. Wrap up warm for the guided tours, since the temperature in the caverns is a cool 61–66 °F (16–19 °C).

The park also offers hiking trails and horseback riding, and visitors can swim and fish in the Chipola River.

Did You Know?

The Apalachicola River by Torreya State Park is great for freshwater fishing.

→

The large pool at the center of the lush Wakulla Springs State Park

A 52-mile (84-km) canoe trail slips through the high limestone cliffs along the river's route south to Dead Lake, just west of Apalachicola National Forest.

 19

Cedar Key

D2 **450 2nd St, Cedar Key, Levy County; www.cedarkey.org**

At the foot of a chain of small bridge-linked keys jutting out into the Gulf of Mexico, Cedar Key is a picturesque, weathered Victorian fishing village. In the 19th century it flourished as the gulf terminal of Florida's first cross-state railroad, and from the burgeoning lumber trade. However, within a few decades its stands of cedar forest had been transformed into pencils, and the logging boom came to an end. A few of the old lumber ware-houses have been turned into shops and restaurants, but the Cedar Key of today is blissfully quiet.

Visitors can take a boat from the docks to an offshore island beach in the Cedar Keys National Wildlife Refuge, or take an enjoyable bird-watching trip along the salt-marsh coast. Various boats run trips from the docks.

Alternatively, visit the entertaining **Cedar Key Historical Society Museum**, in which eclectic exhibits include some fossilized tapir teeth, Native American pottery shards, and crab traps.

Cedar Key Historical Society Museum
⊕ **Corner of D and 2nd sts** ⏰ **1–4pm Sun-Fri, 11am–5pm Sat** **cedarkeyhistory.org**

20

Wakulla Springs State Park

C1 **Wakulla Co 550 Wakulla Park Dr** ⏰ **8am–sunset daily** **floridastateparks.org**

One of the world's largest freshwater springs, the

 INSIDER TIP
Exploring Cedar Key

Blend in with the locals and rent a golf ("gulf") cart - a popular way to get around. Prices start at $25 for two hours with the Gulf Kart Company (www.gulfkartcompany.com).

Wakulla pumps 700,000 gal (2.6 million liters) of water a minute into the large pool which is the big appeal of this park.

Visitors can swim or snorkel in the beautifully clear, limestone-filtered water, or take a ride in a glass-bottom boat. There are also trips on the Wakulla River – look out for alligators, ospreys, and wading birds – and woodland trails to follow.

Do not leave without visiting the Spanish-style Wakulla Springs Lodge hotel and restaurant, built as a hunting lodge in the 1930s. The lobby is the finest part of the hotel, with Tennessee marble decorating the floors, stairwells, and the fantastic bar here. It also houses one of the oldest working Art Deco elevators.

21

St. Joseph Peninsula State Park

⚐B2 ⚑**Gulf County Route 30E** ⏰**8am–sunset daily** 🌐**floridastateparks.org**

At the tip of the slender sand spit that extends north from Cape San Blas to enclose St. Joseph's Bay, this beautifully unspoiled beach park is ideal for those in search of a little peace and quiet. The swimming is excellent, and snorkeling and surf fishing are also popular activities. Birdwatchers should pack their binoculars, since the birdlife is prolific along the shoreline: over 200 species have been recorded here. Guests can stay in cabins overlooking the bay, and there are basic camping facilities, too.

Venture from the beach and explore the saw palmetto and pine woodlands, where you may see deer, raccoons, bobcats, and even coyotes.

22

Manatee Springs State Park

⚐D2 ⚑**11650 NW 115 St, Chiefland** ⏰**8am–sunset daily** 🌐**floridastateparks.org**

Thirty miles (50 km) to the north of Cedar Key is the delightful Manatee Springs State Park, where a spring gushes from a cave mouth 30 ft (9 m) below the surface of an azure pool.

The spring water feeds the Suwannee River, which is as clear as glass and a big draw for both divers and snorkelers. Despite the name of the park, sightings of manatees, which occasionally winter here, are unreliable; however it is easy to spot many other animals, including dozens of turtles, fish, and egrets feeding in the shallows, and the turkey vultures hovering overhead. Visitors can also swim, rent a canoe, take a boat tour, or follow one of the hiking trails; along which they may catch a glimpse of an armadillo in the undergrowth.

23

Apalachicola

⚐C2 ℹ**122 Commerce St, Franklin County; www. apalachicolabay.org**

A riverside customs station established in 1823, Apalachicola saw its finest days during the first 100 years of its existence. It boomed first with the cotton trade, then sponge divers and lumber barons made their fortunes here. Today, a swath of pines and hardwoods still stands as the Apalachicola National Forest, extending from 12 miles (19 km) north of Apalachicola to the outskirts of Tallahassee.

At the end of the lumber boom in the 1920s, the town turned to oystering and fishing in the waters at the mouth of the Apalachicola River. Oyster and other fishing boats still pull up at the dockside, which is lined with refrigerated seafood houses and old brick-built cotton warehouses. Among the seafood houses on Water Street there are several places to sample fresh oysters.

Apalachicola's old town is laid out in a neat grid, with many fine historic buildings dating from the cotton-boom era, including warehouses. A walking map, available from the Chamber of Commerce, takes in treasures as the 1838 Greek Revival Raney House Museum.

Devoted to the town's most notable resident, the **John Gorrie Museum State Park** has a model of Gorrie's patent ice-making machine. Designed to cool

← The Three Soldiers statue in the Vietnam Veterans Memorial Plaza, Apalachicola

← Swimming in the Suwannee River at Manatee Springs State Park, and *(inset)* kayaking at the springs

the sickrooms of yellow fever sufferers, Dr. Gorrie's 1851 invention was the cutting edge of modern refrigeration and air conditioning.

The Veterans Memorial Plaza on Market Street features a resplendent bronze replica of the famous *Three Soldiers* sculpture in Washington DC, honoring veterans of the Vietnam War.

John Gorrie Museum State Park

 🏛 46 6th St (Gorrie Square) ⏰ 9am–5pm Thu–Sat 🌐 floridastateparks.org

---

24

Suwannee River State Park

🅰 D2 🏛 3631 201st Path, Live Oak ⏰ 8am–sunset daily 🌐 floridastate parks.org

Made famous by the song "Old Folks at Home," written by Stephen Foster in 1851, the Suwannee runs 265 miles (425 km) to the Gulf of Mexico.

The river's route through Suwannee River state park offers gorgeous views and some of the best backcountry canoeing in Florida, with an easy flow and low banks, and canoeists have a good chance of seeing a range of wildlife, including herons and turtles.

25

St. Vincent, St. George, and Dog Islands

🅰 C2 ℹ 122 Commerce St, Apalachicola, Franklin County; www.apalachicola bay.org

This string of barrier islands separates Apalachicola Bay from the Gulf of Mexico. St. George is linked by a bridge to Apalachicola. A 9-mile (14-km) stretch of dunes at its eastern end is preserved as the **Dr. Julian G. Bruce St. George Island State Park**. The beaches on St. George are consistently named among the best in the entire country. To the west, the **St. Vincent National Wildlife Refuge** is uninhabited and accessible only by boat; **St. Vincent Island Shuttle and Fishing Charters** runs tours. Visitors can expect to see sea turtles laying their eggs in summer, and migrating waterfowl in winter.

To the east, little Dog Island can be reached only by boat from Carrabelle on the mainland. It has excellent shell hunting.

Dr. Julian G. Bruce St. George Island State Park

🏛 1900 E Gulf Beach Dr, St. George Island ⏰ 8am–sunset daily 🌐 floridastateparks.org

St. Vincent National Wildlife Refuge

🏛 St. Vincent Island ⏰ 24 hours daily 🌐 fws.gov

St. Vincent Island Shuttle and Fishing Charters

🏛 690 Indian Pass Rd, Port St. Joe 🌐 stvincent island.com

> The river's route through Suwannee River state park offers gorgeous views and some of the best backcountry canoeing in Florida, with an easy flow and low banks.

THE GULF COAST

Ever since the Spanish colonization in the 16th century, the focus of activity along the Gulf Coast has been around Tampa Bay, the large inlet in Florida's west coast. The bay was a perfect natural port and became a magnet to pioneers. After the Civil War, the Gulf Coast became a significant center for trade between the US and the Caribbean. This was due in part to Henry Plant, whose rail line from Virginia, laid in the 1880s, helped to fuel both Tampa's and the region's greatest period of prosperity. Pioneers flooded in from all nations and backgrounds, from the Greek sponge fishermen who settled in Tarpon Springs to the circus king John Ringling.

Henry Plant used the promise of winter sunshine to lure wealthy travelers to the Gulf Coast, and the much-advertised average of 361 days of sunshine a year still helps to attract great hordes of tourists to the generous miles of white-sand beaches bathed by the warm, calm waters of the Gulf of Mexico. However, with only a little effort, visitors can kick the sand from their shoes and visit some of Florida's most interesting cities, or explore wilderness areas that have been left virtually untouched by time.

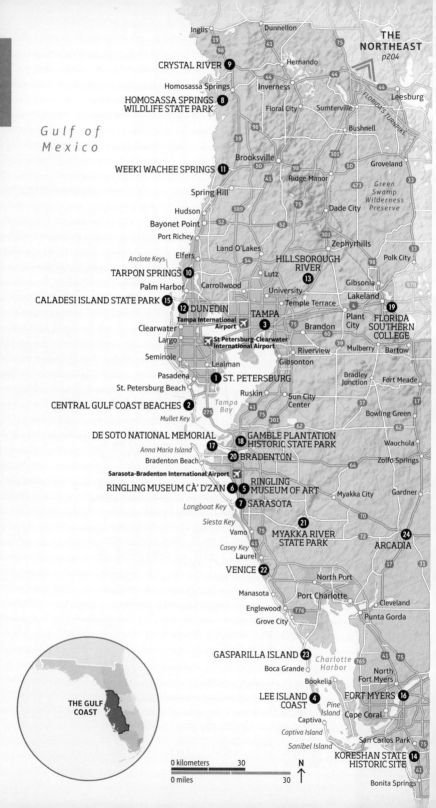

Inglis

Dunnellon

Hernando

CRYSTAL RIVER **9**

Homosassa Springs

HOMOSASSA SPRINGS WILDLIFE STATE PARK **8**

Inverness

Leesburg

Floral City

Sumterville

Bushnell

Brooksville

WEEKI WACHEE SPRINGS **11**

Spring Hill

Ridge Manor

Groveland

Green Swamp Wilderness Preserve

Hudson

Bayonet Point

Port Richey

Dade City

Zephyrhills

Anclote Keys

Elfers

Land O'Lakes

Polk City

TARPON SPRINGS **10**

Palm Harbor

CALADESI ISLAND STATE PARK **15**

12 DUNEDIN

Lutz

University

Carrollwood

HILLSBOROUGH RIVER **13**

Gibsonia

Lakeland

Tampa International Airport

Clearwater

Temple Terrace

TAMPA **3**

FLORIDA SOUTHERN COLLEGE **19**

Largo

St Petersburg-Clearwater International Airport

Brandon

Plant City

Seminole

Lealman

Riverview

Mulberry

Bartow

Pasadena

1 ST. PETERSBURG

Gibsonton

CENTRAL GULF COAST BEACHES **2**

St. Petersburg Beach

Ruskin

Tampa Bay

Sun City Center

Bradley Junction

Fort Meade

Mullet Key

Bowling Green

DE SOTO NATIONAL MEMORIAL

GAMBLE PLANTATION HISTORIC STATE PARK **18**

17

Wauchula

Anna Maria Island

Bradenton Beach

20 BRADENTON

Zolfo Springs

Sarasota-Bradenton International Airport

RINGLING MUSEUM CÀ D'ZAN **6** **5** RINGLING MUSEUM OF ART

7 SARASOTA

Myakka City

Gardner

Longboat Key

Siesta Key

MYAKKA RIVER STATE PARK **21**

Vamo

ARCADIA **24**

Casey Key

Laurel

VENICE **22**

North Port

Manasota

Port Charlotte

Cleveland

Englewood

Grove City

Punta Gorda

GASPARILLA ISLAND **23**

Charlotte Harbor

Boca Grande

North Fort Myers

Bookelia

LEE ISLAND COAST **4**

Pine Island

FORT MYERS **16**

Captiva

Cape Coral

Captiva Island

San Carlos Park

Sanibel Island

KORESHAN STATE HISTORIC SITE **14**

THE GULF COAST

Bonita Springs

0 kilometers 30

0 miles 30

N

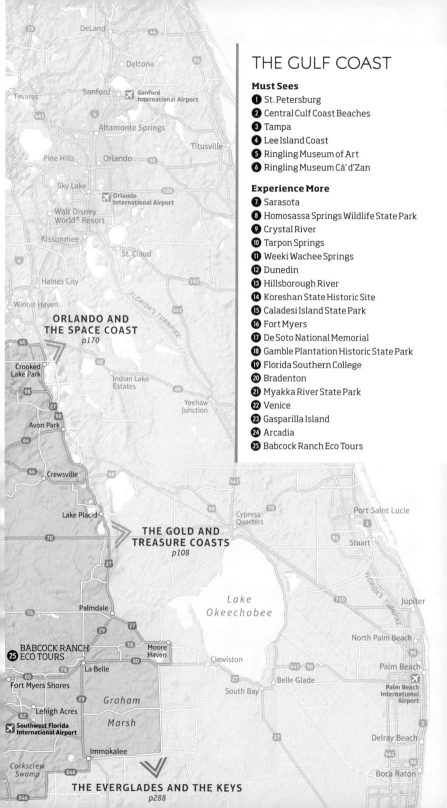

THE GULF COAST

Must Sees

1. St. Petersburg
2. Central Culf Coast Beaches
3. Tampa
4. Lee Island Coast
5. Ringling Museum of Art
6. Ringling Museum Cà' d'Zan

Experience More

7. Sarasota
8. Homosassa Springs Wildlife State Park
9. Crystal River
10. Tarpon Springs
11. Weeki Wachee Springs
12. Dunedin
13. Hillsborough River
14. Koreshan State Historic Site
15. Caladesi Island State Park
16. Fort Myers
17. De Soto National Memorial
18. Gamble Plantation Historic State Park
19. Florida Southern College
20. Bradenton
21. Myakka River State Park
22. Venice
23. Gasparilla Island
24. Arcadia
25. Babcock Ranch Eco Tours

ORLANDO AND
THE SPACE COAST
p170

THE GOLD AND
TREASURE COASTS
p108

THE EVERGLADES AND THE KEYS
p288

1

ST. PETERSBURG

🅐 E4 ✈🚌 🏛 100 2nd Ave N; www.visitstpete clearwater.com

This city of broad avenues grew up in the great era of 19th-century land speculation, and was given its name by an exiled Russian nobleman called Peter Demens. Today, "St. Pete," as it is often dubbed, is best known both for its aging population of sun-seekers and for its rejuvenated downtown area.

1

St. Petersburg Museum of History

🅐 335 2nd Ave NE ⏱ 10am-5pm Mon-Sat, noon-5pm Sun 🌐 spmoh.org

This museum tells the story of St. Petersburg from pre-historic times to the present. Exhibits range from mastodon bones and Native American pottery to an entertaining mirror gallery, which gives visitors a comic idea of how they would have looked in Victorian fashions. A pavilion houses a replica of a sea plane called the Benoist, which marks St. Petersburg as the birthplace of commercial aviation. This aircraft made the first flight with a paying passenger across Tampa Bay in 1914.

2

Florida Holocaust Museum

🅐 55 Fifth St S ⏱ 10am-4pm daily 🌐 flholocaustmuseum.org

This museum, located in downtown St. Petersburg, honors the millions of people who suffered or died during the Holocaust. It played a key role in Florida becoming one of the first US states to mandate Holocaust education in public schools.

→ Visitors examining the powerful exhibits of the Florida Holocaust Museum

↑ St. Petersburg's downtown skyline, reflected in the glassy water of Tampa Bay

A special pavilion houses a replica of a sea plane called the Benoist, which marks St. Petersburg as the birthplace of commercial aviation.

③

The Chihuly Collection

720 Central Ave ◷10am-5pm Mon-Sat, noon-5pm Sun ⓦmoreanartscenter.org/chihuly

The work of world-renowned glass artist Dale Chihuly is displayed in a building designed specifically to show the large-scale works of glass art. Across the street is the Morean Arts Center Glass Studio and Hot Shop where glassblowers create unique pieces, all of which are available for sale.

④

Museum of Fine Arts

255 Beach Dr NE ◷10am-5pm Mon-Sat (to 8pm Thu & Fri), noon-5pm Sun ⓦmfastpete.org

Housed in a striking Palladian-style building overlooking the bay, the Museum of Fine Arts is renowned for its wide-ranging collection of European, American, pre-Columbian, and Asian works. The museum opened to the public in 1965, and was St. Petersburg's first downtown museum. Supreme among the French Impressionist paintings are *A Corner of the Woods* (1877) by Cézanne, and Monet's classic *Parliament, Effect of Fog, London* (1904). Other prominent works are the vivid *Poppy* (1927) by Georgia O'Keeffe, *La Lecture* (1888) by Berthe Morisot, and Auguste Rodin's *Invocation* (1886), which stands in the sculpture garden. A large collection of photographs, dating from the early 1900s to the present, rounds off the collection.

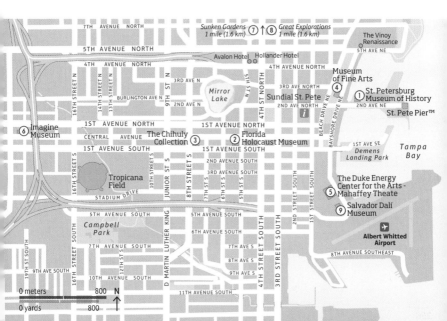

STAY

Avalon Hotel St. Petersburg

This boutique property has a modern Art Deco look, and the interiors explode with retro-chic colors and subtle touches of neon. The nightly cheese and wine social is a charming extra touch.

📍 443 4th Ave N
🌐 avalonst
petersburg.com

$$$ (1)(2)(3)

Hollander Hotel

The highlight of this eclectic hotel is the strikingly elegant outdoor terrace, replete with a well-modeled swimming pool. Shady cabanas and a pool bar complete the look. The sister hotel of the Avalon, the Hollander offers a similarly convenient downtown location.

📍 421 4th Ave N
🌐 hollanderhotel.com

$$$

The Vinoy Renaissance St. Petersburg Resort & Golf Club

The pink exteriors of this historic building, which dates from 1925, complement the harbor skyline. A golf course and deluxe spa are great additions to on-site amenities such as a cute 1920s-style diner.

📍 501 5th Ave NE
🌐 marriott.com

$$$

---

⑤

The Duke Energy Center for the Arts - Mahaffey Theater

📍 400 1st St S 🕐 Daily
🌐 themahaffey.com

This modern, glass-enclosed building provides stunning views across Tampa Bay. It contains a state-of-the-art theater that features a ballroom area and European box-style seating. The theater first opened in 1965, but it was renovated in the late 1980s and renamed for a St. Petersburg family who contributed to the capital campaign. Today, the theater is the city's one-stop-shop for Broadway shows, music and dance events, celebrity entertainers, comedy tours, special exhibitions, and children's theater. It is also home to Florida Orchestra's classical music concerts. The orchestra performs nearly 100 annual concerts in the tri-city area of Tampa, Clearwater, and St. Petersburg, and events in the Mahaffey are always well attended.

---

⑥

Imagine Museum

📍 1901 Central Ave 🕐 10am-5pm Tue-Sat (to 8pm Thu), noon-5pm sun 🌐 imagine museum.com

The popularity of glass art in America began in the 1960s, but there are few museums dedicated to the art form. The Imagine Museum opened in early 2018, thanks to the work of benefactor Trish Duggan, and is focused on the development of studio glass works. Its exhibits examine both work done since the 1960s and in the US, and the museum can guide visitors comprehensively through a particular art scene – from the straightforward early works to the contemporary pieces. Throughout the space, exhibits are lit in atmospheric

Did You Know?

St. Petersburg holds the Guinness World Record for the most consecutive days of sunshine - 768.

↑ Visitors admiring the pale pink flamingo flock in the Sunken Gardens

↑ Enticing exhibits at the Great Explorations interactive museum

galleries. Pieces include everything from the crystalline shapes of Alex Borstein and realism of Brent Kee Young to the more abstract designs of Mark Peiser and William Lequier. New technologies that can be used in an artists' own studio are opening up

this fascinating art form, and there are few better places to receive a full introduction.

⑦

Sunken Gardens

🏛1825 4th St N 📞(727) 551-3102 🕐10am–4:30pm Mon-Sat, noon–4:30pm Sun

Thousands of tropical plants and flowers flourish in this large walled garden, which descends to 10 ft (3 m) below the street outside. The site was once a water-filled sinkhole; its soil is kept dry by a network of hidden pipes. Today it is the city's oldest living museum, having been in place for over 100 years. Wander among the hibiscus and bougainvillea, and visit the extensive orchid garden or eye-catching flamingo flock. Other features include a spectacular walk-through butterfly encounter and a horticulture program.

⑧

Great Explorations

🏛1925 4th Street N 🕐10am–4:30pm Mon-Sat, noon–4pm Sun 🌐great ex.org

"Hands on" is the ethos of this museum, which is aimed at children but is equally fascinating to adults. Youngsters are encouraged to crawl, climb, and touch everything. The popular Orange Grove exhibit, for example, has children picking, packing, and shipping oranges from a mock grove, making pizza, or creating animated videos. The emphasis here is on teamwork. Other highlights include the Lego Wall, "Great Beginnings" which shows how common crops grow, and the Kid Science Lab.

In 2007, Great Explorations also became the first children's museum in America to open a licensed preschool, where their mission of stimulated learning is continued.

The Imagine Museum opened in early 2018, thanks to the work of benefactor Trish Duggan, and is focused on the development of studio glass works.

SALVADOR DALÍ MUSEUM

⌂ 1 Dalí Boulevard, St. Petersburg ▭ 4, 32 ⊙ 10am–6pm Sun–Wed, 10am–9pm Thu–Sat Ⓦ thedali.org

Salvador Dalí is one of the world's most recognizable and feted artists. This museum, known as The Dalí, is dedicated to his iconic Surrealist style as well as earlier works that showcase his versatility.

Although far from the native country of Spanish artist Salvador Dalí (1904–89), this museum holds the most comprehensive collection of his work outside of Spain, spanning his entire career. The first museum opened in 1982, 40 years after Ohio business-man Reynolds Morse and his wife Eleanor saw the first exhibition of Dalí's work, and began collecting his works. After a nationwide search, Morse chose St. Petersburg for the collection because of its resemblance to the artist's childhood summer home of Cadaqués. The museum moved to a spectacular hurricane-proof waterfront location in 2011. In addition to 96 original oil paintings, the museum has more than 100 watercolors and drawings, along with 1,300 graphics, sculptures, and other objects. The works range from Dalí's early figurative paintings to his first experiments in Surrealism, and the biggest collection of mature, large-scale compositions described as his "masterworks."

← The stunning concrete and undulating glass façade of The Dalí

↑ The dramatic helical staircase inside the Salvador Dalí Museum

Early Works

▶ The 1926 oil painting *Basket of Bread* shows the formal influence of Dalí's education before he began experimenting with Surrealism.

Influences

▽ Dalí eschewed the politicism of contemporary Surrealist artists during the 1930s. Paintings like *The Weaning of Furniture Nutrition* (1934) hint at other influences: his childhood home, the symbolism of Freud, and friends such as René Magritte.

Surrealism

▶ Dalí was expelled from the Surrealist movement in 1939, but he remains one of its most prominent figures. The museum houses some of his early attempts, like *Apparatus and Hand* (1927), as well as iconic works.

Nuclear Mysticism

▽ During the 1950s, Dalí became more passionate about profound and complex topics like science and religion. His paintings from this "nuclear mysticism" era explore his new obsessions. In *Nature Morte Vivante* (Living Still Life, 1956), for example, the flying objects reflect the movement of the atom.

A lifeguard tower standing
on the white sands of
Clearwater Beach ↑

2

CENTRAL GULF COAST BEACHES

 E4

With an average of 361 days of sunshine a year, the coast between St. Petersburg and Clearwater encompasses 28 miles (45 km) of superb barrier island beaches. Wherever you are, you can expect high quality sand and water, and a laid-back atmosphere.

① Clearwater Beach

Pinellas County
Clearwater; from Cleveland St 1130 Cleveland St; www.visit clearwaterflorida.com

The satellite of Clearwater city, this lively resort sits amid the long strip of barrier islands that line the Gulf shore. Hotels and bars, often filled with tourists, dominate the waterfront, but Clearwater Beach manages to retain some character. The nightly Sunsets at Pier 60 festival features craft stalls and street performers. The broad strand is consistently voted among the nation's top beach destinations, and the water sports facilities are excellent. Boat trips of all kinds depart from the marina.

② Pass-a-Grille

Pinellas County
Tampa St. Petersburg Tampa Bay Beaches Chamber of Commerce, 6990 Gulf Blvd; www.visitpassagrille.com

At the southern tip of the barrier island group, this sleepy community is a breath of fresh air after the likes of crowded St. Pete Beach. Skirted by the main coastal road, Pass-a-Grille has some lovely homes from the early 1900s, and beaches still in their natural state. A word of warning: take plenty of change for the parking meters.

③

Seaside Seabird Sanctuary

18328 Gulf Blvd, Indian Shores, 33785 (727) 391-6211 8am–4pm daily

Founded in 1971 as the Suncoast Seabird Sanctuary, the organization changed hands and was renamed the Seaside Seabird Sanctuary in 2016. It still operates from the same site – once the largest nonprofit wild bird institution in the US – and admits an average of 2,500 sick or injured wild birds for care every year. The sanctuary is also home to a number of permanent residents; pelicans, owls, herons, egrets, and other species are all on view.

Madeira Beach

🏠 Pinellas County
✈️🚆 Tampa 🚌 St. Petersburg 🛈 Tampa Bay Beaches Chamber of Commerce, 6990 Gulf Blvd; www.visitpeteclear water.org

South of Clearwater and Sand Key Park are a series of small beach communities, which offer quiet beauty and lots of beach access. Madeira Beach is a good place to stay if you prefer a laid-back atmosphere to the buzzing scenes of some of the bigger resorts. John's Pass Village, a re-created fishing village nearby, also offers a quirkier-than-average choice of restaurants and shops. There is also a fishing pier and a marina.

↑ Visitors stroll the boardwalk of John's Pass Village, located near Madeira Beach

Pinellas County Heritage Village

🏠 11909 125th St N
🕐 Tue–Sun 🌐 pinellas county.org/heritage

It is well worth making the diversion inland to Largo, 8 miles (13 km) southeast of Clearwater Beach, to visit the Pinellas County Heritage Village. This consists of 16 historic buildings, brought here from various sites such as the McMullen Log House, which offer a taste of the lifestyle of a wealthy Victorian family. Spinning, weaving, and other skills are demonstrated in the museum.

St. Pete Beach

🏠 Pinellas County ✈️🚆 Tampa 🚌 St. Petersburg 🛈 Tampa Bay Beaches Chamber of Commerce, 6990 Gulf Blvd; www. visitpeteclearwater.org

Located just south of Madeira Beach is St. Pete Beach which is the busiest beach on the Gulf Coast, offering a 7 mile (11 km) strip of white sand and a buzzing scene along the waterfront. At its southern end towers the Don CeSar Resort. Built in the 1920s, the hotel's scale and list of celebrity guests are typical of the grand hotels of that era.

❸

TAMPA

◭E4 ⊠▣▤ ▤ *i* 401 E Jackson St; www.visittampa bay.com

Tampa is one of the fastest-growing cities in Florida. Modern skyscrapers have replaced many original buildings, but vestiges of a colorful history remain – mainly in the historic Latin American quarter, Ybor City. Today, Tampa's big attraction is Busch Gardens, one of the top theme parks in the US, but the Henry B. Plant Museum, the pleasant Riverwalk, and Ybor City itself also offer plenty of interest.

Henry B. Plant Museum

▯ 401 W Kennedy Blvd
◷ 10am–5pm Tue–Sat, noon–5pm Sun ⓦ plant museum.com

The former Tampa Bay Hotel, now home to the University of Tampa, houses the Henry B. Plant Museum. This famous landmark has Moorish minarets that are visible from all over downtown. Henry Plant commissioned the building in 1891 as a hotel for the well-to-do passengers of his newly built railroad. The construction alone cost $3 million, with an additional $500,000 spent on furnishings. The hotel was not a success, however, and it fell into disrepair after Plant's death in 1899. It was bought by the city in 1905 and became part of the university in 1933. The south wing of the ground floor was preserved as a museum. Here, there are special displays dedicated to the Spanish-American War and the life of Plant, as well as a short film providing historical context. Visitors are welcome to walk around what is now the university campus to appreciate the sheer size of the building.

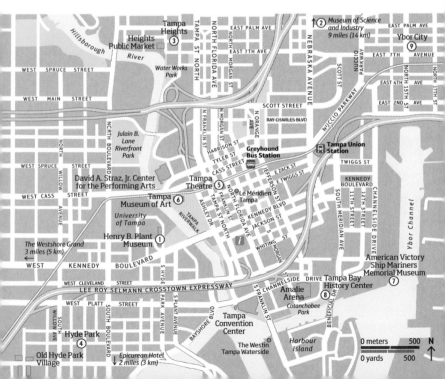

↑ Tampa's skyscrapers looming above the Hillsborough River

Henry Plant commissioned the museum building in 1891 as a hotel for the well-to-do passengers of his newly built railroad.

② **Museum of Science and Industry**

⌂ 4801 E Fowler Ave
🕐 10am–5pm daily
🌐 mosi.org

Two miles northeast of Busch Gardens, the Museum of Science and Industry explores the mysteries of the scientific world, with fun interactive displays, games, and movies. Visitors can explore the moon in the NASA-funded Mission: Moonbase lunar colony, and experience the world of the future in "Connectus."

MOSI is also home to the Saunders Planetarium, which hosts regular astronomical shows. On every Friday and Saturday evening, there are star-viewing sessions at which, weather permitting, telescopes are set up outside so that visitors can observe the night sky.

③ **Tampa Heights**

This historic neighborhood, located north of downtown, lines the east bank of the Hillsborough River. Two food halls opened in late 2017, which house a range of cool spots, including a coffeehouse, meadery, microbrewery, and numerous other activities that attract a diverse mix of entrepreneurial companies. It is also accessible from the Tampa Riverwalk.

④ **Hyde Park**

On the northern edge of the Hillsborough Bay, Hyde Park is a charming historic area in Tampa. Dating from the late 19th century, its houses display a striking mix of architectural styles from Colonial to Gothic Revival (p32). The quiet and peaceful residential streets are best explored on foot. Visitors can park their cars at Hyde Park Village, off Snow Avenue, where you'll find several upscale shops and restaurants. On some days, musicians come out to entertain the shoppers.

THE LEGEND OF GASPAR

José Gaspar was a 19th-century pirate who operated between Tampa and Fort Myers. His stronghold was among the isles of the Lee Island Coast (p270), many of whose modern names – including Gasparilla and Captiva – recall the association. Legend has it that Gaspar was eventually cornered by a US war-ship, and he drowned himself rather than be taken prisoner. Tampa suffered from several of Gaspar's raids, and now holds a Gasparilla Festival each January.

⑤

Tampa Theatre

711 N Franklin St Times vary, check website tampatheatre.org

In its day, the Tampa Theatre was one of the most elaborate movie theaters in America. The building was designed in 1926 by John Eberson in an architectural style known as Florida-Mediterranean. The lavish result was described by the historian Ben Hall as an "Andalusian bonbon."

In an attempt to create the illusion of an outdoor location, Eberson fitted the ceiling with lights designed to twinkle like stars. Other effects included artificial clouds, produced by a smoke machine, and lighting to simulate the rising sun.

The easiest way to visit the beautifully restored theater is to see a movie here. Film festivals, plays, and special events are all held regularly. Guided tours, which take place twice a month, include a 20-minute movie about the theater, and a mini-concert on a traditional 1,000-pipe theater organ.

↑ The historic Tampa Theatre, located on Franklin Street

↑ Children exploring an exhibit at the Tampa Bay History Center

⑥

Tampa Museum of Art

120 W Gasparilla Plaza 10am–5pm daily (10am to 8pm Thu) Easter tampamuseum.org

The Tampa Museum of Art houses a growing collection of world-class art, ranging from Classical Greek, Roman, and Etruscan antiquities; to contemporary American, Cuban, and European works; and world-class traveling exhibitions. The museum houses both permanent and temporary collections of photography, sculpture, paintings, and sketches. The museum building itself is considered a work of art, made with aluminum, glass, and fiber-optic lights. Part of Tampa's scenic Riverwalk, it also hosts outdoor events.

⑦

American Victory Ship Mariners Memorial Museum

705 Channelside Drive Noon–5pm Mon, 10am–5pm Tue–Sun american victory.org

Located behind the Florida Aquarium, this naval museum preserves one of only four fully operational World War II ships in the US. The *SS American Victory* was launched in 1945 to serve as a naval cargo ship, just in time for the last acts of World War II, and later served in the Korean and Vietnam wars. Visitors can explore its cramped interior, restored to its 1940s configuration.

⑧

Tampa Bay History Center

801 Old Water St 10am–5pm daily Thanksgiving & Christmas tampabay historycenter.org

With a beautiful location on the waterfront, the Tampa Bay History Center chronicles the region's past with a series of absorbing exhibits. The diverse collection explores the lives of the first Tocobaga and Timucua inhabitants, pirates like Jack Rackam, the 1920s cigar industry in Ybor City, and the exploits of Teddy Roosevelt.

⑨

Ybor City

Tampa-Ybor 1600 E 8th Ave; www.yborcity online.com

In 1886 a Spanish businessman named Don Vicente Martinez-Ybor moved his cigar business from Key West to Tampa. With ships able to bring a regular supply of tobacco from Cuba to its port, Tampa was ideally located for this cigar industry, and several other huge factories sprang up after Martinez-Ybor moved here. By 1900 Ybor City was producing over 111 million cigars annually.

The legacy of the cigar boom of the late 1800s and early 1900s is still visible in Ybor City. Its main street, 7th Avenue, with its Spanish-style tiles and wrought-iron balconies, looks much as it did then. Often compared to trendy spots Little Havana (p84) and Key West (p298), modern-day Ybor is a multi-cultural neighborhood hosting Tampa's hippest party scene. What were once cigar factories and workers' cottages now house shops, restaurants, and clubs. Quiet during the day, Ybor City comes to life in the evening.

STAY

Le Méridien Tampa

Located as it is in a former courthouse, there's an immediate grandeur to this central hotel. Guests can enjoy the architecture along with a pool and a French-inspired bistro.

🏠 601 N Florida Ave
ⓦ marriott.com

$ $ $

Epicurean Hotel

As the name suggests, this hotel has a culinary emphasis. Their signature steakhouse is a regal affair, and a further two well-regarded restaurants lie in wait for foodies to enjoy.

🏠 1207 S Howard Ave
ⓦ epicureanhotel.com

$ $ $

The Westin Tampa Waterside

This contemporary hotel with modern rooms is located on a private island in Hillsborough Bay. The on-site Blue Harbour Eatery + Bar has lovely bay views.

🏠 725 South Harbour Island Blvd ⓦ marriott.com

$ $ $

The Westshore Grand

A modern and luxurious hotel in the heart of Tampa. The rooftop pool is a great place to soak up the Florida sun.

🏠 4860 West Kennedy Blvd ⓦ westshore grand.com

$ $ $

Did You Know?

In 1919, Babe Ruth hit his longest ever home run in Tampa – it flew a whopping 587 ft (179 m).

↑ A street in popular Ybor City, lined with eateries and boutiques

Turquoise waters and a white sand beach on Sanibel Island ↑

4

LEE ISLAND COAST

△E5 **✕♿** **ℹ1159 Causeway Rd, Sanibel; (239) 472-1080**

The Lee Island Coast offers an irresistible combination of sandy beaches (famous for their shells), exotic wildlife, lush vegetation, and stupendous sunsets. Most visitors head for the chic resorts of Sanibel and Captiva islands, but the remote beauty of less developed islands is equally appealing.

①

Sanibel and Captiva Islands

Within easy reach, Sanibel and Captiva have a laid-back, Caribbean air, and are famous for their shells. Most visitors soon get drawn into the shell-collecting culture, which has given rise to the expressions "Sanibel Stoop" and "Captiva Crouch" for the posture adopted by avid shell hunters.

Two areas of Sanibel are protected as preserves. The **Sanibel Captiva Conservation Foundation** oversees the protection of a chunk of Sanibel's interior wetland, with 4 miles (6 km) of tranquil boardwalk trails nearby. An observation tower provides a perfect vantage point. Most of Sanibel's beaches with public access are along Gulf Drive, the best being Turner and Bowman's beaches.

Captiva is less developed than Sanibel, but you'll still find the odd resort, including the South Seas Island Resort, with its busy marina – a starting point for boat trips to Cayo Costa.

Another site well worth visiting is the **Bailey-Matthews National Shell Museum**. The centerpiece Great Hall of Shells includes displays grouped according to habitat, from the Everglades to barrier islands. It claims to have a third of the world's 10,000 shell varieties.

J.N. "Ding" Darling National Wildlife Refuge occupies two-thirds of Sanibel. Resident wildlife, including raccoons, alligators, and birds such as bald eagles, are surprisingly

SHELLS AND SHELLING

The beaches of Sanibel and Captiva are among the best in the US for shelling. There is no offshore reef to smash the shells, and the warm, shallow waters have a flat bed, which also encourages growth. Live shelling is subject to severe restrictions, so collect only empty shells. Go early, and search where the surf breaks. Shelling is best in winter or just after a storm.

> INSIDER TIP
> **Pine Island**
> This island, fringed with mangrove rather than beaches, provides a useful access point to nearby islands. Arrange any boat trips at the marina in Bokeelia, but allow time to enjoy the range of fishing piers.

easy to spot. The popular 5-mile (8-km) "Wildlife Drive" can be covered by bike or by car, and there are trolley tours, too. Canoes, fishing boats, and bikes can be rented.

Sanibel Captiva Conservation Foundation
Mile Marker 1, Sanibel-Captiva Rd May-Nov: Mon-Fri; Dec-Apr: Mon-Sat sccf.org

Bailey-Matthews National Shell Museum
3075 Sanibel-Captiva Rd 10am-5pm daily shell museum.org

J.N. "Ding" Darling National Wildlife Refuge
1 Wildlife Dr 9am-4pm daily fws.gov/dingdarling

②

Cabbage Key

cabbagekey.com

This island was chosen by the novelist Mary Roberts Rinehart for her home in 1938. Her house, built in the shade of two 18th-century Cuban laurel trees, is now the Cabbage Key Inn. This is best known for its restaurant, which is decorated with around 30,000 autographed one-dollar bills. The first bill was left by a fisherman anxious to make sure he had funds to buy drinks on his next visit. When he returned, he had money to spare and left the bill where it was. Other visitors then took up the idea.

A 40-ft (12-m) water tower nearby provides a lovely view of the small island, and there

↑ Dollar bills lining the walls and ceiling of Cabbage Key Inn

is also a nature trail. Tropic Star from Pine Island, and Captiva Cruises from Captiva Island run the most regular trips to the Cabbage Key.

③

Cayo Costa State Park

Cayo Costa Island
(941) 964-0375
8am-sunset daily

Cayo Costa Island is one of the state's most unspoiled barrier islands. Much of it is planted with non-native Australian pine and Brazilian pepper trees. These were originally imported during the 1950s for their shade and wood, but are now gradually being cleared to let domestic species take over. There are miles of dune-backed beach and several mangrove swamps. Inland, there is a mix of pine flatwoods, grassy areas, and hammocks. The island offers plenty of bird-watching opportunities and excellent shelling, especially in winter. Boat trips take visitors to Cayo Costa all year round, and a trolley links the bayside dock to the gulf side.

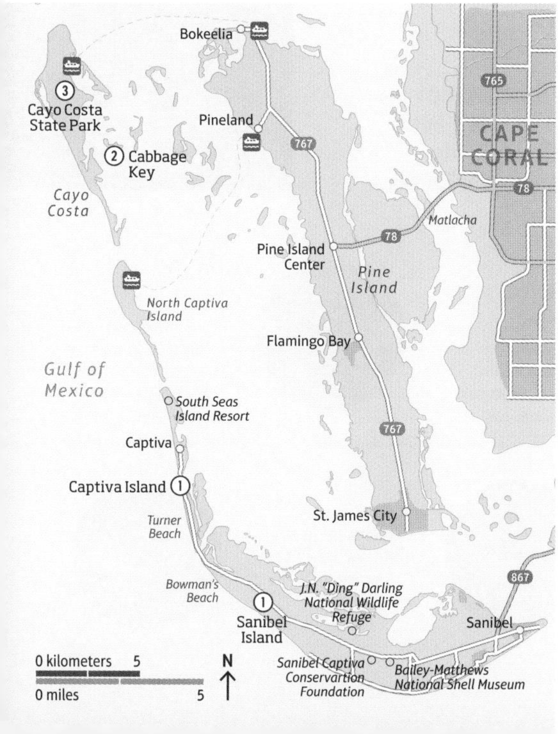

5

RINGLING MUSEUM OF ART

E4 5401 Bay Shore Rd, Sarasota 10am-5pm daily (to 8pm on Thu) ringling.org

The Ringling Circus is a globally famous enterprise, and the wealthy lifestyle of this well-known family is on display at the Ringling Estate, the centerpiece of which is the Ringling Museum of Art.

John Ringling was an Iowa-born circus owner whose phenomenally successful show made him a multimillionaire. In 1925, he decided to build an art collection and a museum to house it – both as a memorial for himself and his wife, Mable, and as a gift to the people of Florida. He spent the next six years amassing a remarkable collection of European paintings, including Italian and Flemish Renaissance and Baroque artworks. There is also a dedicated Center for Art, whose opening in 2016 revitalized the museum and ushered in a new era for this important cultural center.

> **In 1925, Ringling decided to build an art collection and a museum to house it, both as a memorial for himself and his wife, Mable, and as a gift to the people of Florida.**

Museum Highlights

Center for Asian Art

▼ The Dr. Helga Wall-Apelt Gallery of Asian Art is dedicated to historical and contemporary Asian cultures.

Bayfront Gardens

▼ The Ringling sits on the shores of Sarasota Bay. The grounds contain Mable Ringling's Rose Garden, planted in 1913.

Spanish Gallery

▲ This gallery contains Spanish works of the 17th century, including paintings by El Greco and Velázquez.

Astor Rooms

▲ These lavish 19th-century interiors came from a mansion in New York.

↑ Renaissance paintings and sculpture on display in the Ringling Museum of Art, and the gardens (inset)

The Ulla R. and Arthur F. Searing wing

▽ Houses contemporary art special exhibitions.

Statuary

▲ The Renaissance-style courtyard is dotted with bronze casts of Classical sculpture.

THE ULLA R. & ARTHUR
SEARING WING

GALLERY GUIDE

The galleries are arranged around a sculpture garden. Starting with the galleries to the right of the entrance hall, the rooms roughly follow a chronological order counterclockwise, ranging from late medieval painting to 20th-century European art; 16th and 17th-century Italian painting is well represented. Modern art and special exhibitions are displayed in the Searing Wing. The Visitors Pavilion is home to the Historic Asolo Theater, a splendid horseshoe-shaped theater built in 1798 in Asolo near Venice, dismantled in 1930, and shipped to Sarasota.

RINGLING MUSEUM CÀ D'ZAN

🅐E4 🅝5401 Bay Shore Rd, Sarasota 🅞10am–5pm daily (to 8pm Thu) 🅦ringling.org/ca-dzan

With the glamor and style of a fantasy palace, this Italian-inspired mansion was Ringling's winter estate. Restored to its original glory in 1996, Cà d'Zan is full of beautiful original interiors to admire.

The Ringlings' love of Italy, nurtured during frequent visits to Europe, was displayed for all to see in the building's design. Set off by a marble terrace and crowned by a distinctive tower, Cà d'Zan took two years to build and was finished in 1926. The ballroom, court,

formal dining room, and bedrooms all provide glimpses into the life of the American super-rich of the period.

As well as the nearby Museum of Art (p272), the Ringling estate complex is also home to the fun and interactive Circus Museum.

Did You Know?

Cà d'Zan means "House of John" in Venetian.

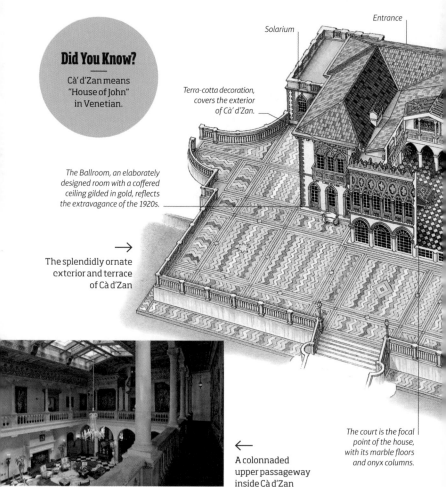

Solarium

Entrance

Terra-cotta decoration, covers the exterior of Cà d'Zan.

The Ballroom, an elaborately designed room with a coffered ceiling gilded in gold, reflects the extravagance of the 1920s.

→ The splendidly ornate exterior and terrace of Cà d'Zan

The court is the focal point of the house, with its marble floors and onyx columns.

← A colonnaded upper passageway inside Cà d'Zan

→

An aerial view of the mansion, with its terrace reaching down to the water

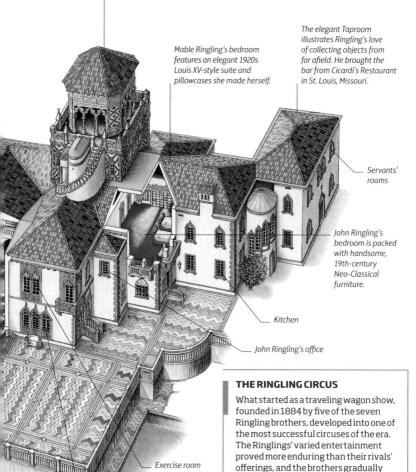

The tower, was lit up when the Ringlings were at home.

Mable Ringling's bedroom features an elegant 1920s Louis XV-style suite and pillowcases she made herself.

The elegant Taproom illustrates Ringling's love of collecting objects from far afield. He brought the bar from Cicardi's Restaurant in St. Louis, Missouri.

Servants' rooms

John Ringling's bedroom is packed with handsome, 19th-century Neo-Classical furniture.

Kitchen

John Ringling's office

Exercise room

The Breakfast room was used mainly for informal family occasions.

THE RINGLING CIRCUS

What started as a traveling wagon show, founded in 1884 by five of the seven Ringling brothers, developed into one of the most successful circuses of the era. The Ringlings' varied entertainment proved more enduring than their rivals' offerings, and the brothers gradually bought up their competitors. Their first director, A. Everett Austin, Jr., established the Circus Museum in 1948. It was the first museum in the country to document the history of the circus. In 2006, the Tibbals Learning Center opened and houses the Howard Bros. Circus Model, a miniature replica of the Ringlings' circus.

Sun worshippers at Siesta Key Beach, on an island off the coast of Sarasota ↑

EXPERIENCE MORE

Sarasota

🅰E4 🚌 🛈1945 Fruitville Rd, Sarasota County; www.visitsarasota.com

This city is sometimes known as Florida's cultural center, perhaps because of circus owner, real estate developer, and art collector John Ringling, who poured money into the area in the early 1900s. Ringling's legacy is seen everywhere, though nowhere more so than in his house (p274) and fine art collection (p272), which are the city's biggest attractions.

Other must-see spots to visit on a trip to Sarasota include the **Sarasota Classic Car Museum**, which is home to over 75 classic cars. Highlights of the permanent collection include a vintage Alfa Romeo, Bentley, Cadillac, Edsel, and Ferrari models. Exhibits rotate through the year.

Set inside the historic Sarasota High School and operated by Ringling College of Art + Design, **Sarasota Art Museum** focuses on 20th and 21st century art with exhibition spaces, an auditorium, and an outdoor sculpture garden. Though there isn't a permanent collection, the temporary shows here are always excellent – exhibitions in 2021 featured German artist Janaina Tschäpe and architect Carl Abbott.

You needn't be a gardener to appreciate the **Marie Selby Botanical Gardens**, the former home of wealthy local residents William and Marie Selby. Set among laurel and banyan trees overlooking Sarasota Bay, the estate was designed in the early 1920s as an escape from the modern world. The gardens have more than 20,000 tropical plants, including a famous collection of orchids and epiphytes. The **Mote Aquarium and Mote Marine Laboratory** is located on City Island, between Lido and Longboat keys. It has a bay walk with an excellent view of the Sarasota skyline, but the real attractions can be found inside. Among the most popular exhibits is a huge shark tank, complete with underwater observation windows, and the exhibit "Otters & Their Waters," featuring North American river otters Huck, Pippi, and Jane.

Sarasota's nearby barrier islands – Longboat Key, Lido Key, and Siesta Key – have superb sandy beaches facing the Gulf of Mexico, and they are understandably popular. Development has been intense, but there are several quieter areas, too. The beach in South Lido Park, on Lido Key, is peaceful during the week and has a pleasant woodland trail. On Siesta Key, the broad Siesta Key Beach is lively at any time. A quieter scene can be found at Turtle Beach. Longboat Key is well-known for its golf courses. Wherever you are, the water-sports are excellent.

> **Sarasota's nearby barrier islands - Longboat Key, Lido Key, and Siesta Key - have superb sandy beaches facing the Gulf of Mexico, and they are understandably popular.**

Did You Know?

Towles Court Artist Colony *(www. towlescourt.com)* in Sarasota hosts monthly art walks.

Sarasota Classic Car Museum

✧ ⓣ 🏛 📍5500 N Tamiami Trail 🕙9am–6pm daily
ⓦsarasotacarmuseum.org

Sarasota Art Museum

✧ ⓣ 🏛 📍1001 S Tamiami Trail 🕙10am–5pm Wed–Mon
ⓦsarasotaartmuseum.org

↑ Vintage cars on display at the Sarasota Classic Car Museum

Marie Selby Botanical Gardens

✧ ⓣ 🏛 📍811 S Palm Ave 🕙10am–5pm daily
ⓦselby.org

Mote Aquarium and Mote Marine Laboratory

✧ ⓣ 🏛 📍1600 Ken Thompson Parkway 🕙9:30am–5pm daily
ⓦmote.org

8

Homosassa Springs Wildlife State Park

🅐E3 📍4150 South Suncoast Blvd, Homosassa 🕙9am–5:30pm daily
ⓦfloridastateparks.org

One of the best places to see manatees is at Homosassa Springs Wildlife State Park, where a floating observatory enables visitors to get up close to the animals. Injured manatees are treated and rehabilitated here before being released back into the wild. There are often half a dozen in the recovery pool, and more outside the park fence in winter: in cold weather manatees are attracted by the warm spring water.

EAT

Owens Fish Camp

A gift to seafood lovers. Have the catches of the day ("Naked Fish") cooked to your liking.

🅐E4 📍516 Burns Ct, Sarasota 🕙Lunch
ⓦowensfishcamp.com

$ $ $

Dry Dock Waterfront Grill

Eat dockside at this diner with great views and fresh seafood. There are choices aplenty beyond fish.

🅐E4 📍412 Gulf of Mexico Dr, Longboat Key
ⓦdrydockwater frontgrill.com

$ $ $

The Cottage

Asian influences feature on the seafood-rich menu, as attested by the tuna tacos and lobster maki roll.

🅐E4 📍153 Avenida Messina, Sarasota 🕙Lunch Sun–Thu
ⓦcottagesiestakey.com

$ $ $

⑨ Crystal River

ⒶE3 🚌 ℹ28 NW US 19, Citrus County; www. crystalriverfl.org

Between January and March, people come to Crystal River to watch the manatees, which gather in herds of up to 300 to bask in the warm local springs. You need to make a reservation with one of the boat operators in the area for an early-morning trip around the **Crystal River National Wildlife Refuge**, which was set up specifically to protect the manatees. Manatees are active only in the very early morning hours, and the clear water makes spotting them easy.

A year-round attraction is the brilliant **Crystal River Archaeological State Park**, a complex of six mounds 2 miles (3 km) west of the town. The site, now a National Historic Landmark, is thought to have been occupied for 1,600 years, from 200 BC to AD 1400, one of the longest continually occupied sites in Florida. An estimated 7,500 Native Americans visited the complex every year for ceremonial purposes.

> Between January and March, people come to Crystal River to watch the manatees, which gather in herds of up to 300 to bask in the warm local springs.

Excavation of 400 of the possible 1,000 graves at the site has also revealed that local tribes had trade links far to the north of Florida.

Climb up to the observation deck for a bird's-eye view of the site. Just below is the main temple mound, built in around AD 600. Beyond, two stelae, or carved ceremonial stones, erected in around AD 440, can be seen flanking two of the site's three burial mounds. These stones are typical of the pre-Columbian cultures of Mesoamerica, but no evidence exists to link them with Crystal River. On the western edge of the site is an area marked by two midden mounds on a midden ridge. A model of the site in the visitor center has examples of the pottery found.

Crystal River National Wildlife Refuge

Ⓐ1502 SE Kings Bay Drive Ⓒ8am–4pm daily (May-Oct: Mon-Fri) Ⓦfws.gov/crystalriver

Crystal River Archaeological State Park

🚻 Ⓐ3400 N Museum Point Ⓒ8am–sunset daily Ⓦfloridastateparks.org

---

⑩ Tarpon Springs

ⒶE4 🚌 ℹ1 N Pinellas Ave #B, Pinellas County; www.tarponspring chamber.com

This town on the Anclote River is famous as a center of Greek culture – the legacy of the immigrant fishermen lured here at the start of the 20th century by the prolific local sponge beds. Visitors will find restaurants specializing in Greek food, an Athens Street, and a Poseidon gift shop.

Alongside Dodecanese Boulevard are the Sponge Docks, which are busy once more – thanks to the recovery of the nearby sponge beds, which were decimated by bacterial blight in the 1940s.

Climbing up the main temple mound in Crystal River Archaeological State Park ↑

↑ Shopping for gifts at the Spong Exchange in Tarpon Springs

Boat trips organized by local fishermen include a demonstration of sponge diving.

The **Spongeorama** museum and shopping village is housed in former dockside sheds, and the Sponge Exchange is an upscale complex with galleries, boutiques, and quaint restaurants.

Two miles (3 km) south rises **St. Nicholas Greek Orthodox Cathedral**. The Byzantine Revival church, a replica of St. Sophia in Istanbul, was erected in 1943 using marble transported from Greece. It is the starting point for the Epiphany Festival.

Spongeorama

🕐 🏠 510 Dodecanese Blvd
🕐 10am–6pm daily
🌐 spongeorama.com

St. Nicholas Greek Orthodox Cathedral

🏠 36 N Pinellas Ave at Orange St 🌐 stnicholastarpon.org

Weeki Wachee Springs

🅰 E3 🏠 6131 Commercial Way, Spring Hill, Junction of US 19 & SR 50, Hernando County 🚌 Brooksville 🕐 9am–5:30pm daily 🌐 weekiwachee.com

This long-standing and quirky theme park is built on one of the largest and deepest freshwater springs in Florida. In the 1940s, former Navy frogman Newton Perry came up with the idea of employing women swimmers to play the impressive part of "live mermaids" while performing a kind of underwater ballet. A theater was built 15 ft (5 m) underwater with strategically placed air pipes for the swimmers to take in air when needed.

Other attractions on site include a water park, an interpretive exhibit on Florida wildlife, and a popular wilderness river cruise that offers the opportunity to see local wildlife, such as bald eagles, turtles, and herons.

Dunedin

🅰 E4 🚌 🛈 301 Main St, Pinellas County; www.visitdunedinfl.com

Dunedin was founded by a Scotsman, John L. Branch, who in 1870 opened a store to supply ships on their way down the Gulf Coast to Key West. Passing sea and rail routes brought trade and prosperity, and this soon attracted a number of his compatriots. Dunedin's Scottish heritage is still expressed in its annual Highland Games festival held in late March or early April.

The renovated properties on and around Main Street have the flavor of early 20th-century, small-town Florida. The **History Museum** in the former railroad station houses photographs and artifacts from the town's early days. Nearby Railroad Avenue is now part of the Pinellas Trail, a paved walking and cycling path running for 47 miles (76 km) from Tarpon Springs to St. Petersburg.

History Museum

♿ 🏠 349 Main St 🕐 11am–4pm Tue–Sat, noon–4pm Sun 🌐 dunedinmuseum.org

> ### THE MANATEE IN FLORIDA
>
> Once plentiful, manatees were hunted for meat and sport until the early 1900s; since then, habitat destruction and boats have done more damage. Numbers are recovering – from 2,500 a decade ago to around 6,300 in 2020. The manatee grows to an average length of 10 ft (3 m). This gentle creature lives in shallow coastal waters, rivers, and springs, spending about five hours a day feeding – seagrass is its favorite food.

A mermaid performer at Weeki Wachee Springs State Park

13

Hillsborough River

🅰E4 🅷Hillsborough County

Extending through the countryside northeast of Tampa, the Hillsborough River provides a pleasant respite from the hustle and bustle of the city. It is flanked on both sides by dense backwoods of live oak, cypress, magnolia, and mangrove trees, which once covered great swathes of Florida's terrain.

One of the best ways to experience the Hillsborough River is by canoe: **Canoe Escape** organizes trips along a stretch of the river about 15 minutes' drive from downtown Tampa. Located just beyond the city line, the area is surprisingly wild, and there is a good chance of spotting a great variety of wildlife, including herons, egrets, alligators, turtles, and otters. Canoeing conditions are ideal for beginners. Visitors can choose from three main itineraries, each of which covers about 5 miles (8 km). All journeys involve roughly two hours' paddling, which allows plenty of time to absorb the surroundings. Longer day trips are also available.

A section of the river is protected as **Hillsborough River State Park**. Canoeing is a popular way to explore this stretch; there are also walking trails, and the chance to swim and fish. The park has a large and popular campground, which is open all year round, and there are a range of great picnic sites.

Developed in 1936, the Hillsborough River State Park became one of Florida's earliest state parks partly due to the historic significance of Fort Foster, built during the Second Seminole War (p45) to guard a bridge at the confluence of the Hillsborough River and Blackwater Creek. The fort and bridge have been reconstructed, and a battle is reenacted here annually in December. Tours visit the fort every weekend and on holidays; a shuttle bus runs to it from the park's entrance.

Canoe Escape

 🅐John B. Sargeant Park 12702, US 301, Thonotosassa ⏱Times vary, check website 🆆canoeescape.com

Hillsborough River State Park

 🅐15402 US 301 N, 12 miles (19 km) NE of Tampa ⏱8am–sunset daily 🆆floridastateparks.org

14

Koreshan State Historic Site

🅰E5 🅐3800 Corkscrew Rd, Estero, 14 miles (23 km) S of Fort Myers ⏱8am–sunset daily 🆆floridastateparks. org

In 1894, Dr. Cyrus Teed had a vision telling him to change his name to Koresh (Hebrew for Cyrus) and to move to southwest Florida, where he was to establish a great utopian city. He chose this beautiful location on the Estero River, where members of the Koreshan Unity sect pursued a communal lifestyle, with equal rights for women and shared ownership of property.

The Koreshan Unity sect had a mere 250 followers at its peak, and membership dwindled after Teed's death in 1908. The last four members donated the site to Florida in 1961. Twelve of the sect's 60 buildings and their gardens survive; they include Cyrus Teed's home.

The park has canoe and nature trails, camping facilities, opportunities for fresh- and saltwater fishing, and also arranges guided tours.

15

Caladesi Island State Park

🅰E4 🅐1 Causeway Blvd ⏱8am–sunset daily 🆆floridastateparks.org

One of the few unspoiled islands on the Gulf coast, Caladesi Island State Park has 3 miles (5 km) of pristine beach fronting the Gulf of Mexico. Shore birds and sea turtles grace its sands. The beach gives way to dunes fringed by sea oats, and there is a 3-mile (5-km) nature trail through cypress and mangrove woods.

It is reached by a 20-minute passenger ferry journey from the largely undeveloped

↑ Paddling a canoe on the tranquil, wildlife-rich Hillsborough River

The museum at the Edison Winter Home and the estate's guest house *(inset)* ↑

Next to the Edison home (and viewable on the same ticket) is the small estate bought in 1916 by the car manufacturer Henry Ford, who was great friends with Edison. The rooms have been faithfully re-created with period furnishings and still have the homey air favored by Clara Ford. Some early Ford cars are displayed in the garage.

Edison and Ford Winter Estates

⊛ ⊛ 🏠 🚗 2350 McGregor Blvd 🕙 9am–5:30pm daily 🌐 edisonfordwinter estates.org

barrier island of **Honeymoon Island State Park**, an osprey nesting site 3 miles (5 km) north of Dunedin, or from Clearwater Beach *(p264)*.

Honeymoon Island State Park

⊛ ⊛ 🏠 🚗 Route 586, 3 miles (5 km) NW of Dunedin 🕙 8am–sunset daily 🌐 floridastateparks.org

---

16

Fort Myers

🅰 E5 🚗🚆🚌 🛈 11000 Terminal Access Rd #8640, Lee County; www.fort myers-sanibel.com

The approach to Fort Myers across the Caloosahatchee River is stunning, a fine introduction to a city that still has an air of old-time Florida. Following the sweep of the river is McGregor Boulevard, lined with ranks of royal

palms. The old downtown area around First Street, with its wide variety of shops and restaurants, is worth exploring; a trolley service runs regularly through the downtown area linking the main sights.

It was inventor Thomas Edison (1847–1931) who put Fort Myers on the map in the 1880s, when it was just a small fishing village, and his house – part of the **Edison and Ford Winter Estates** – is Fort Myers' most enduring attraction. Edison built the estate in 1886, and the house, laboratory, and splendid botanical gardens are much as he left them. The two-story home and adjoining guest house were among the first prefabricated buildings in the US, built in sections to Edison's specifications in Maine, and shipped to Fort Myers by schooner. Edison was the holder of more than 1,000 patents, and his laboratory, on the opposite side of McGregor Boulevard from the house, contains some of his original equipment.

17

De Soto National Memorial

🅰E4 **🏠8300 De Soto Memorial Hwy, Bradenton** **🕐9am–5pm daily** **🌐nps. gov/deso**

Situated 5 miles (8 km) west of central Bradenton *(p285)*, the De Soto National Memorial commemorates the landing near here in 1539 of the Spanish explorer Hernando de Soto. He and his 600 men embarked on an epic four-year, 4,000-mile (6,500-km) trek into the southeastern US in search of gold. They reached the Mississippi, but the trek was disastrous, resulting in the death of de Soto and half his army.

A monument recalls the luckless explorers and marks the start of the De Soto Trail, which follows part of the route they took during their fateful expedition in the 16th century. The park also has a fascinating replica of de Soto's base camp. This is staffed by costumed volunteers, who give a memorable insight into the daily routines of the Spanish conquistadors. A visitor center has a museum, a bookstore, and exhibits of 16th-century weapons and armor. There is also a half-mile (1-km) nature trail through mangroves.

18

Gamble Plantation Historic State Park

🅰E4 **🏠3708 Patten Ave, Ellenton, Manatee County** **🕐Times vary, check website** **🌐floridastate parks.org**

This state park is home to the Gamble Mansion, the only antebellum home left in southern Florida. Built for Major Robert Gamble between 1845–50, the whitewashed mansion on the main road into Bradenton is regarded as a sight of significant architectural importance. Nearly 200 enslaved people lived and worked here in the early 1850s before the plantation was sold in 1859. The property was bought by the United Daughters of the Confederacy and given to the state of Florida in 1925.

The Gamble Mansion is furnished just as it was in the past, and the garden, flourishing with live oak trees draped with Spanish moss, is pure Deep South. Only a fraction of the sugar plantation's original 3,500 acres (1,416 ha) remains, however. The site of the enslaved peoples' quarters, for instance, is now a school.

Did You Know?

Frank Lloyd Wright laid the groundwork for today's sustainable design movement.

19

Florida Southern College

🅰E4 **🏠111 Lake Hollingsworth Dr, Lakeland, Pol County** **🚉🚌Lakeland** **🕐9:30am–4:30pm daily** **🌐flsouthern.edu**

This small college holds the world's largest collection of buildings designed by Frank Lloyd Wright. Amazingly, the college president managed to persuade Wright (one of the most eminent architects of his day), to design the campus at Lakeland with the promise of little more than the opportunity to express his ideas – and payment when the money could be raised. Work began in 1938 on what Wright, already famous as the founder of organic architecture, termed his "child of the sun."

His aim of blending buildings with their natural surroundings made special use of glass to bring the outdoor light to the interiors. The original plan was for 18 buildings, but only seven had been completed by the time Wright died in 1959 – five were finished or added later.

The Annie Pfeiffer Chapel is a particularly fine expression of Wright's ideas. Windows of stained glass break the monotony of the building blocks, and the entire edifice is topped by a spectacular tower in place of the traditional steeple; Wright called it a "jewel box."

As a whole, the campus exudes the light and airy feel that Wright sought to achieve. The buildings are linked to each other by the Esplanades – a covered walkway, stretching for 1.5 miles (2 km), in which light, shade, and variations in height draw attention from one building to the next.

Visitors can wander around the campus at any time, but the interiors can be explored only during the week. The Sharp Family Tourism and Education Center (open 9:30am–4:30pm daily) is a visitor center and exhibition space for the permanent display of drawings and

↑ A family enjoying the exhibits in the Bishop Museum of Science and Nature, Bradenton

furniture by Wright, as well as photographs of the building work. It also offers self-guided and docent tours.

___

⑳
Bradenton

🅰E4 ✈🚌 ℹ**1 Haben Blvd, Palmetto, Manatee County; www.bradentongulf islands.com**

Bradenton is best known as the home of the Nick Bollettieri Tennis Academy, the renowned school that has nurtured the early promise of such world-famous tennis stars as Andre Agassi and Pete Sampras.

The local beaches are a big attraction, but a couple of sights deserve a visit before heading off to the beach. **Manatee Village Historical Park** recounts the story of the Florida frontier a century ago through a fascinating collection of restored buildings. These include a boathouse, a general store, and an early settler's house, and all have been furnished as they would have originally looked.

The **Bishop Museum of Science and Nature** is both

educational and fun. "Florida from Stone Age to Space Age" is the theme, and exhibits range from dinosaur dioramas to life-size replicas of 16th-century Spanish-style buildings and early cars. Laser shows add excitement to the Bishop Planetarium. The Parker Manatee Rehabilitation Habitat provides a temporary home for manatees that will be released back into the wild after having received medical treatment.

Manatee Village Historical Park
🏠1404 Manatee Ave E
🕐9am-4pm Mon-Fri (2nd and 4th Sat of every month)
🌐manateevillage.org

Bishop Museum of Science and Nature
⊛ 🏠201 10th St W 🕐10am-5pm Tue-Sat, noon-5pm Sun 🚫Nov: 1st Sat 🌐south floridamuseum.org

🔍 HIDDEN GEM
Anna Maria Island

Two bridges link Bradenton to Anna Maria Island, whose sandy shoreline, backed by dunes, attracts many surfers. There are a few small resorts and a picturesque pier.

←
Shaded trail along the Manatee River in the De Soto National Memorial

21 Myakka River State Park

E4 🏞 13207 SR 72, 9 miles (14 km) E of Sarasota 🕗 8am-sunset daily 🌐 floridastateparks.org

In the Myakka River State Park you can imagine how the region must have looked to its first settlers. Dense oak, palm thickets, pine flatwoods, and an expanse of dry prairie are interspersed with marshland, many swamps, and lakes.

The parkland's 28,000 acres (11,300 ha), which stretch along the Myakka River and around Upper Myakka Lake, form an outstanding wildlife sanctuary. More than 200 species of bird have been recorded here, including egrets, blue herons, vultures, and ibis, all of which are plentiful, as well as much rarer ospreys, bald eagles, and wild turkeys. Alligators and deer can also be seen. Observation platforms, from which you can view the wildlife, are dotted throughout the park. Ambitious explorers can

→

The Venice Little Theater, built in the late 1920s

take to the park's 39 miles (63 km) of marked hiking trails or 15 miles (24 km) of bridle trails. Alternatively, there are guided tours by trolley between December and May, the best time to visit, and narrated river tours by airboat all year round.

22 Venice

E5 🚌 ℹ 597 S Tamiami Trail, Sarasota County; www.visitvenicefl.org

Situated slightly off the beaten track, this sleepy seaside town is awash with flowers and palm trees, which line the center of the main shopping street, Venice Avenue. The town has a fine collection of carefully restored historic buildings, including

the Venice Little Theater on Tampa Avenue, which dates from 1927.

Caspersen Beach, fringed by sea oats and palmettos, lies at the southern end of Harbor Drive. It is a popular place to swim, to fish, and to collect shells, although the main shelling beaches are farther south (p270). The area is famous for the fossilized sharks' teeth brought in by the tide. Brohard Paw Park on Harbor Drive South is a haven for dog lovers.

23 Gasparilla Island

E5 🚌 Venice ℹ 5800 Gasparilla Rd, Boca Grande, Charlotte County and Lee County; www.bocagrande chamber.org

Colonized by fishermen, and later by the wealthy who were fleeing northern winters, Gasparilla is a perfect island

← The expansive wetlands of the Myakka River State Park, and a little blue heron *(inset)*

hideaway midway between Sarasota and Fort Myers.

Activity is centered around the community of Boca Grande, which is joined by a causeway to the mainland. The restored former railroad station and the grand Gasparilla Inn are eloquent reminders of times past. Many old wooden buildings have been saved and freshly painted, giving the place a pleasant, tropical feel. Fishing has been big business here for a long time – Boca Grande is known as the "tarpon capital of the world" – and there are a number of marinas where you can arrange boat trips, some of which go to nearby barrier islands *(p270)*. Another great way to explore is to follow the bike trail that runs down Gasparilla Island.

At the island's southern tip, the **Gasparilla Island State Park** has some lovely quiet beaches where visitors can fish and swim as well as hunt for shells. A squat late 19th-century lighthouse has a museum and visitor center, but its function is fulfilled by the more modern Range Light.

Gasparilla Island State Park

⊛ 🏠 880 Belcher Rd, Boca Grande 🕐 8am–sunset daily 🌐 florida stateparks.org

㉔
Arcadia

🄰 E4 🚌 🛈 16 S Volusia Ave, De Soto County; www. desotochamber.net

It is a pleasure to stroll around the old cattle ranching town of Arcadia. Although these days local cowboys are more likely to ride around in a pick-up truck than on horseback, the horse is still an integral part of the local culture. Cowboy fever reaches a peak twice a year, in March and July, when competitors and devotees come for the All-Florida Championship Rodeo, the oldest rodeo in the state.

Arcadia's flamboyant architecture recalls the prosperity and confidence of the 1920s. The best examples are the Florida Mediterranean-style Koch Arcade Building, on West Oak Street, and the Schlossberg Plaza Hotel building, on West Magnolia Street.

Many earlier buildings were destroyed by a fire in 1905. Only a few from the late 1800s survive, and these can be seen by arrangement with the Chamber of Commerce.

㉕
Babcock Ranch Eco Tours

🄰 E5 🏠 8502 FL-31, Punta Gorda, Charlotte County 🕐 9:30am–3pm daily 🌐 babcockrancheco tours.com

The huge Crescent B Ranch was originally owned by Pittsburgh lumber baron E.V. Babcock, who bled the cypress swamp for timber in the 1930s. It is still run by the wealthy Babcock family, and part of the 90,000-acre (36,420-ha) working ranch is open as the Babcock Ranch Eco Tours. During 90-minute trips led by trained naturalists, swamp buggies take visitors through deep woods and a dense patch of cypress swamp, offering the opportunity to see a wide variety of wildlife. Panthers, which are bred successfully here, are in a specially designed paddock; alligators cruise just a short distance away. The ranch's herds of horses and Cracker cattle are also on view. These tours are very popular and must be reserved in advance.

> **Cowboy fever reaches a peak twice a year at Arcadia, in March and July, when competitors and devotees come for the All-Florida Championship Rodeo.**

THE EVERGLADES AND THE KEYS

The mainland of southwest Florida was not settled until the mid-19th century, with the establishment of what is now the thriving coastal resort of Naples. The first road to open up the area by linking the Atlantic and Gulf coasts was the Tamiami Trail, built in 1928. Pioneer camps located off it, such as Everglades City and Chokoloskee, mark the western entrance of the Everglades National Park. This broad expanse of wetland, dotted with tree islands, possesses a peculiar beauty and is a paradise for its thrilling and prolific wildlife.

Running southwest off the tip of the Florida peninsula are the Keys, a chain of jewel-like islands protected by North America's only coral reef. In the early 20th century, Henry Flagler's Overseas Railroad was built to connect the mainland and the Keys, all the way to the southernmost settlement at Key West. The railroad has since disappeared and has been replaced by the Overseas Highway –the route of one of the country's classic road trips. The farther south you travel, the easier it is to agree with the saying that the Keys are more about a state of mind than a geographical location.

THE EVERGLADES AND THE KEYS

Must Sees

1. Everglades National Park
2. Key West

Experience More

3. Naples
4. Marco Island
5. Big Cypress Swamp
6. Key Largo
7. John Pennekamp Coral Reef State Park
8. Islamorada
9. Indian and Lignumvitae Keys
10. Marathon
11. Pigeon Key
12. Lower Keys
13. Miccosukee Indian Village
14. Ah-Tah-Thi-Ki Museum
15. Florida Keys National Wildlife Refuges
16. Dry Tortugas National Park
17. Tavernier

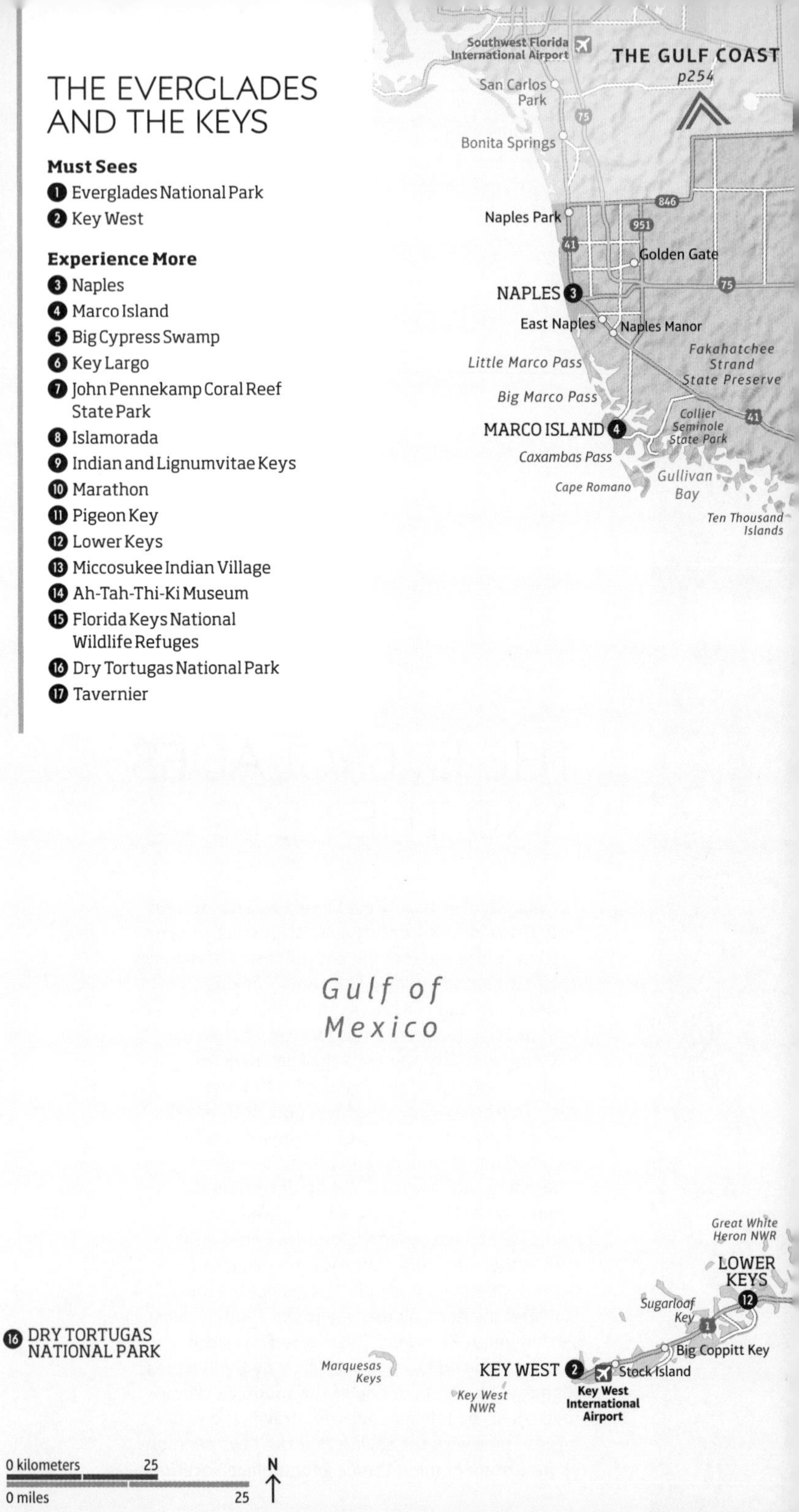

Southwest Florida International Airport
THE GULF COAST p254
San Carlos Park
75
Bonita Springs
846
Naples Park
951
41
Golden Gate
NAPLES 3
East Naples
Naples Manor
Fakahatchee Strand State Preserve
Little Marco Pass
Big Marco Pass
MARCO ISLAND 4
Collier Seminole State Park
Caxambas Pass
Cape Romano
Gullivan Bay
Ten Thousand Islands
Gulf of Mexico
Great White Heron NWR
LOWER KEYS 12
Sugarloaf Key
1
Big Coppitt Key
16 DRY TORTUGAS NATIONAL PARK
Marquesas Keys
KEY WEST 2
Stock Island
Key West NWR
Key West International Airport
0 kilometers 25
0 miles 25
N

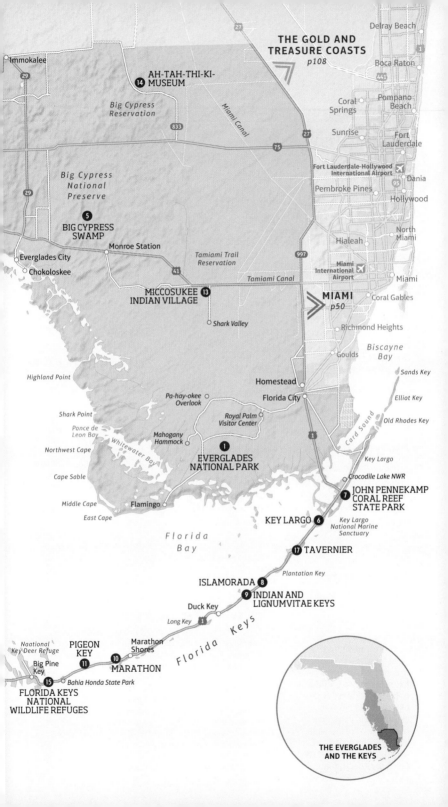

EXPERIENCE **The Everglades and the Keys**

EVERGLADES NATIONAL PARK

⌖F6 **ℹ40001 State Road, Homestead** **Ⓦnps.gov/ever**

The Everglades are one of the most immediate and enduring images of Florida, and the Everglades National Park is the ideal place to explore this famous natural wonder. There are trails for walking and cycling as well as plenty of opportunities for boat trips.

Everglades City

ℹ815 Oyster Bar Lane; (239) 695-3311

This city is the self-proclaimed "Gateway to 10,000 Islands," and is a common starting point for kayakers who want to explore the national park. Kayak fishing is a particularly popular activity in this part of the Everglades, and exciting excursions through the backcountry feel like a behind-the-scenes glimpse of nature. There are a smattering of perfectly fine accommodation and eating options for overnight (or longer) stays.

Royal Palm Visitor Center

⌂40001 State Road
🕑9am–4:15pm daily
Ⓦnps.gov

The highly informative Royal Palm Visitor Center is a great place to learn more about the national park during your trip to this unique landscape.

Two nearby boardwalk trails are located on the site of Florida's first state park, created in 1916. The popular Anhinga Trail, passing over Taylor Slough, contains slightly deeper water than the surrounding terrain; in the dry winter months it attracts wildlife to drink. Its open site provides better photo

---

THE EVERGLADES UNDER THREAT

The Everglades' ecosystem and Florida's human population are in direct competition for this priceless commodity: irrigation canals and roads disrupt the natural through-flow of water from Lake Okeechobee (p128), and the drainage of land for development has also had detrimental effects on wildlife. Agriculture in central Florida uses vast amounts of water, and high levels of chemical fertilizers promote the unnatural growth of swamp vegetation. The state and federal governments are studying how best to protect the area and return water flow to its natural state.

← Sunrise at Long Pine Key in the Everglades National Park

 INSIDER TIP
The Two Seasons

The seasons in the Everglades is split into two polar opposites: the wet season and the dry season. The wet season lasts through summer and fall, and visitors should expect a lot of insects at this time. The dry season lasts from around December through to mid-May.

opportunities and fewer insects, but the intense sun can be hazardous. Alligators generally congregate near the beginning of the trail, and a wide range of fauna, including raccoons, deer, and the splendid anhinga bird, can also be seen. The Ernest F. Coe Visitor Center is nearby.

③
Long Pine Key

⌂ **Main Park Rd** Ⓦ **nps.gov**

The camp ground here occupies a stunning position and is one of the main reasons that people stop at Long Pine Key. Several pleasant, shady trails lead off from it, but remember not to stray from the path: the limestone bedrock contains "solution holes" created by rain eroding away the rock. These can be deep and difficult to spot.

This area takes its name from a large stand of slash pines that are unique to southern Florida. Insect- and rot-proof, they have been a popular building material for many years.

↑ A great blue heron, one of the many birds of the Everglades

0 kilometers   25
0 miles   25
N ↑

Must See

Carnestown
Big Cypress National Preserve
Monroe Station
997
① Everglades City
Chokoloskee
41
Olympia Heights
Shark Valley ⑥
Kendale Lakes
Everglades National Park
South Miami Heights
Highland Point
Pa-hay-okee Overlook ⑦
Homestead
Ernest F. Coe Visitor Center
Shark Point
Long Pine ③ Key
② Royal Palm Visitor Center
Mahogany ⑤ Hammock Trail
⑧ Main Park Road
Cape Sable
9336
1
④
Flamingo
Key Largo
Florida Bay
Florida Keys
1

④

Flamingo

🏠 1 Flamingo Lodge Hwy, Homestead; www.flamingo everglades.com

The settlement of Flamingo lies 38 miles (60 km) from the main park entrance. In the late 1800s, it was a remote outpost and hideaway for hunters and fishermen. These days, a few park rangers are the only long-term residents.

Flamingo's position on Florida Bay offers visitors a wide choice of activities such as hiking, fishing, boating, and watching wildlife. An over-night stay at the campground is recommended – especially for bird-watching, which is most rewarding in the early morning and late afternoon. Apart from countless species of birds and animals, the bay and creeks around Flamingo contain manatees *(p279)* and the endangered American crocodile. This is easily distinguished from

↑ A tour boat from Flamingo taking visitors down the scenic Buttonwood Canal

the alligator by its gray-green color and the fact that the teeth of both jaws show when its mouth is shut. You may spot one in this area. Flamingo's visitor center provides wildlife guides and information about local ranger-led activities. These include evening slideshows and talks, and day-time "slough-slogs" – intrepid walks through the swamp.

⑤

Mahogany Hammock Trail

🚗 20 miles (32 km) from Ernest Coe Visitor Center
🌐 nps.gov

The popular – yet unspoiled – 0.5-mile (800-m) Mahogany Hammock Trail leads through one of the park's largest hammocks. This area is home to a wide variety of fauna and flora, including the largest living mahogany tree in the US and huge bromeliads. The jungle-like vegetation is especially dense during the wet season (mid-May through November).

⑥

Shark Valley

🏠 Highway 41; www. nps.gov

Shark Valley is a much more hospitable place than it sounds, and has a well-paved, 15 mile (24 km) looped trail. The wildlife that most people come to see is very accessible, with a

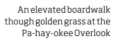
→ An elevated boardwalk though golden grass at the Pa-hay-okee Overlook

SAFETY TIPS

Protection against biting insects is vital, especially during the summer months. Follow the advice given by rangers and on information boards, and respect all wildlife: alligators can jump and move quickly on land; some trees and shrubs like the Brazilian pepper tree are poisonous, as are some caterpillars and snakes. If planning to go off the beaten path, let someone know your itinerary. Always drive slowly: much wildlife can be seen from the road - and may also venture onto it.

diversity of birdlife and 'gators that nap close to the trail. It's perfect for a bike ride – the only other traffic you'll encounter is the slow-moving trolley service, which runs around four times a day.

Pa-hay-okee Overlook

⏹13 miles (12 km) from Ernest Coe Visitor Center
Ⓦnps.gov

The open expanse of sawgrass prairie that can be viewed from the elevated Pa-hay-okee Overlook is the epitome of the Everglades. The observation tower here is a perfect spot from which to watch the fluid light changes, especially in the late afternoon. Tree islands or hammocks break the horizon, and you will see wading birds, hawks, and snail kites, whose only food – the apple snail – lives on the sawgrass. This prairie is also home to cattails and other wetland plants.

Main Park Road

⏹Main Park Rd
Ⓦnps.gov

A popular excursion in Everglades National Park involves stopping at the different boardwalk trails along the Main Park Road (Route 9336). There are some less-visited trails located off the southern part of the road, between Mahogany Hammock and Flamingo; try the West Lake Trail or the Snake Bight Trail, which ends on Florida Bay. Information boards abound to help you identify the flora and fauna. Make sure to bring insect repellent and protection against the sun.

 Must See

TOP 3 ACTIVITIES IN THE EVERGLADES

Hiking
There are hiking trails for casual hikers as well as seasoned pros.

Kayaking or Canoeing
Some backcountry trails can be done in an hour, while others need a whole week.

Cycling
As well as paved routes, there are shaded pineland trails through beautiful wooded areas.

The open expanse of sawgrass prairie that can be viewed from the elevated Pa-hay-okee Overlook is the epitome of the Everglades.

THE ECOSYSTEM OF THE EVERGLADES

The Everglades is a vast sheet river system – the overspill from Lake Okeechobee that moves across a flat bed of peat-covered limestone. Some 200 miles (322 km) long and up to 50 miles (80 km) wide, its depth rarely exceeds 3 ft (1 m). Tropical air and sea currents act on this temperate zone to create unique combinations of flora. Clumps of vegetation, such as cypress domes and bayheads, break the tract of sawgrass prairie. There are hundreds of animal species – some 350 species of birds, for which the area is particularly renowned.

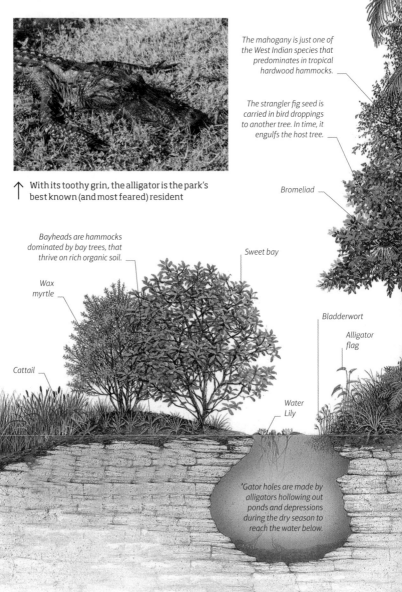

↑ With its toothy grin, the alligator is the park's best known (and most feared) resident

The mahogany is just one of the West Indian species that predominates in tropical hardwood hammocks.

The strangler fig seed is carried in bird droppings to another tree. In time, it engulfs the host tree.

Bromeliad

Bayheads are hammocks dominated by bay trees, that thrive on rich organic soil.

Sweet bay

Wax myrtle

Bladderwort

Alligator flag

Cattail

Water Lily

'Gator holes are made by alligators hollowing out ponds and depressions during the dry season to reach the water below.

Royal Palm

The wading Great
Blue Heron perched
on a branch

Hammocks or tree islands are
areas of elevated land found
in freshwater prairies.

The gumbo-limbo's bark
is red and peeling, hence its
nickname the "tourist tree."

Red mangrove trees
are recognized by their
distinctive roots.

Saw palmetto

Peat

Did You Know?

In South Florida, some
Great Blue Herons have
plummage which is
completely white.

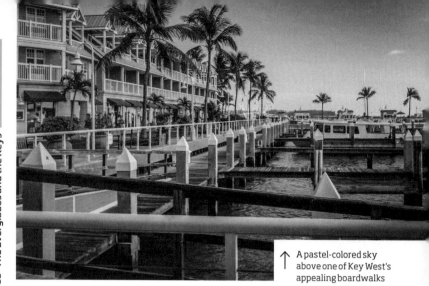

↑ A pastel-colored sky above one of Key West's appealing boardwalks

2

KEY WEST

 F7 ⊠⊟⊟ *i* 402 Wall St; www.fla-keys.com

The southernmost settlement in the continental US, Key West is a city like no other. Most of the sights are either on or within two or three blocks of Duval Street, which links the Gulf of Mexico with the Atlantic, and is the main axis of Old Key West. Take the Conch Train or Old Town Trolley tour, rent a bicycle, or just wander around the back streets. In the south of the island, there are plenty of beautiful, sandy beaches.

1

Fort East Martello Museum

🏛 3501 S Roosevelt Blvd
🕙 10am–4pm daily
🌐 kwahs.org

Located in the east of the island, the East Martello tower was begun in 1861 to protect

Did You Know?

Beloved author Judy Blume is a long-time resident of Key West.

Fort Zachary's defensive position. It was never completed, because its design quickly became outmoded.

Today, the squat tower is an informative museum, opened by the Key West Art and Historical Society in 1950. The museum provides visitors with an excellent introduction to Key West and its checkered past. Everything is included here, from stories about Key West's many literary connections, to the island's changing commercial history. Visitors can also see one of the flimsy rafts used by Cubans to flee Castro's regime (p47).

The tower itself offers fine views over the island, and houses works of art by a number of local artists.

2

Fort Zachary Taylor Historic State Site

🏛 Southard St 📞 (305) 292-6713 🕙 8am–sunset daily

As part of the national coastal defense system begun in the mid-19th century, this brick fort was completed in 1866. During the Civil War, Union troops were stationed here

THE BUSINESS OF WRECKING

In the late 1700s, the waters off the Keys were fished mainly by Bahamians of British descent, who patrolled the reef in order to salvage shipwrecks. In this way, goods from around the world ended up in the Keys, ranging from basics such as timber to luxury goods like lace, wine, and silver. This scavenging was known as "wrecking." It grew so popular that in 1825 an act of the US Congress legislated for tighter control and decreed that only US residents could have salvage rights.

to keep the island loyal to the north. Originally, the three-story fort had toilets that were flushed by the tides.

Today, the fort houses a museum with a fine collection of Civil War artifacts. Visitors can also explore the grounds and observation deck. Nearby is Key West's best public beach, which has shady picnic areas.

③

Hemingway Home

☐ 907 Whitehead St ☐ 9am–5pm daily ☐ hemingwayhome.com

Probably the town's major (and most hyped) attraction, this Spanish colonial-style house built of coral rock is where Ernest Hemingway lived from 1931 to 1940. Above the carriage house is the room where the novelist penned several works; *To Have and Have Not* was the only book set in Key West. Hemingway's library and mementos from his travels are displayed, as are memorabilia such as the cigar-maker's chair upon which he sat and wrote. Guides describe the hard-living writer's nonliterary passions of fishing and hell-raising in Sloppy Joe's *(p302)*. Descendants of his six-toed cats still prowl around the house and its luxuriant garden.

④

Key West Lighthouse

☐ 938 Whitehead St ☐ (305) 294-0012 ☐ 10am–4pm daily

Across the road from Hemingway House stands the town's lighthouse, built in 1848. The keeper's cottage at its foot houses a modest museum, which contains artifacts relating to the lighthouse and other areas of local history.

The greatest attraction at this site is the tower itself. Make the 88-step climb for panoramic views across the island and out over the ocean, as well as the chance to step inside and look through the old lens, once capable of beaming light some 25 miles (40 km) out to sea.

↑ The pristine tower of Key West's lighthouse, wreathed in foliage

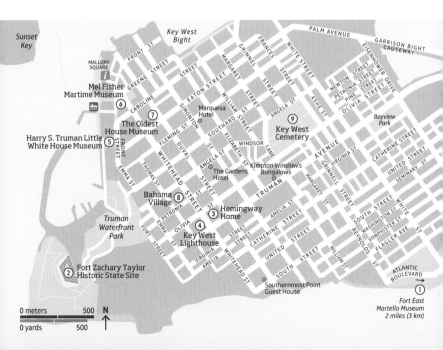

STAY

Marquesa Hotel

The four buildings that comprise this boutique hotel date back to the 19th century. They're built around two pools surrounded by lush foliage.

⌂ 600 Fleming St
ⓦ marquesa.com

⑤⑤⑤

Southernmost Point Guest House

The house itself is well over a century old, and its half-dozen units are cozy, with outdoor patios, hammocks, and a small pool. Breakfast is served al fresco on the sunny veranda.

⌂ 1327 Duval St
ⓦ southernmost point.com

⑤⑤⑤

Kimpton Winslow's Bungalows

This larger guest house has a choice of styles to enjoy, with motel-style units around the pool or individual cottages. The buzz of Duval Street is nearby, but is not intrusive.

⌂ 725 Truman Ave
ⓦ kimptonkeywest.com

⑤⑤⑤

The Gardens Hotel

Once a private estate with botanical gardens, plenty of greenery remains here. Each of the 21 rooms features hardwood floors and four-poster beds.

⌂ 526 Angela St
ⓦ gardenshotel.com

⑤⑤⑤

↑ The impressive exterior of the Harry S. Truman Little White House Museum

⑤

Harry S. Truman Little White House Museum

⌂ 111 Front St Ⓞ 9:30am–4:30pm daily ⓦ truman littlewhitehouse.com

This comparatively modest home was built in 1890 for naval officers, but is best known for being the winter White House of President Harry S. Truman (from 1946 to 1952). It's been intermittently used by presidents and former presidents ever since, and was also the location of peace talks between the presidents of Armenia and Azerbaijan in 2001. Tours take place in the main restored rooms of the house, amid an immense array of memorabilia, while guides offer entertaining stories about Truman's life in Key West.

⑥

Mel Fisher Maritime Museum

⌂ 200 Greene St Ⓞ 10am–4pm Tue–Sun ⓦ mel fisher.com

A plain stone exterior belies the opulence of this museum's treasures. The late Mr. Fisher grabbed the headlines in 1985 when he discovered the wrecks of the Spanish galleons *Nuestra Señora de Atocha* and *Santa Margarita*. Inside were 47 tons of gold and silver bars, and 70 lbs (32 kg) of raw emeralds that sank with them in 1622.

Items on display include jewelry, coins, and crucifixes, and the story of the salvage operation is also told.

⑦

The Oldest House Museum

⌂ 322 Duval St Ⓞ 10am–4pm Thu–Mon ⓦ oldest housemuseum.com

Originally the home of, Francis B. Watlington, captain of a

←

An antique diver's helmet, on display in the Mel Fisher Maritime Museum

crew of wreckers, this is thought to be the oldest house in Key West. Built in 1829, its design reveals some rather idiosyncratic maritime influences, such as the hatch used for ventilation in the roof. The house is stuffed with nautical bric-a-brac and documents concerning wrecking – the industry that first made Key West (and Captain Watlington) rich. Visitors are greeted by volunteer staff, whose anecdotes make the house's history come alive.

Don't miss the backyard kitchen house, the oldest of the few examples that still remain in the Keys. Located away from the main building, it minimized the risk of fire and helped lower the temperature in the rest of the house.

KEY WEST ARCHITECTURE

The architecture of Key West is primarily striking for its simplicity, a response to the hot climate, and the limited materials available – principally salvaged or imported wood. Early 19th-century "conch" houses were often built by ships' carpenters who introduced elements they had seen on their travels. From the Bahamas came devices to increase shade and ventilation against the Florida sun. Later, Classical Revivalism filtered in from the north, while the late 1800s Victorian style introduced a decorative influence. Key West's prosperous inhabitants favored extravagant gingerbread details, but carvings also adorn humbler dwellings. Since the town's architectural legacy was properly acknowledged in the 1970s, many houses have been renovated, but their essential flavor remains.

North America. The typical shotgun houses have largely escaped the enthusiastic renovations found elsewhere.

Key West Cemetery

 701 Passover Lane
📞 (305) 292-8177 ⏰ 7am-7pm daily (winter: to 6pm)

Due to the proximity of the limestone bedrock and water table, most of the tombs here are above ground. There are separate areas for Jews and Roman Catholics, while many of the Cuban crypts are topped with a statue of a chicken, probably associated with the Santería religion. There is even a special burial area devoted to pets.

A statue commemorates the loss of 252 crewmen on the battleship USS *Maine*, sunk in Havana's harbor at the onset of the Spanish-American War *(p44)*. Stroll around to read the witty inscriptions, "I told you I was sick" among others. Many of the town's early settlers were known by their first names or nicknames, and this informality followed them to their graves. There are references to Bunny, Shorty, Bean, and so forth.

---

⑧

Bahama Village

 Petronia St

Named after Key West's earliest settlers, this is a historic neighborhood on the western fringe of the old town. Life here is lived outside, with streetside domino games and chickens wandering freely – a taste of the Caribbean in

↑ Cyclists pedaling through the colorful streets of Bahama Village

A SHORT WALK
KEY WEST

Distance 1.5 miles (2 km) **Time** 25 minutes

Key West is a magnet for people who want to leave the rest of Florida, and even America, behind. This is a place to join in with locals busy dropping out, and to indulge in the laid-back, tropical lifestyle.

First recorded in 1513, the island soon became a haven first for pirates and then for "wreckers," both of whom preyed on passing merchant ships and their precious cargos. Key West grew to be the most prosperous city in Florida, and the opportunistic lifestyle on offer lured a steady stream of settlers from the Americas, the Caribbean, and Europe. Visitors will find their legacy in the island's unique architecture, cuisine, and spirit. A large LGBT+ community, writers, and New-Agers are among the more recent arrivals who have added to Key West's cultural cocktail.

The opulent 19th-century **The Curry Mansion** reflects the wealth of Key West's wreck captains.

DUVAL STREET

GREENE STREET

CAROLINE STREET

Sloppy Joe's was Ernest Hemingway's favorite haunt. The bar moved here from its former site on Greene Street in 1935.

START

WHITEHEAD STREET

Audubon House, built in the 1840s, contains period pieces and ornithological prints by John James Audubon.

All sorts of shipwreck treasures, and the gear used to find them, are displayed in the excellent **Mel Fisher Maritime Museum**.

Key West's main thoroughfare, **Duval Street** is lined with souvenir shops and is often busy with tourists. Several of the Old Town's sights are located here.

← Visitors enjoying live music in Sloppy Joe's bar

Did You Know?

Key West was first called "Cayo Hueso," or "Island of Bones."

The Oldest House Museum

→ The bright white Episcopal Church towering over Key West

The 1912 **St. Paul's Episcopal Church** *is dedicated to the patron saint of shipwrecked sailors. Some of its 49 stained-glass windows feature nautical imagery.*

Jimmy Buffet, the Floridian singer, owns **Margaritaville,** *a cafe with an adjoining shop, where T-shirts and memorabilia are sold.*

EATON STREET

The **San Carlos Institute** *was founded by Cubans in 1871. Today it occupies a beautiful Baroque-style building, which functions as a Cuban heritage center.*

WHITEHEAD STREET

SOUTHARD STREET

FLEMING STREET

○ **FINISH**

THOMAS STREET

0 meters 100
0 yards 100

N

EXPERIENCE MORE

❸

Naples

 E5 🚗🚌 **ℹ 2390 Tamiami Trail N, Collier County; www.paradisecoast.com**

An affluent beach city, Naples prides itself on its manicured appearance and on its 55 golf courses: it has the greatest per capita concentration of courses in the state.

Downtown, most of what is called "historic" Naples dates from the early 20th century, and, with its pastel-colored buildings, is a pleasant area to explore. Many of the 19th-century houses were destroyed by hurricane Donna in 1960, which also claimed the original 1887 pier. Rebuilt in 1961, this is now a popular spot

Did You Know?

Naples's Third Street South Farmers Market takes place on Saturdays from 7:30am.

for both anglers and pelicans; the latter are a common sight perched upon the railings.

A beautiful white sandy beach stretching for 10 miles (16 km) is flanked mostly by condos, but it offers easy public access and safe swimming in warm Gulf waters.

The **Collier Museum at Government Center** focuses on local history, with exhibits ranging from ancient Indigenous tribal artifacts to those connected with the region's pioneering past and the building of the Tamiami Trail (US 41), on which the museum stands.

Collier Museum at Government Center

🏛 3331 Tamiami Trail E
🕐 9am–4pm Tue–Sat
🌐 colliermuseums.com

❹

Marco Island

 F6 ℹ 1102 N Collier Blvd, Collier County; www. marcoislandonline.com

Developed as a resort since the 1960s, Marco Island is

the most northerly of the Ten Thousand Islands chain, and it is an excellent base from which to explore the western fringe of the Everglades. A number of outstanding archaeological items, some 3,500 years old, were found here. Although these are now kept in museums elsewhere, it is still possible to see the remains of midden mounds – giving clues to the lifestyle of the ancient Calusa people.

❺

Big Cypress Swamp

 F6 🏛 Collier County, Monroe County 🌐 nps.gov

Home to several hundred species, including the endangered Florida panther, this vast, shallow wetland basin is not, in fact, a true swamp. It features a range of habitats, determined by only slight differences in elevation, which include sandy islands of slash pine, wet and dry prairies, and hardwood hammocks. One-third of the swamp is

The pier in the charming city of Naples, a great spot to watch the sun set

INSIDER TIP
Learning about the Swamp

Ranger-led activities in Big Cypress Swamp include nature walks, information sessions on local wildlife, and canoeing excursions. Be sure to make your reservations up to two weeks in advance (*www.nps.gov/bicy.*)

covered by cypress trees, growing in belts and long narrow forests known as "strands." It is the scale of these strands as opposed to the size of the trees that gives the area its name.

The swamp functions as a wet season water storage area for the greater Everglades system and as a buffer zone for the Everglades National Park (*p292*). Completed in 1928, the Tamiami Trail, also known as US 41, cuts through the swamp and has opened up the area. The road skirts the Everglades and stretches from Tampa to Miami, hence its name. Today, such engineering feats are environmentally questionable, because they block the natural movement of water and wildlife essential to the fragile balance of southern Florida's unique ecosystem.

Big Cypress National Preserve is the largest of the protected areas. Most visitors here enjoy the views from US 41, and stop at the Oasis Visitor Center for information.

On the western edge of the swamp is the **Fakahatchee Strand Preserve State Park**, one of Florida's wildest areas.

A huge natural drainage ditch, or slough (pronounced "slew"), it is 20 miles (32 km) long and 3–5 miles (5–8 km) wide.

Logging ceased here in the 1950s, having destroyed a shocking 99 percent of old-growth cypresses. The preserve's only remaining examples, some dating from the 15th century, are found at Big Cypress Bend. Here, a short trail passes through a mosaic of plant communities, including magnificent orchids and nestlike epiphytes. Here too is the US's largest stand of native royal palms.

Route 846, running northeast from Naples, takes you to the popular **Audubon of Florida's Corkscrew Swamp Sanctuary**. Here, a 2-mile (3-km) boardwalk traverses various habitats, including Florida's largest stand of old growth cypress trees. The sanctuary is famous for its many birds, and it is known as an important nesting area for endangered wood storks, which visit during the winter.

Big Cypress National Preserve

♿ 🚻 📍Tamiami Trail E, Ochopee 🕐24 hours daily
ℹ️ 33000 Tamiami Trail E, Ochopee; www.nps.gov

Fakahatchee Strand Preserve State Park

♿ 📍137 Coast Line Dr, Copeland 🕐8am–sunset daily 🌐floridastateparks.org

Audubon of Florida's Corkscrew Swamp Sanctuary

♿ 🚻 📍375 Sanctuary Rd W 🕐7am–5:30pm daily
🌐corkscrew.audubon.org

Alligator at Big Cypress National Preserve, part of Big Cypress Swamp

6

Key Largo

🅰 G6 ☒ 🅸 106000
Overseas Hwy, Key Largo;
www.fla-keys.com

The first of the inhabited Keys, this is the largest island in the chain and was named "long island" by Spanish explorers. Key Largo's proximity to Miami makes it also the liveliest, especially on weekends, when it is crowded. The island's greatest attractions are the diving and snorkeling opportunities along the coral reef found just offshore, in the John Pennekamp Coral Reef State Park (*p307*). For those who simply want to relax here, Key Largo is also a beautiful place to watch the sunset.

Another attraction at Key Largo is the **African Queen**, the boat used in the 1951 movie of the same name. The boat makes short pleasure trips between extensive periods of restoration. It is moored at MM 100, which is also the base for several boat charters including *Key Largo Princess Glass Bottom Boat*.

Key Largo is also home to the **Dagny Johnson Key Largo Hammock Botanical State Park**, which encompasses one of the largest tracts of West Indian tropical hardwood hammock in the US. Over 6 miles (9 km) of trails lead through the forest, providing sightings of the local crocodiles and rich birdlife.

One of the most unusual places to stay in the Keys is Jules' Undersea Lodge, set in shallow water in a mangrove lagoon off Key Largo – guests have to scuba dive to get to the "moon pool" entrance.

↑ A marina full of fishing boats at Key Largo in the Florida Keys

FLORIDA'S CORAL REEF

North America's only live coral reef system extends 200 miles (320 km) along the length of the Keys, from Miami to the Dry Tortugas. A complex and extremely delicate ecosystem, it protects these low-lying islands from storms and heavy wave action emanating from the Atlantic Ocean. Coral reefs are created over thousands of years by billions of tiny marine organisms known as polyps. Lying 10–60 ft (3–18 m) below the surface, the reef is an intricate web of countless cracks and cavities, and is home to a multitude of plants and diverse sea creatures, including more than 500 species of fish.

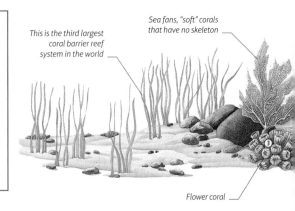

📷 PICTURE PERFECT
Christ of the Deep

The Key Largo Dry Rocks reef at the John Pennekamp Coral Reef State Park is home to the *Christ of the Deep* statue, a popular photo spot, which lies submerged at 20 ft (6 m). Access it through snorkeling tours.

This is the third largest coral barrier reef system in the world

Sea fans, "soft" corals that have no skeleton

Flower coral

It has two private bedrooms and a common room, and even has Wi-Fi.

African Queen
🏠 99701 Overseas Hwy
🕐 Times vary, check website
Ⓦ africanqueenflkeys.com

Dagny Johnson Key Largo Hammock Botanical State
♺ 🏠 County Road 905, MM 106 🕐 Sunrise–sunset daily
Ⓦ floridastateparks.org

John Pennekamp Coral Reef State Park

🅰 G6 🏠 102601 Overseas Hwy, Key Largo 🕐 8am–sunset daily Ⓦ florida stateparks.org

About 95 percent of this park is in the ocean, but the part that's on land is still well-equipped. Its facilities include

a visitor's center, a small museum on the ecology of the reef, woodland trails, and lots of picnicking spots with barbeque grills. But this park is best known for its fabulous underwater reaches, which extend 3 miles (5 km) east from Key Largo, and provide a great glimpse of the vivid colors and extraordinary forms of coral reef life.

There are canoes, dinghies, and motorboats for rent, as well as snorkeling and scuba gear. Snorkeling and diving tours can easily be

arranged, and there is a diving school that offers certified courses. Those who are less inclined to get wet can take a glass-bottom boat trip. Most tours visit destinations that are actually located in the neighboring section of Key Largo National Marine Sanctuary, which extends 3 miles (5 km) farther out to sea.

Some parts of the reef here are favored by snorkelers, such as the shallow waters of White Bank Dry Rocks, with its impressive array of corals and colorful tropical fish. Nearby Molasses Reef offers areas for both snorkelers and divers, who may encounter a wide variety of fish such as snapper and angelfish. Farther north, at French Reef, divers can swim through plenty of caves to find darting shoals of glassy sweepers.

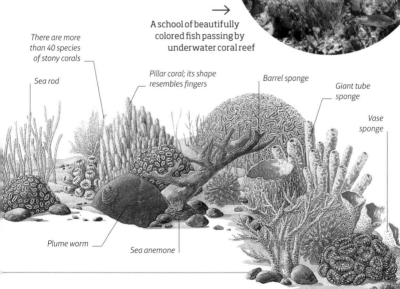

A HARD CORAL POLYP

This type of coral polyp secretes a limescale skeleton to protect its fleshy body. Coral heads and branches are eventually formed by the growth cycles of countless polyps. Microscopic plants, which live in the polyps' tissues, determine the color of the coral.

→

A school of beautifully colored fish passing by underwater coral reef

There are more than 40 species of stony corals

Sea rod

Pillar coral; its shape resembles fingers

Barrel sponge

Giant tube sponge

Vase sponge

Plume worm

Sea anemone

Dining under palm trees at a seafront restaurant on Islamorada ↑

8

Islamorada

 G7 🚌 ℹ 87100 Overseas Hwy, Monroe County; www.islamorada chamber.com

Proudly declaring itself "The Sport Fishing Capital of the World," Islamorada, pronounced "Eye-luh-mo-rada," encompasses seven islands and is best known for its outstanding big game fishing.

Whale Harbor Marina in the town of Islamorada, on Upper Matecumbe Key, bristles with impressive deep-sea charter craft used to catch deep-water fish. Fishing party boats based here take people of all levels of experience, so even those who are not dedicated anglers can enjoy half a day out at sea on one of these trips. Back in town at MM 82, the Art Deco

Hurricane Monument marks the grave of 500 people killed by a tidal surge in the hurricane of 1935.

9

Indian and Lignumvitae Keys

 G6 🚌 Lower Matecumbe Key ℹ 106240 Overseas Hwy, Key Largo; www. floridastateparks.org

These uninhabited islands, located on opposite sides of the Ocean Highway, are accessible only by boat or kayak.

Tiny Indian Key has a surprising amount of history for its size. Once occupied by Indigenous peoples, it was settled in 1831 by Captain J. Houseman, an opportunistic wrecker (p299). A small community flourished under his rule, but in 1840 Seminoles attacked, and all the settlers

> INSIDER TIP
> ### What Is Lignum Vitae?
>
> Lignum vitae ("the wood of life" in Latin) is among the densest and heaviest woods on Earth. This endangered tropical hardwood can be found, naturally, on Lignumvitae Key.

were killed. The Key was abandoned, and today only the outlines of the village and its cisterns remain, amid vegetation impressive for both its variety and rampant growth. An observation tower provides splendid views.

Larger Lignumvitae Key, which can be explored only on a guided tour, is of even greater botanical interest. It boasts 133 native tree species, including its namesake, a blue-flowering tree that can live for 1,000 years. Scientists believe that other vegetation here is as old as 10,000 years. Notable wildlife includes some colorful tree snails (and impressively large spiders). Be prepared for mosquitoes.

> **Whale Harbor Marina in the town of Islamorada, on Upper Matecumbe Key, bristles with impressive deep-sea charter craft used to catch deep-water fish.**

FISHING IN THE FLORIDA KEYS

There are three main fishing zones in South Florida, each offering its own type of experience and rewards. Near the warm Gulf Stream, offshore gamefish such as marlin abound in conditions excellent for deep-sea (or blue-water) angling. The Atlantic coastal waters up to and including the coral reef itself contain tropical species such as snapper and grouper. To the north of the Keys, the shallow backcountry flats of the Gulf are home to game fish such as tarpon. Islamorada, Marathon, and Key West are the area's major fishing centers, and small marinas throughout the region have boats for rent.

WHERE TO GO

There are a number of companies that will organize deep-sea fishing excursions; for good freshwater fishing you should head to Amelia Earhart Park or Lake Okeechobee (p128).

The Keys are a paradise for deep-sea fishing. With the Gulf Stream nearby, these waters offer the most varied fishing imaginable. Boat trips are easy to come by; try Key West Fishing Club.

WHAT YOU NEED

Bait and tackle shops are found along the Overseas Highway and in marinas. They not only rent and sell equipment and licenses, but are often the best places to find out about guides and fishing trips offered locally.

Flat-bottom skiffs are available to rent and can be poled through inshore waters. However, motors can sometimes become snarled up in the seagrass.

Fishing party boats are a popular and economical way to fish around the reef. The per-person price usually includes a fishing license, tackle, and bait, as well as the crew's expertise.

Note that weather conditions and seasonal variations determine the available species.

DEEP-SEA VERSUS BACKCOUNTRY

Deep-sea fishing, one of the most exhilarating options available, appeals to the Hemingway spirit of the trophy angler. Renting a sports boat, however, is expensive. Skiffs fish the tranquil and scenic back-country reaches, where cunning and stealth help to secure a catch.

Fishing boats moored in the still, reflective waters of Islamorada ↑

10

Marathon

AF7 **🚗🚌** **ℹ**12222 Overseas Hwy; www.floridakeys marathon.com

Marathon was originally named Vaca ("cow") Key by the Spanish settlers, probably for the herds of manatees, or sea cows (p279), once found offshore. It was renamed in the early 1900s by the men who laid the Overseas Railroad.

The main center of the Middle Keys, this island is heavily developed. Marathon's principal appeal lies in its fishing grounds, and those under the bridges where the Atlantic Ocean and the Gulf of Mexico meet are said to be particularly fertile.

Visitors can choose from a broad range of angling techniques. These include spearfishing (illegal in the Upper Keys but allowed here), and line-fishing off what may be the longest pier in the world – a 2-mile (3-km) stretch of the old 7-Mile Bridge. There are several pleasing waterfront resorts with small beaches, created artificially from imported sand. Turn south off the Overseas Highway for these.

Definitely worth a visit is Crane Point Hammock, consisting of a large area of tropical hardwood forest and wild mangrove wetlands.

There are nature trails and a traditional conch-style house built out of tabby – a type of local homemade concrete, made of burned seashells and coral rock. The entrance to the hammock is via the **Crane Point Museum**, whose collection explains the history, geology and the ecology of the islands.

Around two miles beyond Crane Hammock, the Overseas Highway passes the **Turtle Hospital**, a rescue, rehabilitation, and release facility for injured turtles recovered from all over the keys. Guided tours (mandatory) take in the hospital and rehab sections, with stories of some of the current patients.

Crane Point Museum

⊛⊛⊕ **A**5550 Overseas Hwy **🕑**9am-5pm Mon-Sat, noon-5pm Sun **w**cranepoint.net

Turtle Hospital

⊛⊛⊕ **A**2396 Overseas Hwy **🕑**9am-6pm daily **w**turtlehospital.org

---

11

Pigeon Key

AF7 **ℹ**2010 Overseas Hwy, Marathon; www. pigeonkey.net

This tiny Key was once the construction base for Henry Flagler's 7-Mile Bridge, completed in 1912. Seven wooden structures, originally used by building crews, are now part of a marine research and educational foundation.

There is a historical museum in the Bridge Tender's House, but many people visit simply to enjoy the island's tranquil surroundings. The old bridge, running parallel to the "new" 7-Mile Bridge built in 1982, provides a stunning backdrop to the island. The old bridge is currently closed for repairs and will reopen at a future date. Until then, you can reach Pigeon Key via the "new" 7-mile bridge or on a boat tour from Marathon. No cars

↑ Bridge Tender's House, now the home of Pigeon Key's historical museum

↑ Idyllic white-sand beach in Bahia Honda State Park, part of the Lower Keys

Did You Know?

Near the Blue Hole quarry is the beautiful looped Jack Watson Nature Trail, less than a mile (1 km) long.

are allowed on the Key, so go by foot or bicycle, or take the shuttle bus from the foundation's visitor center at MM 47.5.

12

Lower Keys

F7 **www.fla-keys.com**

Once beyond the 7-Mile Bridge, the Keys appear to change. The land is wider and less developed than in the Upper Keys, and the vegetation is more wooded.

Just 37 miles (60 km) from Key West is **Bahia Honda State Park**, a protected area that boasts the finest beach in all the Keys. Brilliant white sand is backed by a dense, tropical forest crossed by trails. Here, find unusual species of tree, such as silver palm and yellow satinwood, and many birds. The usual watersports equipment is available to rent, but

be aware that the current here can be very strong.

Trips out to the Looe Key National Marine Sanctuary are also available from the park. This 5-mile (8-km) section of the reef is spectacular, with unique coral formations and abundant marine life.

From Bahia Honda, the highway swings north and reaches the second largest island in the chain, Big Pine Key. The Lower Keys' main residential community, this is the best place to see the tiny Key deer, most often spotted at dusk or in the early morning. Take the turning for Key Deer Boulevard near MM 30 to reach the Blue Hole, a flooded quarry set in woodlands. Watch from the viewing

platform as the deer and other wildlife come to drink.

One Keys icon worth seeking out is **No Name Pub**, tucked away in Big Pine Key, north of the Overseas Highway (it sits just before the causeway to No Name Key). The bar and restaurant began life as a 1930s general store, which added the pub in 1936. It's best known for its dollar-bill smothered walls and its famous "pub pizza."

Bahia Honda State Park

♿ ⌂ 36850 Overseas Hwy
🕐 8am–sunset daily
ⓦ floridastateparks.org

No Name Pub

⌂ 30813 Watson Blvd
ⓦ nonamepub.com

KEY DEER

Related to the white-tailed deer, Florida's endangered Key deer are found only on Big Pine Key and the surrounding islands. They swim between these keys, but are more often sighted around the slash pine woodlands. Despite the strict enforcement of speed restrictions, about 50 deer are killed in road accidents each year.

Decorative
animal skull
at Miccosukee
Indian Village

EXPERIENCE The Everglades and the Keys

13

Miccosukee Indian Village

🅰F6 🅖Mile Marker 36, US 41, 25 miles (40 km) W of Florida Turnpike 🕘9am–5pm daily 🌐village. miccosukee.com

Most of the Miccosukee Tribe live in small settlements along US 41. The best way to find out more about them is to visit the Miccosukee Indian Village near Shark Valley (p295).

Here, visitors can see *chickees* (traditional homes) and crafts like basket-weaving, dollmaking, and beadwork. Native American artifacts, clothing, paintings, and cooking utensils are displayed at the Miccosukee Museum. There is also a luxurious resort and gaming facility, which offers spa facilities, a golf course, and a country club.

> At the Miccosukee Indian Village, visitors can see *chickees* (traditional homes) and crafts like basket-weaving and dollmaking.

14

Ah-Tah-Thi-Ki Museum

🅰F5 🅖34725 West Boundary Road, Big Cypress Seminole Indian Reservation 🕘9am–5pm daily 🌐ahtahthiki.com

The Ah-Tah-Thi-Ki Museum is located on 64 acres (26 ha) of the Big Cypress Reservation. On site is a traditional village where Seminole Tribe members tell stories and demonstrate crafts. The museum is dedicated to the understanding of Seminole culture and history; Ah-Tah-Thi-Ki means "a place to learn." There is an impressive 180-degree, five-screen orientation film. It also houses more than 180,000 artifacts and items to explore, as well as a fantastic library.

15

Florida Keys National Wildlife Refuges

🅰F7 🕘Times vary, check website 🅘30587 Overseas Hwy, Big Pine Key, Monroe County; www.fws.gov

This nature complex comprises four different national wildlife refuges (NWRs) set up to protect the birds and wildlife endemic to the Keys: the National Key Deer Refuge; the Great White Heron NWR; the Crocodile Lake NWR; and the Key West NWR. The National Key Deer Refuge protects this species of white-tailed deer, as well as 21 other threatened animal and plant species. The great white heron and the American crocodile are similarly protected in their respective refuges.

The Key West NWR is based in Big Pine Key, but covers the Marquesas Keys and 13 other keys west of Key West itself, which are only accessible by boat. Home to some 250 species of bird, this refuge is also important as a nesting site for sea turtles.

16

Dry Tortugas National Park

🅰E7 🅖Fort Jefferson, Key West 🕘24 hours daily 🌐www.nps.gov/drto

The Dry Tortugas consists of seven reef islands lying 68 miles (109 km) west of Key West. Of these reef islands, Garden Key is the most visited as it is the site

12

of Fort Jefferson, the largest brick fortification in the United States. The hexagonal design included a moat 70 ft (21 m) wide, and walls up to 8 ft (2.5 m) thick and 50 ft (15 m) high.

It was originally envisaged that the fort would control the Florida Straits with a garrison of 1,500 men and 450 cannons. Beginning in 1845, construction continued for the next 30 years; however, the fort was never completed and was not involved in any battle. During the Civil War, after being occupied by Union forces, it was actually downgraded to a prison for captured deserters.

The only access is by boat or seaplane. Most people come on organized trips from Key West, which often include an opportunity to snorkel. The birdwatching is especially good between March and October, when the islands are home to migrant and nesting birds, such as boobies, sooty terns, and magnificent frigatebirds with their 7-ft (2-m) wingspan.

❶⑦

Tavernier

🅐G6 🅘87100 Overseas Hwy, Islamorada; (305) 451-1414

An unincorporated community to the south of the town of Key Largo, Tavernier is known for its history and wildlife. Henry Flagler's railroad reached this part of the Keys in the early 20th century. Today, a number of buildings, constructed in the 1920s and 1930s as the settlement grew, are located around MM 92. The most notable attraction in Tavernier is the **Florida Keys Wild Bird Rehabilitation Center**. Here, sanctuary is offered to injured birds, most of which have been harmed by humans, usually involving vehicles or fishing tackle. Barn owls, merlins, and crows recuperate in spacious cages set in tranquil surroundings, contrasting with the bustle of the rest of the island.

Florida Keys Wild Bird Rehabilitation Center

🕐 🅐92080 Overseas Hwy
🅞 Sunrise-sunset daily
🆆 keepthemflying.org

↑ Relaxing on the beach beside Fort Jefferson, on Garden Key, Dry Tortugas National Park

NEED TO KNOW

The Overseas Highway connecting the Keys

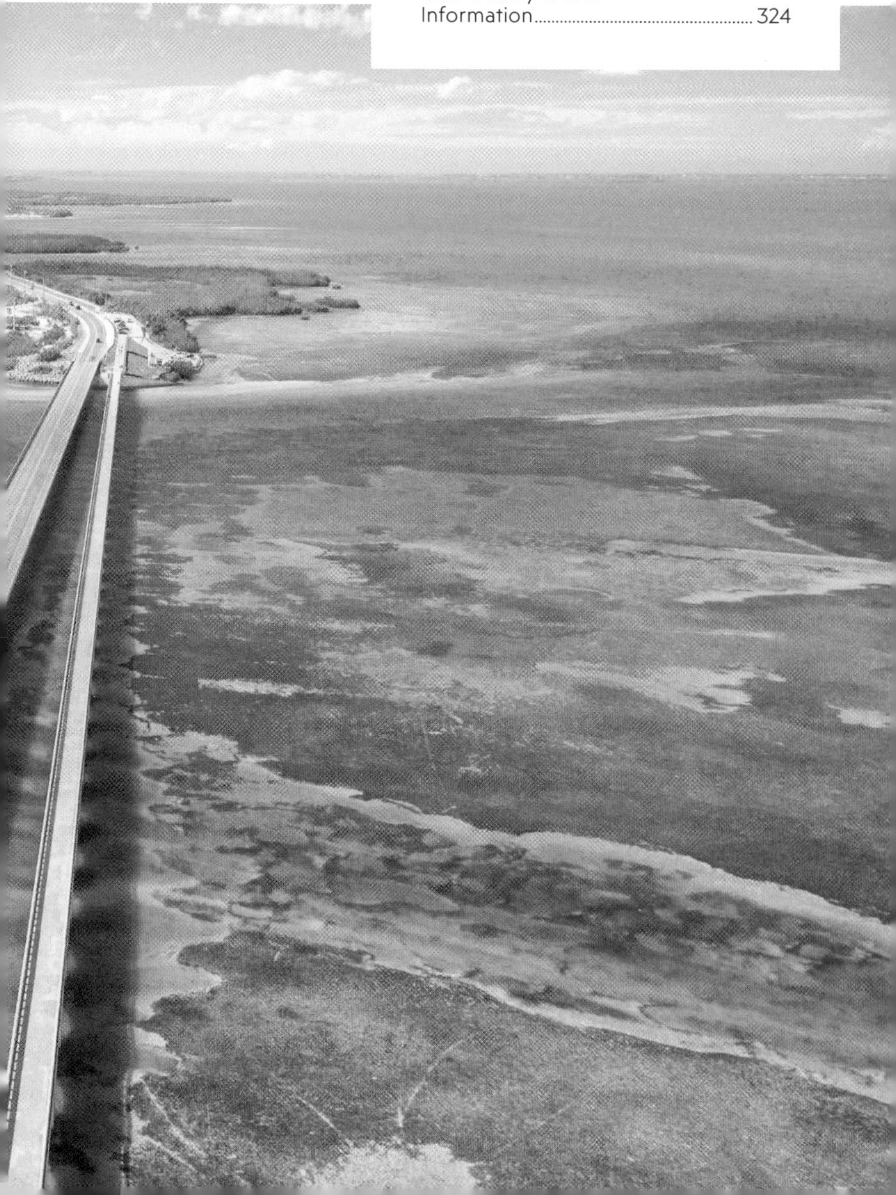

BEFORE
YOU GO

Things change, so plan ahead to make the most of your trip. Be prepared for all eventualities by considering the following points before you travel.

AT A GLANCE

CURRENCY
Dollar (USD)

AVERAGE DAILY SPEND

SAVE	SPEND	SPLURGE
$80	**$150**	**$250**

BOTTLED WATER	COFFEE	BEER	DINNER FOR TWO
$2	**$2.80**	**$5**	**$55**

CLIMATE

Summers are long, hot and fairly humid. Temperatures in July hit 82°F (28°C).

Winters are mild. Temperatures can sink to 61°F (16°C) in January.

Short, sharp downpours are the norm in the wet season (May–Sep). Hurricane season is from June to November.

ELECTRICITY SUPPLY

The standard US electric current is 110 volts and 60 Hz. Power sockets are type A and B, fitting plugs with two flat pins.

Passports and Visas

For entry requirements, including visas, consult your nearest US embassy or check with the **US Department of State**. All travelers to the US should have a passport that is valid for six months longer than their intended period of stay. Citizens of the UK, Australia, New Zealand, and the EU do not need a visa, but must apply to enter in advance via the Electronic System for Travel Authorization (**ESTA**). Applications must be made at least 72 hours before departure, and applicants must have a return airline ticket. Visitors from all other regions will require a visa.
ESTA
W esta.cbp.dhs.goc/esta
US Department of State
W travel.state.gov

Government Advice

Now more than ever, it is important to consult both your and the US government's advice before travelling. The US Department of State, the **UK Foreign and Commonwealth Office**, and the **Australian Department of Foreign Affairs and Trade** offer the latest information on security, health and local regulations.
Florida is occasionally at risk from hurricanes. Advance warnings are activated if there is any danger and **Ready** lists safety precautions.
Australian Department of Foreign Affairs and Trade
W smartraveller.gov.au
Ready
W ready.gov/hurricanes
UK Foreign and Commonwealth Office
W gov.uk/foreign-travel-advice

Customs Information

You can find information on the laws relating to goods and currency taken in or out of the US on the **Customs and Border Protection Agency** website. All travelers need to complete a Customs and Border Protection Agency form.
US Customs and Border Protection Agency
W cbp.gov

Insurance

We recommend that you take out a comprehensive insurance policy covering theft, loss of belongings, medical care, cancellations and delays, and read the small print carefully. All medical treatment is private and US health insurers do not have reciprocal arrangements with other countries.

Vaccinations

No inoculations are needed for the US.

Reserving Accommodations

An extensive list of accommodations can be found on the Visit Florida website (p322). Room rates vary enormously depending on the time of year. In south Florida, the high season runs from mid-November through Easter, while in the Panhandle and the Northeast, hotels charge their highest rates in spring and summer.

Money

Most establishments accept major credit, debit, and prepaid currency cards. Contactless payments are becoming increasingly common, but cash is usually required for smaller items, bus tickets, and tips. Tipping is an important local custom (p323). Waiters and taxi drivers will expect to be tipped 15 per cent of the total bill, while hotel porters and housekeeping should be given $5 per bag or day.

Travelers with Specific Requirements

US federal law demands that all public buildings be accessible to people in wheelchairs, although some old buildings are exempt.

A number of groups offer general advice for travelers with disabilities, including **Mobility International USA** and Visit Florida (p322). **Lighthouse Central Florida** is a useful resource for visually impaired travelers and **Florida Disabled Outdoors Association** lists recreational activities throughout the state. Staying in one place? **Visit Florida Keys** provides island-specific advice, while Walt Disney World® Resort has an accessible park guide.

When it comes to getting around, a few car rental companies, including **Accessible Vans of America**, have vehicles adapted for people with disabilities, and some buses have "kneeling" wheelchair access – look for a sticker on the windshield or by the door.

Accessible Vans of America
w accessiblevans.com
Florida Disabled Outdoors Association
w fdoa.org
Lighthouse Central Florida
w lighthousecfl.org
Mobility International USA
w miusa.org
Visit Florida Keys
w fla-keys.com/travelers-with-disabilities

Language

The official language of Florida is English, but parts of Miami are home to large Latin American communities, where Spanish is also spoken.

Opening Hours

> **COVID-19** Increased rates of infection may result in temporary opening hours and/or closures. Always check ahead before visiting museums, attractions, and hospitality venues.

Monday Some museums are closed.
Sunday Most banks close in the afternoon and smaller businesses close for the day.
Federal and State Holidays Museums, public attractions, and many businesses close.

FEDERAL HOLIDAYS

Jan 1	New Year's Day
Mid-Jan	Martin Luther King Day
Late May	Memorial Day
Jul 4	Independence Day
Early Sep	Labor Day
Nov 11	Veterans Day
Late Nov	Thanksgiving Day and Thanksgiving Friday
Dec 25	Christmas Day

GETTING
AROUND

Whether you are visiting for a short city break or relaxed beach holiday, discover how best to reach your destination and travel like a pro.

AT A GLANCE

PUBLIC TRANSPORTATION

MIAMI

$2.25

Single Ticket
Metrorail

ORLANDO

$2.00

Single Ticket
Lynx

TALLAHASSEE

$1.25

Single Ticket
StarMetro

SPEED LIMIT
Speed limits in the US are set by individual states. The limits in Florida are as follows:

FREEWAYS

70 mph
(110 km/h)

RURAL ROADS

55 mph
(85 km/h)

RESIDENTIAL AREAS

30 mph
(45 km/h)

NEAR SCHOOLS

20 mph
(30 km/h)

Arriving by Air

Florida's major airports are Miami, Orlando, Tampa, and Fort Lauderdale. These are all served by national carriers from around the world. In addition there are hundreds of charter flights during the winter months.

Be sure to allow plenty of extra time at the airport, both at arrival and departure, as there are often long lines for passport control and thorough security checks.

For a list of transportation options, approximate journey times, travel costs for traveling between each of Florida's major airports and cities, see the table opposite. Note that public buses are cheaper than shuttle buses. The fare from Miami International Airport to Miami Beach is $2.65 on an express bus, for example.

Train Travel

Amtrak, the national passenger rail company, serves Florida from the east coast. There is one daily service from New York City. This Silver Service takes up to 28 hours (with sleepers and meals available), and runs via Washington D.C., down through Jacksonville and Orlando, terminating in Miami or Tampa. The Palmetto serves the same route and offers a business-class service. When traveling overnight, you can choose between the seats of coach class or a cabin. Both options have decent meal services on longer stretches.

If you want to travel by train to Florida but take your own car to drive once you get there, book a ticket on Amtrak's Auto Train, which runs daily from Lorton in Virginia to Sanford, Florida – 30 miles (48 km) north of Orlando. The journey takes about 18 hours.

Amtrak trains serve only a limited number of towns and cities in Florida. Other than Tampa, the Gulf Coast is linked only by Amtrak buses, known as "Thruway" buses. These run from Winter Haven, near Orlando, to Fort Myers via St. Petersburg and Sarasota, with guaranteed connections with Amtrak rail services.

If you are planning to make more than a couple of trips by train, it is worth considering

GETTING TO AND FROM THE AIRPORT

Airport	Destination	Distance	Taxi Fare	Shuttle Bus Fare
Miami	Miami Beach	10 miles (16 km)	$35	$20–30
Orlando	Walt Disney World®	18 miles (28 km)	$60-70	$49
	Universal Orlando Resort™	15 miles (24 km)	$55-60	$40-60
	Downtown Orlando	14 miles (22.5 km)	$45-50	$38
Sanford	Walt Disney World®	40 miles (64 km)	$100-110	$20-50
Tampa	Downtown Tampa	9 miles (14 km)	$30	$19
Fort Lauderdale	Fort Lauderdale	8 miles (13 km)	$17-20	$13-15
	Miami	30 miles (48 km)	$80-90	$25

buying a rail pass, which gives unlimited travel on Amtrak's network during a set period of time. The pass must be bought before you arrive – either online with Amtrak or through a travel agent that deals with Amtrak. Rail fares do not compete well with those of buses, but trips are more comfortable and relaxing.

Another train service is the south Florida regional **Tri-Rail**, which links 15 stations between Miami airport and West Palm Beach, including Fort Lauderdale and Boca Raton. Although primarily for commuters, these trains can also be useful for tourists.

Amtrak
w amtrak.com
Tri-Rail
w tri-rail.com

Long-distance Bus Travel

Whether you are traveling from other parts of the country or within Florida, **Greyhound** buses offer the cheapest way to get around. Some services are "express," with few stops en route, while others serve a greater number of destinations. A few routes have "flag stops", where a bus may stop to deposit or collect passengers in places without a bus station. To reserve in advance visit the Greyhound website. You can also go to a Greyhound agent – usually found in a local store or post office – or pay the driver directly.

Passes provide unlimited travel for set periods of time (between four and 60 days), but you may only find them particularly useful if you have a very full itinerary. Overseas visitors should also note that passes cost less if bought from a Greyhound agent outside the US.

Timetables, information about the different types of ticket, and details of baggage limits are available on the Greyhound website.

Red Coach runs smaller, premium buses – offering movies, Wi-Fi, and reclining seats – from Miami to Orlando, Tampa, Tallahassee, and Gainesville.

Greyhound
w greyhound.com
Red Coach
w redcoachusa.com

Public Transportation

Most Florida cities have good public transportation networks, though the vast majority of people do rely on a car to get around. There are various modes of transportation to choose from, including trains and buses, which are often used by visitors who don't have access to their own vehicle. Safety and hygiene measures, timetables, ticket information, transport maps, and more can be obtained at tourist information centers, stations, and individual operators' websites.

Tickets

Each city provides different public transportation services. Most cities only offer buses, while Miami also has the Metrorail and Metromover. There are often discounted passes for multiple trips as well as reduced rates for children.

If you plan to take local city buses, make sure that you have cash and remember that you should buy tickets from the driver. It is recommended that you pay with the exact fare, as drivers can't always provide change.

Bus

All of Florida's major cities have city bus networks. **Metrobus** runs throughout Miami-Dade County. A single ride costs $2.25 and transfers are free. A 24-hour unlimited pass costs $5.65, while a seven-day pass is $29.25. There is a 60 cent fee to transfer between bus and train services.

You can get by in Orlando without a car thanks to the **Lynx** buses. While some residential areas have few or no bus routes, the main tourist areas of downtown Orlando, International Drive (including Universal Studios Florida™ and SeaWorld®), and Walt Disney World® Resort are quite well served. The free **Lymmo** service (run by Lynx) travels within downtown Orlando, with rides to and from the Amway Center sports arena and through the dining and nightlife area.

Metrobus
W miamidade.gov/global/transportation
Lynx and Lymmo
W golynx.com

Metrorail and Metromover

Miami has two additional rail-based public transportation services. **Metrorail** is a 25-mile (40-km) rail line between the northern and southern suburbs of Miami. It provides a useful link between the most popular tourist areas of Coral Gables, Coconut Grove, and the downtown area. Services run daily every 10 minutes or so from 6am until midnight. You can transfer free from Metrorail to the Tri-Rail line in Hialeah, and also to the Metromover system at Government Center and Brickell stations.

Miami's free **Metromover** monorail has three loops, connecting the heart of downtown with the Omni entertainment and Brickell financial districts on separate elevated lines. There are 20 stations in total. The Inner Loop provides a quick way to see the downtown area. Cars operate from 5am to midnight daily, arriving every 90 seconds during rush hours and every three minutes during off-peak hours.

Metrorail and Metromover
W miamidade.gov

Taxis

Taxis are a comfortable though expensive way of getting around. Due to the popularity of Lyft and Uber ride-hailing services, taxicabs are becoming increasingly scarce, though cabs can still be picked up at taxi ranks and hotels in larger city centers, as well as at airports. They can also be booked by telephone. Most have a "TAXI" sign on the roof; this is illuminated if the taxi is free.

Water Taxi

Water taxis are found in Jacksonville, Tampa, Fort Lauderdale, and the islands around Fort Myers. Routes are generally geared to tourists, and as a result they are fairly limited in scope – linking hotels, restaurants, and stores, for example. However, they are great for sightseeing and often offer special fares.

Driving

Driving in Florida is, by and large, the most efficient way to get around urban areas and travel between cities. It's also very straight-forward: most highways are well-paved, gasoline is relatively inexpensive, and car rental rates are the lowest in the US.

Car Rental

Rental car companies are located at airports and other locations in major towns and cities. It is usually cheaper to rent a vehicle at the airport rather than from a downtown outlet.

All you need to rent a car is your driver's license, passport, and a credit card. If you present a debit card, you may be required to allow a large deposit to be charged. The minimum age for car rental is 21, but drivers under 25 may need to pay a surcharge.

The state of Florida requires that you carry a copy of the rental agreement in the car. It is recommended to store it safely out of sight.

Make sure your car rental agreement includes Collision Damage Waiver (CDW) – also known as Loss Damage Waiver (LDW) – or you'll be liable for any damage to the car, even if it was not your fault. Rental agreements include third-party insurance, but this is rarely adequate. It is advisable to buy additional or supplementary Liability Insurance, just in case something unexpected happens.

Most companies add a premium if you want to drop the car off in another city, and all impose high charges for gas: if you return the car with less fuel than it had initially, you will be required to pay the inflated fuel prices charged by the rental agencies. Be aware that the gas stations nearest airports are particularly expensive.

Driving in Florida

You must have a valid driver's license in order to drive a car in Florida.

While there are many state and federal regulations on the equipment requirements of cars, there are very few that pertain to occupants. There is no requirement to carry warning triangles or safety flares for instance. Drivers and passengers can be fined for not wearing seatbelts, and at certain times of the year state-wide campaigns make violations particularly expensive; heavy fines can be levied at checkpoints by the Florida Highway Patrol.

If you want to explore off-road trails on a motorbike, be aware that riders younger than

16 years are required to wear eye protection, over-the-ankle boots, and a safety helmet.

Parking

Finding a parking space is rarely a problem at theme parks and other major tourist attractions, shopping malls, or in most downtown districts. Parking near city beaches is more difficult.

You will find small and multi-level parking lots or parking garages in cities, but usually you will have to use parking meters. Feed the meter generously: the fee varies from 50¢ to $2 per hour. Overstay and you risk a fine or the possibility of your car being clamped or towed away.

Be sure to read parking signs carefully. Restrictions may be posted on telephone poles, street lights, or roadside walls. Cars parked within 10 ft (3 m) of a fire hydrant will be towed.

Roads and Tolls

Florida has an excellent road network. The fastest and smoothest routes are the interstate highways, referred to with names such as "I-10" and "I-75". These usually have at least six lanes with rest areas generally located about 45 minutes' apart. Interstates form part of the expressway system of roads (sometimes called "freeways"), to which access is permitted only at specified junctions or exits.

The main toll roads are BeachLine Expressway (between Orlando and the Space Coast) and the Florida Turnpike, which runs from I-75 northwest of Orlando, to Florida City. The toll you have to pay is dependent on the distance covered. Tolls can be paid to a collector in a booth or – if you have the correct change and do not need a receipt – dropped into a collecting bin.

There are several toll roads throughout Florida that now feature all-electronic tolling. Note that most sections of the Turnpike have been converted to an electronic collection system and cash is no longer accepted. Tolls are collected via Sunpass transponders or from having your license plate photographed at each toll booth; your rental car agency can provide information regarding this.

Other routes include the US highways, which are usually, but not always, multi-lane. These are slower than expressways and often less scenic, because they are lined with motels and gas stations. Highways can also get congested during morning and evening rush hours.

Take care when approaching exits, which can be on both sides of the highway; most accidents occur when making left turns.

State Roads and County Roads are smaller but better for casual touring by car. Unpaved routes exist in some of Florida's more rural areas; note that some car rental companies may not permit you to drive on these.

Breakdown Assistance

If your car breaks down, pull off the road, turn on the emergency flashers, and wait for the police. On expressways you can make use of one of the Motorist Aid Call Boxes. It is advisable to always carry a cell phone in case of emergencies. If you have rented a car, you will find an emergency number on the rental agreement. In the event of a serious breakdown, the rental agency will provide a new vehicle. The American Automobile Association (**AAA**) will assist its members. Alternatively, call the Florida Highway Patrol (511) or the free Road Ranger service (*347).

AAA
w aaa.com

Rules of the Road

Follow these rules to stay safe. Drive on the right-hand side of the road. Seat belts are compulsory for both drivers and passengers, and children under three must sit in a child seat.

Drinking and driving is illegal. Driving under the influence can result in a fine, having your driver's license suspended, or imprisonment.

Passing is allowed on both sides on any multilane road, including interstate highways. It is illegal to change lanes across a double yellow or double white solid line.

If a school bus stops on a two-way road to drop off or pick up children, traffic traveling in both directions must stop. On a divided highway, only traffic traveling in the same direction need stop.

Cycling

Cycling is not a good way to get around the major cities (with the exception of some parts of Miami Beach), but smaller towns are usually quiet enough to be safely explored by bicycle.

For longer excursions there are miles of marked cycle paths along the coast, and long-distance bike trails crisscross the state's interior. The **Florida Coast-to-Coast Trail** connects Titusville with St Petersburg, while the Pinellas Trail connects St Petersburg with Tarpon Springs. The Florida Keys Overseas Heritage Trail runs along US–1 to Key West.

Florida Coast-to-Coast Trail
w fgtf.org/projects/coast-to-coast-connector

Walking

Florida's cities are not particularly pedestrian-friendly, and the hot and humid summers make exploring cities on foot pretty uncomfortable. But, outside urban areas, Florida has some lovely hiking trails. The **Florida Trail Association** provides information, including maps.

Florida Trail Association
w floridatrail.org

PRACTICAL
INFORMATION

A little local know-how goes a long way in Florida. Here you will find all the essential advice and information you will need during your stay.

AT A GLANCE

EMERGENCY NUMBER

GENERAL EMERGENCY

911

TIME ZONE
EST (Eastern Standard Time - except for Panhandle - CST - Central Standard Time).

TAP WATER
Unless otherwise stated, tap water in Florida is safe to drink.

WEBSITES
www.visitflorida.com
Florida's national tourist board
www.nhc.noaa.gov
National Hurricane Center
www.aaa.com
American Automobile Association
www.amtrak.com
The US rail network
www.greyhound.com
America's national bus network

Personal Security

Florida is a relatively safe place to visit, but it is still advisable to take precautions. As in any urban area, there are parts of Miami, Orlando, Jacksonville, and other Florida towns where you should stay alert. Plan your routes in advance, look at maps discreetly, walk with confidence, and avoid deserted areas at night. If you need directions, ask hotel or shop staff, or the police.

Make sure your credit cards, cell phones, and cash are kept in a safe place. If you have anything stolen, report the crime as soon as possible to the nearest police station. Get a copy of the crime report in order to claim on your insurance. Most credit card companies have toll-free numbers for reporting a loss, as do Thomas Cook and American Express for lost cash cards.

Contact your embassy or consulate if you have your passport stolen, or in the event of a serious crime or accident.

As a rule, Floridians are accepting of all people, regardless of their race, gender or sexuality. The state has a big Latin American and African American population. Following the Black Lives Matter protests sparked by the killing of George Floyd in the summer of 2020, some confederate statues have been removed, and buildings and squares named after historical figures have been renamed.

Florida has a long history as an LGBT+-friendly vacation destination. Miami is world-famous for its dynamic LGBT+ scene, and Key West, Orlando, Fort Lauderdale, and Tampa have long supported the community. Key West elected one of the country's first openly gay mayors in 1983. This attitude, however, does not always extend to the state's more rural areas. If you do feel unsafe, the **Safe Space Alliance** pinpoints your nearest place of refuge.
Safe Space Alliance
W safespacealliance.com

Health

Healthcare in the US is costly. Ensure you have full medical coverage prior to your visit, and keep receipts to claim on your insurance if needed.

Hospitals accept the majority of credit cards, as do most doctors and dentists. Those without insurance may need to pay in advance.

Anyone on prescribed medication should take a supply with them and ask their doctor to provide a copy of the prescription in case of loss, or the need for more.

Large cities as well as some smaller towns may have 24-hour walk-in medical and dental clinics, where minor ailments can be treated. For less serious complaints, many drugstores such as Walgreens and CVS (some of which stay open late or for 24 hours) have registered clinics.

Smoking, Alcohol, and Drugs

Florida has a partial smoking ban, with lighting up prohibited in most enclosed spaces and on public transportation. Users of e-cigarettes follow the same rules.

You must be over 21 to buy and drink alcohol, and to buy tobacco products. It is advisable to carry valid ID at all times, as you will not be permitted to enter bars or order alcoholic beverages in restaurants without ID.

The possession of narcotics is strictly prohibited and could result in prosecution and a prison sentence.

Local Customs

Tipping is an important custom in Florida, as in the rest of the US. Anyone who provides a service expects to receive a "gratuity," and this needs to be calculated in the price of things like meals and taxi journeys (p317).

Visiting Churches and Cathedrals

Always dress respectfully when visiting places of worship: cover your torso and upper arms. Ensure shorts and skirts cover your knees.

Cell Phones and Wi-Fi

The main US network providers are AT&T, Sprint, T-Mobile US, and Verizon. Most of these offer prepaid, pay-as-you-go phones and US SIM cards, starting at around $30 (plus tax), which you can purchase upon arrival. Inexpensive cell phones can also be purchased at supermarkets, convenience stores (such as 7-Eleven), and big-box electronic and discount department stores, including Target, Walmart, and Best Buy.

Triband or multiband cell phones from around the world should work in the US, but your service provider may have to unlock international roaming. It is worth checking this with your provider before you set off.

Calls within the US are cheap, but making international calls may be pricey.

Free Wi-Fi is ubiquitous in hotels and just about everywhere else. Cafés and restaurants are often happy to permit the use of their Wi-Fi if you make a purchase.

Taxes

The state sales tax in Florida is 6 per cent. Local authorities can add additional levies up to a maximum 2.5 per cent. Tampa charges the full 8.5 per cent, Miami adds 1 per cent and Orlando's tax rate is 6.5 per cent.

Post

Post office opening hours vary but are usually 9am to 5pm on weekdays, with some offices opening on Saturday mornings. There are 24-hour Automated Postal Centers inside post office lobbies, which dispense stamps and postage for larger packages. Drugstores, supermarkets, and hotels often sell stamps, but may charge more than the post office.

Private courier services, such as UPS and Federal Express, can be used for both domestic and international mail, while DHL is for overseas packages; they can offer next-day delivery to most places, but the service is expensive.

Discount Cards

Discount cards can potentially save you a lot of money in Florida, but it's important to check the small print and to be realistic about how much you'll use them – most cards only save money if they are used to the maximum extent. The **Sightseeing Day Pass** and **Go City** offer discounted admissions in Miami and Orlando.

Go City
w gocity.com

Sightseeing Day Pass
w sightseeingpass.com

WALT DISNEY WORLD®
INFORMATION

A lot goes into planning a trip to Walt Disney World® Resort. Here are the key things to consider when organizing your dream vacation.

AT A GLANCE

AVERAGE DAILY SPEND FOR A FAMILY OF FOUR

SAVE	SPEND	SPLURGE
$160	$220	$350

BUSY SEASONS
US Federal holidays (p317).
US Spring Break & Easter.
June, July, and early August.
Last week in November (Thanksgiving).

NEW ATTRACTIONS
Remy's Ratatouille Adventure, Harmonious, and Space 220 all debuted at Epcot® in 2021; Guardians of the Galaxy: Cosmic Rewind is likely to open in 2022.

OPENING HOURS
These vary by park, by day, and by season. All parks extend their opening hours during the summer months.

WEBSITES AND APPS
Walt Disney World® Resort
 disneyworld.disney.go.com
Guests with Disabilities
 disneyworld.disney.go.com/guest-services/guests-with-disabilities
Disney Play App
 disneyworld.disney.go.com/guest-services/play-app
Park Calendar
 disneyworld.disney.go.com/calendars
Park Map
 disneyworld.disney.go.com/maps
Ticketed Events
 disneyworld.disney.go.com/events-tours

Tickets

Guests can buy tickets to visit a single park, or Park Hopper® tickets that provide access to multiple parks and other areas of the resort. There are also options for multiple days as well as admission for a single day.

Guests booking a vacation package through Walt Disney World® Resort can take advantage of promotions such as free dining or discounted park ticket rates.

Throughout the year Walt Disney World® Resort offers many special ticketed events. These require the purchase of a separate ticket as well as park entry.
Park Tickets
 disneyworld.disney.go.com/admission

Accommodation

Walt Disney World® Resort offers four different categories of accommodations for guests, ranging from Value resorts (starting at $99 per night) to Deluxe Villa resorts (from $335 per night). Value resorts are further away from the theme parks, with only buses available to transport guests to the parks, whereas Deluxe Villa accommodations are closer, with more transportation options.

There are lots of accommodations options outside Walt Disney World® Resort hotel, but staying at a resort hotel offers many perks, including advance FastPass+ reservation, Extra Magic Hours, and access to Disney dining plans. Resort guests also receive airport transportation, and MagicBands.
List of Accommodations
 disneyworld.disney.go.com/resorts

Transportation

Getting To and From the Resort
The nearest major airport to Walt Disney World® resort is Orlando International (MCO). The journey time between the airport and the resort can range from 25 minutes to an hour, depending on traffic. Guests staying at a Walt Disney World® Resort hotel can use the

complimentary Disney's Magical Express Service, which travels between the airport and the resort's hotels. Other visitors can make use of taxis and shuttles from the airport (p319).

Disney's Magical Express Service,
W disneyworld.disney.go.com/guest-services/magical-express/

Driving

There are many rental car companies available at Orlando International Airport. It is also possible to rent a vehicle at the resort's Car Care Center, located near the Magic Kingdom® Theme Park.

Parking at Walt Disney World® Resort hotels for registered guests is not complimentary, and prices range from $15 to $25 per vehicle per night based on hotel category.

Renting a Car from Disney World
W disneyworld.disney.go.com/guest-services/car-rental-services

Traveling Between the Parks

The theme parks and hotels at Walt Disney World® Resort are up to 6 miles (11 km) apart, with little or no designated walking paths. Traveling is kept simple as Disney operates several modes of transportation that go to guest areas, including buses, monorails, boats, and the Skyliner gondolas. You can also rent "Minnie Vans" using the the Lyft app (p320).

Disney's Transportation System
W disneyworld.disney.go.com/guest-services/resort-transportation/

Dining

Many restaurants at the resort accept reservations 120 days in advance, and guests are recommended to book well ahead, especially for unique experiences such as character dining, fireworks dessert parties, and popular restaurants like Be Our Guest.

Guests can bring their own food and drinks (except alcoholic beverages) into the parks, provided they do not need to be heated. Please note that glass containers are prohibited, with the exception of baby food jars.

Dining Option
W disneyworld.disney.go.com/dining

Disney Dining Plans

A convenient choice for guests staying at the Walt Disney World® Resort hotels is the Disney Dining Plan, which can be added to vacation packages. As dining plans are pre-purchased, guests know what is being spent on food in advance (excluding gratuities). There are three different dining plans available for purchase, depending on your tastes and budget.

Disney Dining Plans
W disneyworld.disney.go.com/dining/plans

Additional Features

My Disney Experience App

It is highly recommended that guests download the My Disney Experience app, available for free on both Google Play and the App Store. The app allows guests to create FastPass+ reservations, look up wait times for rides and show times for parades, explore Walt Disney World® Resort with the help of a GPS-enabled map, reserve dining, and search for merchandise across the parks, among many other useful tools. Wi-Fi is available throughout the resort so guests can use the app anywhere.

FastPass+

FastPass+ allows guests to pre-book their spot in line at many of Walt Disney World® Resort's most popular attractions. All that is needed is valid theme park admission and a My Disney Experience account. Guests can make FastPass+ reservations on the My Disney Experience app, the Walt Disney World® website, or via kiosks throughout the park.

Guests staying in a Walt Disney World® Resort hotel can make their FastPass+ selections 60 days before the first day of their visit, for the duration of their stay. Other guests will be able to make their selections 30 days before their visit. Selections are made on a first come, first served basis, so guests are recommended to make their selections as early as possible.

FastPass+ Information
W disneyworld.disney.go.com/fastpass-plus

MagicBands

MagicBands are wristbands that serve as a guest's park ticket and entry into FastPass+ queues. For guests staying at a Walt Disney World® Resort hotel, MagicBands can also function as a hotel room key and – with a credit card on file – a convenient way to pay for merchandise and food. MagicBands are complimentary with any Walt Disney World® Resort reservation.

MagicBands
W disneyworld.disney.go.com/plan/my-disney-experience/bands-cards/

Memory Maker

Memory Maker allows guests to pay one price for unlimited digital downloads of all pictures taken at the park, including attraction photos, select character dining experiences, and those taken using the PhotoPass® service.

PhotoPass® photographers are stationed at key picture points throughout the parks, ready to take photos for guests using professional cameras, or the guests' own cameras.

MemoryMaker
W disneyworld.disney.go.com/memory-maker

INDEX

Page numbers in **bold** refer to main entries.

ACKNOWLEDGEMENTS

DK would like to thank the following for their contribution to the previous edition: Eleanor Berman, Marc Di Duca, Jennifer Ferguson, Gabrielle Innes, Adrian Mourby, Paul Oswell, Carlye Wisel, Ruth and Eric Bailey, Richard Cawthorne, David Dick, Guy Mansell, Fred Mawer, Emma Stanford, Phyllis Steinberg, Ian Williams

The publisher would like to thank the following for their kind permission to reproduce their photographs:

Key: a-above; b-below/bottom; c-centre; f-far; l-left; r-right; t-top

© 2018 Universal Orlando. All Rights Reserved: 174cl, 179clb, 182cra, 183b, 184cl, 184-5tc.

2018 – Salvador Dalí Museum, Inc., St. Petersburg, FL.: 262-3bl, 263tl; *Basket of Bread*, 1945 / © Salvador Dali, Fundació Gala-Salvador Dalí, DACS 2019 263tr; *The Weaning of Furniture Nutrition*, 1934 / © Salvador Dali, Fundació Gala-Salvador Dalí, DACS 2019 263cra; *Apparatus and Hand*, 1927 / © Salvador Dali, Fundació Gala-Salvador Dalí, DACS 2019 263cr; *Nature Morte Vivante*, 1956 / © Salvador Dali, Fundació Gala-Salvador Dalí, DACS 2019 263br.

4Corners: Pietro Canali 17ca, 108-9; Susanne Kremer 8cl, 8-9, 21ca, 288-9.

Alamy Stock Photo: 24BY36 41br; AF archive 48bc, 49crb; age fotostock / Alvaro Leiva 76bl; All Canada Photos 14clb; Alpha and Omega Collection 162crb; Andreoletti 242bl; Jon Arnold Images Ltd 27cl, 237cr; Art Directors & TRIP 190cb; Bill Bachmann 224br, 244t; Lori Barbely 142-3tc; Andrew Barker 151bc, 152-3bl, 162fclb, 162fbr, 165t, 184b; Mark J. Barrett 252-3tc; Pat & Chuck Blackley 221tl; blickwinkel 37bl; steve bly 309cra; Jason Bryan 69crb; Roman Budnyi 191crb; Buff Henry Photography 104t; Pat Canova 250t, , 252bl, 253tr; Yvette Cardozo 35cr; Peter Carroll 163fbr; Charles O. Cecil 85br; Tonya Civiello-Bixler 148bl; Lucy Clark 159br, 160t; Collection Christophel 49bl; Bruce Corbett 248bl; Creative Touch Imaging Ltd. 312tl; Cultura Creative (RF) 131b; Ian Dagnall 228-9b, 264t, 269b, 296cla, 302bl; Danita Delimont 105bl, 270t; David R. Frazier Photolibrary, Inc. 297tr; Teila K. Day Photography 22t; Songquan Deng 143tr, 166-7tl; Reinhard Dirscherl 229crb; Disney Magic 155bc, 169b; dmac 144-5tc, 150t; Education & Exploration 3 42tr; Education & Exploration 4 132-3; Richard Ellis 46bl; Everett Collection Historical 46crb; EyeVisualEyesIt 199br; Findlay 13crb, 30-31tc, 142tl, 168-9tl, 180bc, 181t; Frank Fell 63cla; Fotan 157cl; Gabbro 305br; The Granger Collection 44bl; Richard Green 148-9tr,

166clb, 167crb; Jeffrey Isaac Greenberg 5+ 59br; Jeffrey Isaac Greenberg 9+ 268tr; Hemis 59cla; Dan Highton 163fclb; Historic Images 101br; History and Art Collection 272fclb; Robert Hoetink 19t, 170-71; Hendrik Holler 308t; Hum Images 190bl; IamKai / Stockimo 145cl; imageBROKER 293bl; Images-USA 218t, 272ca, 273bc; Paul Jacobs 162bl; Brian Jannsen 190crb, 304-5t; JeffG 91br, 189bl, 273clb; John Kellerman 79br; Dzmitry Kliapitski 174t; Russell Kord 92-3b, 97cb, 100bl; Lazyllama 74t; Rick Lewis 245cr, 246t; Littleny 70cra, 72tr, 168br; LMR Group 313tc; LOOK Die Bildagentur der Fotografen GmbH 303tr; lovethephoto 31cla; Lucky-photographer 102-3b; Patrick Lynch 127tl; Dennis MacDonald 78tr, 227br; Ilene MacDonald 125tl; dov makabaw 129bl; Thomas Marchessault 143cla; mauritius images GmbH 116bc; Patti McConville 42br; Ball Miwako 177cla; Dawna Moore 219b, 222clb; Moviestore Collection Ltd 48bl; Glenn Nagel 33tr; NASA Image Collection 191bl; Natural History Library 40tl; Nature Picture Library / Alex Mustard 279br; Newscom / BJ Warnick 223b; Nikreates 94t; NJphoto 153tr; North Wind Picture Archives 45tr; M. Timothy O'Keefe 136-7t, 165br; Sean Pavone 19bl, 176-7tl, 201bl, 204-5; Andrew Pearson 22cr; Douglas Peebles Photography 15cr; Peter Ptschelinzew 123bc; James Quine 216bl; robertharding / Michael Runkel 312-13b; Grant Rooney 197bl; Dominic Romer 29b; RosalreneBetancourt 10 61tr, 200tr, 285tr; RosalreneBetancourt 13 73tr, 93tr, 174bl; RosalreneBetancourt 3 / *Chairman Mao series*, 1972 / © 2019 The Andy Warhol Foundation for the Visual Arts, Inc. / Licensed by DACS, London 119bl; RosalreneBetancourt 6 43bl, 124-5b; RosalreneBetancourt 7 / *Inflammatory Essays, 1979-82* / Jenny Holzer © ARS, NY and DACS 2019, London 2019 24-5ca; RosalreneBetancourt 9 222br; Tom Rose 181br; Jorge Royan 18ca, 138-9; RSBPhoto 237tl; RSBPhoto1 30-31bl, 151tr, 179br; Stephen Saks Photography 25tr, 105tr, 235tr, 237cra; James Schwabel 25tl, 135bl, 202br, 236-7bl, 260-61bc, 265bl, 277bl, 282bl, 283t, 283cla, 284-5b, 286br, 286-7t, 294tr, 294-5br; Science History Images 194cra; stephen searle 158b, 200bc; Helen Sessions 145b, 147cl, 150cra, 152cl; Martin Shields 270br; Sinibomb Images 174crb; Don Smetzer 226bc; Solarsys 31crb; Tom Stack 40-41bl, 278b, 309b; Felix Stensson 58b; Johnny Stockshooter / © Bradley Dooley 240br; SuperStock 208br; Tasfoto 71cra; Torontonian 95clb; Travel Pictures 182t; Tribune Content Agency LLC 42tl; A. Robert Turner 163crb; United Archives GmbH 49clb; VIAVAL 196t; Stephen Vincent 228tl; Joe Vogan 136cra; gary warnimont 237br; WaterFrame_mus 130bl; Mark Waugh 198t; Tim E White 178-9tl; Jennifer Wright 272bl; WS Collection 46tl; ZealPhotography 144b; ZUMA Wire / Mario Houben 28-9tr, / Scott A. Miller 42bl;

The Bass, Miami Beach: Zachary Balber / The Haas Brothers: *Ferngully,* December 5, 2018 – April 21, 2019 76-7tc.

WonderWorks, Orlando: 38br , 198cla.

The Wolfsonian–FIU: World Red Eye 75bl.

The Wynwood Walls: Photo courtesy of Goldman Properties 103tr.

Front Flap
Alamy Stock Photo: Danita Delimont t; EyeVisualEyesIt cla; Hendrik Holler cb; **Getty Images:** cra; Jeff Greenburg br; **iStockphoto. com:** EditorBRo bl.

Cover images
Front and spine: **Dreamstime.com:** Aiisha.
Back: **4Corners:** Susanne Kremer c; **Dreamstime. com:** Aiisha b, Kmiragaya cla, Sean Pavone tr.

For further information see: www.dkimages.com

Illustrators: Richard Bonson, Richard Draper, Chris Orr & Assocs, Pat Thorne, John Woodcock.

This edition updated by
Contributors Stephen Keeling, Manu Velasco
Senior Editor Alison McGill
Senior Designers Laura O'Brien, Stuti Tiwari
Project Editors Dipika Dasgupta, Rebecca Flynn
Project Art Editor Bharti Karakoti
Editor Nayan Keshan
Picture Research Coordinator
Sumita Khatwani
Assistant Picture Research Administrator
Vagisha Pushp
Jacket Coordinator Bella Talbot
Jacket Designer Ben Hinks
Senior Cartographer Mohammad Hassan
Cartography Manager Suresh Kumar
DTP Designer Tanveer Zaidi
Senior Production Editor Jason Little
Production Controller Rebecca Parton
Deputy Managing Editor Beverly Smart
Managing Editors Shikha Kulkarni,
Hollie Teague
Managing Art Editor Bess Daly
Senior Managing Art Editor Priyanka Thakur
Art Director Maxine Pedliham
Publishing Director Georgina Dee

First edition 1997

Published in Great Britain by Dorling Kindersley Limited, DK, One Embassy Gardens, 8 Viaduct Gardens, London SW11 7BW

The authorised representative in the EEA is Dorling Kindersley Verlag GmbH. Arnulfstr. 124, 80636 Munich, Germany

Published in the United States by DK Publishing, 1450 Broadway, Suite 801, New York, NY 10018

Copyright © 1997, 2021 Dorling Kindersley Limited
A Penguin Random House Company
21 22 23 24 10 9 8 7 6 5 4 3 2 1

A CIP catalog record for this book is available from the British Library.

A catalog record for this book is available from the Library of Congress.

ISSN: 1542 1554
ISBN: 978 0 2415 4429 7

Printed and bound in China.

www.dk.com

A NOTE FROM DK EYEWITNESS
The rapid rate at which the world is changing is constantly keeping the DK Eyewitness team on our toes. While we've worked hard to ensure that this edition of Florida is accurate and up-to-date, we know that opening hours alter, standards shift, prices fluctuate, places close and new ones pop up in their stead. So, if you notice we've got something wrong or left something out, we want to hear about it. Please get in touch at travelguides@dk.com